The Political Economy of Exchange Rate Policy-Making

The Political Economy of Exchange Rate Policy-Making

From the Gold Standard to the Euro

Steven Kettell

palgrave
macmillan

First published 2004 by
PALGRAVE MACMILLAN
Houndmills, Basingstoke, Hampshire RG21 6XS and
175 Fifth Avenue, New York, N. Y. 10010
Companies and representatives throughout the world

PALGRAVE MACMILLAN is the global academic imprint of the Palgrave
Macmillan division of St. Martin's Press, LLC and of Palgrave Macmillan Ltd.
Macmillan® is a registered trademark in the United States, United Kingdom
and other countries. Palgrave is a registered trademark in the European
Union and other countries.

ISBN13: 978-1-4039-2071-3
ISBN10: 1-4039-2071-0

This book is printed on paper suitable for recycling and made from fully
managed and sustained forest sources. Logging, pulping and manufacturing
processes are expected to conform to the environmental regulations of the
country of origin.

A catalogue record for this book is available from the British Library.

Library of Congress Cataloging-in-Publication Data
Kettell, Steven, 1973–
    The political economy of exchange rate policy-making : from the gold
standard to the euro / Steven Kettell.
        p. cm.
    Includes bibliographical references and index.
    ISBN 1-4039-2071-0 (cloth)
        1. Foreign exchange–Government policy–Great Britain. 2. Gold
standard–Great Britain–History–20th century. 3. Great Britain–Economic
conditions–20th century. I. Title.
HG3943.K48 2004
332.4'5'0941–dc22   2004043620

10   9   8   7   6   5   4   3   2   1
13   12   11   10   09   08   07   06   05   04

For my son,
Elliott

Contents

Acknowledgements

This book is based on Ph.D. research conducted at my time in the Department of Politics and International Studies at the University of Warwick from 1999 to 2003, and which was funded by ESRC award number R00429934243. My acknowledgements and thanks must go first of all to Tony Tant at the University of Plymouth, whose enthusiasm and verve whetted my appetite for further study, to Werner Bonefeld at the University of York, without whom this project would never even have started, and to Wyn Grant at the University of Warwick, for all the useful help and advice given throughout the duration of the thesis. I would also like to extend my thanks and appreciation to all my colleagues at the Department of Political Science and International Studies at the University of Birmingham, especially Peter Kerr, Colin Hay, Matthew Watson, and David Marsh, whose comments and advice on the writing of this book (whether consciously intended or otherwise) have all been gratefully received.

A very special mention must of course go to Peter Burnham, who supervised the Ph.D. thesis, who was at all times an invaluable and seemingly limitless source of comments, ideas, and reflections, and for whose guidance and assistance I shall remain deeply indebted. I would also like to extend many thanks to all the archive staff at the Modern Records Centre for their patience, assistance, and file-finding-finesse, and as well as to Amanda Watson at Palgrave, and Shirley Tan at EXPO whose help, advice, and relaxed attitude at all stages of this project have been much appreciated. A big thank-you must also go to the Trades Union Congress, to the Confederation of British Industries, and to the Bank of England for granting their kind permission to access and cite their archives.

On a personal level, I would also like to take this opportunity to express the incalculable debt, both financially and emotionally, that I owe my parents Dot and John for all their help and support throughout the years. The greatest thanks of all however, must go to my wife, Marie, to whom I shall be forever indebted in a way that words can never express.

Preface

This book examines the political economy of exchange rate policy-making from a theoretical and an empirical perspective. It argues that conventional means of understanding this subject are problematic, and it develops an alternative framework of analysis based on an 'open Marxist' methodology. This contends that exchange rate policy-making needs to be analysed and understood as a component part of a wider governing strategy that is made by the core executive with a view to containing class struggle, to providing favourable conditions for capital accumulation, and to ensuring a sufficient degree of governing autonomy for the pursuit of high political aims. These theoretical claims are empirically substantiated through an examination of three key episodes of exchange rate policy-making in Britain: the return to the gold standard in 1925, membership of the Exchange Rate Mechanism from 1990 to 1992, and the present situation concerning New Labour's attitude towards the single European currency. In contrast to traditional interpretations of these episodes, these are seen to have been designed to address long-term economic and political difficulties in the British state through the imposition of financial discipline and through the 'depoliticisation' of economic conditions and policy-making, and with the exception of the single currency are also considered to have been relatively successful in achieving these aims.

List of Abbreviations

ABCC   Association of British Chambers of Commerce
BE   Bank of England
CBI   Confederation of British Industries
EAC   Economic Advisory Council
EC   European Community
ECB   European Central Bank
EEA   Exchange Equalisation Account
EMU   Economic and Monetary Union
ERM   Exchange Rate Mechanism
EU   European Union
FBI   Federation of British Industries
FRBNY   Federal Reserve Bank of New York
G7   The Group of Seven Industrialised Nations
GDP   Gross Domestic Product
ILP   Independent Labour Party
LRD   Labour Research Department
MAIE   Manchester Association of Importers and Exporters
MAGB   Mining Association of Great Britain
MFGB   Miners' Federation of Great Britain
MPC   Monetary Policy Committee
MRC   Modern Records Centre
MTFS   Medium Term Financial Strategy
NCEO   National Confederation of Employers Organisations
TNA   The National Archives
TUC   Trades Union Congress
TUCGC   Trades Union Congress General Council

1
Introduction: Themes, Schemes, and Exchange Rate Regimes

Where are we now?

On first impressions the subject of exchange rate policy-making appears to be one that is more soporific than stimulating. Anyone wishing to engage with this issue is immediately confronted by a world filled with obscure technical jargon and debates whose contents seem penetrable only to the trained economist, while the lack of any clearly defined core literature on the matter only adds to the sense of confusion and exclusivity. As a topic of study then, exchange rate policy-making would seem to deserve its place at the margins of political-economic analysis. Such a view however is more understandable than reasonable. As the principal means by which national states are integrated into the global economy, the process of exchange rate policy-making is of fundamental importance for a wide variety of both national and international factors. Levels of economic output, employment, prices, and trade are all intimately affected by the operation of the exchange rate system, as are political relations within and between states themselves. An analysis of exchange rate policy-making then is of no small concern, but is of central importance to any full understanding of high-level political and economic developments.

More concrete evidence to illustrate this point is provided by the evolution of the international monetary system itself. The first truly global 'exchange rate regime' (the set of official institutional arrangements, mechanisms and tools that are used to influence or control the value of the national currency on the foreign exchange markets) was the 'classical' gold standard. This emerged during the latter half of the nineteenth century as the world's major trading nations undertook to fix the value of their national currencies in terms of gold. The system was underpinned by the global dominance of sterling, as the world's primary currency, and provided a level of stability and certainty to world trade that was not only essential for the smooth expansion of the international economy, but which also helped to secure political stability by ensuring that national rates of inflation were maintained at broadly similar levels. While this proved to be a highly successful regime, the classical gold standard was shattered by the First World War, and efforts to secure its reconstruction were not completed until the mid-1920s, by which time global political and economic conditions had been severely strained by a high level of monetary disorder and exchange rate volatility. Although the eventual return of the gold standard in a reformed guise, known as the 'gold exchange standard', therefore seemed to augur a return to the harmonious days of the previous century, such hopes were doomed to disappointment. By the end of the 1920s the failings of the restored system, which included a high degree of inflexibility, a lack of co-operative mechanisms, and a core of inappropriately valued exchange rates, were contributing to renewed instability within the world economy. As this degenerated into the worst depression in the history of global capitalism, the international monetary system again collapsed, and was now replaced by a series of fragmented and competitive 'monetary blocs', adding further to the prevailing political and economic chaos.

The world economic crisis of the 1930s was ultimately 'resolved' by the Second World War. This was followed by a restoration of international monetary stability through the Bretton Woods system of fixed-but-adjustable exchange rates. Now underpinned by the global dominance of the US dollar, this provided the lynchpin for a new economic expansion and presided over the greatest boom the world has ever seen. By the late 1960s however, the shortcomings of this new regime (most notably the lack of any constraints on the American balance of payments deficit) were also becoming increasingly apparent. Combined with growing difficulties in the world economy itself, by the early 1970s the attempt to maintain a global system of fixed exchange rates had once again been abandoned, and while many developing countries continued to maintain their link to the dollar, the industrialised world now moved to a system of floating exchange rates.

In the third of a century since the demise of Bretton Woods the international monetary system has contained a mixture of exchange rate regimes. At the present time around a quarter of countries operate on the basis of a floating exchange rate, more than a third are committed to the use of a fixed regime, while the remainder utilise a combination of the two by seeking to manage, but not control any movements in their exchange rate. Despite this eclecticism however, the impact of exchange rate policy-making nonetheless remains keenly felt. Countries using a floating regime are open to difficulties posed by exchange rate fluctuations, which can significantly alter the price of imports and exports, while countries seeking to avoid such problems through the use of a fixed or managed exchange rate are subject to potentially greater difficulties should domestic economic conditions become incompatible with the maintenance of the regime, or should the regime itself come crashing down. The recent currency crises which engulfed Asia and Latin America from 1997 for example, bear clear testimony to the economic and political havoc that such developments can wreak. Indeed, even the most successful application of a fixed exchange rate regime is not without its difficulties. The road to monetary union in Western Europe for instance, was neither smooth nor simple. Early moves in this direction were plagued by the problems of exchange rate instability following the collapse of the Bretton Woods system; the entire project itself came under threat following a series of speculative attacks during the early 1990s; and even the successful realisation of European monetary union has failed to put an end to the problems associated with this process. Economic difficulties within the newly established Eurozone coupled with an underlying weakness of the euro itself have proved to be a key source of tensions, while political uncertainty continues to surround the future direction of those European Union member states that have yet to participate fully in the project.

The argument and structure of the book

While exchange rate policy-making is clearly of central importance to an analysis of political and economic developments, existing theoretical approaches to this subject – which are defined here as the 'rational choice', the 'country characteristics', and the 'interest group' approaches – are considered to be methodologically problematic. In particular, their failure to address the fundamental question of 'social form', namely why society itself should assume the particular organisational composition that it does, is thought to impose significant restrictions on their understanding of the policy-making process. The key reason for this is that existing approaches take their starting point for analysis to be the various 'components' of society themselves (namely its division into apparently separate and autonomous 'public'

and 'private' agents, 'political' and 'economic' structures, and sectorally defined interest groups), and proceed in a positivist fashion by
examining the interactions between them in order to construct a systematised model of policy developments. The main problem with such
an approach however, is that treating the constituent parts of society
in an unquestioned, unchanging, and taken-for-granted manner,
means that any analysis must therefore be based on causal factors
whose very existence remains unaccounted for. As such, existing theories are unable to fully conceptualise the fundamental constraints that
the organisational composition and development of society itself
imposes upon the process of exchange rate policy-making.

In contrast, this book argues that a more useful explanatory framework of analysis can be derived from an 'open Marxist' methodology.
Starting with the question of social form, this alternative approach
conceptualises society as a unified whole, and seeks to understand how
and in what way its various component parts are derived from, and are
related to its organisational composition. This leads to an understanding of society as an ongoing process that is conditioned by the development of an indeterminate class struggle, and thereby provides a
means of analysis that is grounded in a wider social theory than is
offered by existing approaches. On this basis, exchange rate policy-
making is not seen as the result of a dynamic interaction between
equally rational 'public' and 'private' actors, as something that is determined by the economic or political 'structural characteristics' of the
country involved, or as the result of interest group pressure, but is
instead seen to be a component part of a wider governing strategy that
is designed by state managers with a view to containing class struggle,
ensuring favourable conditions for capital accumulation, and securing
a sufficient degree of governing autonomy for the pursuit of 'high
political' aims and ambitions.

This alternative theory of exchange rate policy-making is substantiated through an empirical examination of three key policy episodes in
Britain: the return to the gold standard in 1925, membership of the
European Exchange Rate Mechanism from 1990 to 1992, and the
current situation with regards to Britain's participation in the single
European currency. It is the first of these which provides the main
component of the book. For this, there are three main reasons. Firstly,
the return to the gold standard has received extensive scholarly attention, is widely regarded as a classical example of exchange rate policy-
making, and therefore offers a well-developed case-study against which
to set an alternative analysis of the policy-making process. Secondly,

the historical nature of the policy itself forms a useful backdrop against which to contrast more contemporary policy-making episodes, and thus provides a firm platform on which wider generalisations can be established. Thirdly, the availability of extensive archival documentation for this period enables the internal debates and decision-making processes involved to be examined in a way that is not possible for more contemporary instances of exchange rate policy-making, and thereby provides a crucial body of first-hand empirical evidence with which to corroborate or invalidate an alternative theoretical view.

The analysis of Britain's return to the gold standard in 1925 begins with a critique of the 'conventional narrative' that has developed to explain this policy episode. This argues that the return to gold was the result of an eclectic mix of factors, including national pride and prestige, a desire to return to prewar conditions, the political self-interest of state officials, and a policy-making bias in favour of Britain's financial sector. In terms of its impact, this decision is widely regarded as having been a complete disaster, with a mistaken overvaluation of the pound and/or the existence of unpropitious global conditions being thought to have exacerbated Britain's postwar economic difficulties, to have led to chronically high levels of unemployment, and to have produced a surge in labour unrest, the apogee of which was a general strike during 1926.

In contrast, this book contends that Britain's gold standard policy was chiefly developed to address long-term economic and political difficulties, and that in this it proved to be relatively successful. During the last third of the nineteenth century Britain began to experience increasing problems associated with the onset of relative economic decline, a growing dependency on industries of diminishing international importance, and a progressive rise in labour dissatisfaction and radicalism. These difficulties were compounded during the First World War, which led to a politicisation of economic conditions and policy-making, and which raised the expectations of capital and labour as to what the postwar state could be expected to achieve. Against this background, a return to gold at the prewar exchange rate of $4.86 was seen by Britain's state managers as the key element of a governing strategy designed to deal with these problems by imposing a firm anti-inflationary discipline on capital and labour, and by displacing any adverse social and political consequences of this process away from the state through a 'depoliticisation' of economic conditions and policy-making. Linking the pound to an internationally constituted fixed exchange rate regime backed by the mass of domestic opinion would provide a useful mechanism for ensuring that British prices remained internationally competitive, for locking in the general direction of economic policy as a whole, and for enabling officials to legitimately disclaim responsibility, and hence accountability, for key economic policy decisions.

The initial attempt to implement this strategy however was unsuccessful. The introduction of deflationary measures needed to force down prices and raise the value of the pound after the war was delayed for fear of acute social unrest, while the development of a fierce economic boom during 1919 further exacerbated Britain's political and economic difficulties by producing even higher inflation, growing class disquiet, and a further maladjustment of the British economy in relation to the changing composition of world trade. By 1920, with the danger of severe unrest believed to be in decline, officials were finally able to impose tight economic policies designed to prepare the way for a return to gold. The introduction of deflation however now coincided with the onset of a severe slump, putting state officials under growing pressure. By the end of 1922 this had forced the governing authorities to suspend their deflationary approach, and had led to the adoption of a 'waiting strategy' based on the hope that a rise in sterling could be achieved in a less disruptive fashion through a rise in American inflation and a subsequent fall in the dollar. This approach though proved to be short-lived, and as hopes of US inflation began to recede, officials began to adopt a different strategy. By mid-1924 Britain's state managers were increasingly of the view that a return to the gold standard at what would clearly now be an overvalued exchange rate given the relative level of British prices, could itself be used as a deliberate means of imposing deflationary pressure on capital and labour, forcing them to become more competitive and to move into newer and more advanced lines of production. At the same time, the depoliticising aspects of the regime would also enable the authorities to displace any unpalatable social and political pressures resulting from this process by shifting responsibility for economic conditions and policy-making onto the gold standard itself.

In contrast to conventional assessments of this policy decision, from this alternative perspective Britain's return to the gold standard at $4.86 can also be interpreted as having been a relative success for the governing authorities. Although it did not manage to overcome the entrenched resistance of capital and labour to economic modernisation, and although it did not therefore lead to any substantial economic adjustment or breakthrough in competitiveness, the strategy nevertheless proved to be largely successful in providing officials with a credible and a depoliticised framework for economic policy management. Although political difficulties persisted, disquiet from capital and labour over economic conditions was now largely displaced away from the state, and Britain's governing authorities were now under less pressure than they had been under the politicised regime in operation since the war.

Despite the relative success of the strategy however, towards the end of the 1920s a combination of growing international difficulties and a lack of domestic economic adjustment increased the pressure on the British state. In September 1931 this culminated in a speculative attack on the pound, and in the eventual collapse of the gold standard strategy. The underlying aims of the authorities though were not abandoned, and Britain's exit from the regime was followed by the construction of a new economic policy framework based on the principles of encouraging an improved economic performance while minimising the economic involvement and responsibilities of the state. Moreover, until the latter half of the 1930s officials also remained anxious to secure another return to the gold standard at the old exchange rate of $4.86, though such a move now proved to be impossible. The increasingly unstable nature of the international situation and the high degree of domestic hostility to what was now a discredited policy regime both precluded any attempt to re-link the pound to gold, and by the latter years of the decade the governing authorities were finally forced to abandon their efforts in this direction.

This in-depth analysis of Britain's return to the gold standard also provides a solid foundation for demonstrating the utility of an open Marxist approach to other episodes of exchange rate policy-making. On this basis, the examination of the return to gold is followed by an empirical analysis of Britain's membership of the Exchange Rate Mechanism (ERM) from 1990 to 1992. While this too is commonly perceived to have been a major policy disaster, with officials being thought to have joined at an overvalued exchange rate and to have thereby added to the difficulties facing the British economy, from an open Marxist approach it is also possible to interpret this episode in a markedly different manner. As with the return to gold, Britain's membership of the ERM is again considered to have been the central component of a wider governing strategy designed to address long-running economic and political difficulties within the British state through the imposition of anti-inflationary discipline, buttressed by the deliberate use of a relatively high exchange rate, and through the depoliticisation of monetary and economic policy.

Furthermore, this strategy is also considered to have been relatively successful for the governing authorities. Although membership of the ERM again failed to overcome the resistance of capital and labour, although it too failed to produce any significant improvement in Britain's relative economic performance, and although the eventual collapse of the policy in September 1992 played a large part in destroying the political fortunes of the Conservative Party, it nonetheless provided officials with a credible and a largely depoliticised regime of economic management during its time of operation. This enabled the governing authorities to successfully contain class discontent, to effectively displace much of the responsibility for economic conditions and policy-making away from the state (despite the fact that Britain was locked into a severe recession), and to enjoy a greater level of governing autonomy than would otherwise have been possible.

The arguments underpinning these analyses of Britain's return to the gold standard and its membership of the ERM can also be extended to illuminate the present debate surrounding Britain's potential entry into the single European currency. In broad terms, it is argued that British membership of the euro would provide the New Labour government with a useful means of extending and strengthening its existing 'rules-based' and depoliticised framework of economic management. Handing control of interest rates over to the European Central Bank (ECB) would enable the governing authorities to impose tighter discipline on capital and labour, especially if combined with a relatively high exchange rate, while at the same time this would also enhance their freedom of high political manoeuvre by further distancing key economic policy issues from the sphere of democratic accountability. In contrast to the gold standard and the ERM strategies however, it remains unlikely that membership of the single European currency would be able to deliver these economic and political benefits. The resistance of capital and labour to greater competitive pressure is likely to remain strong, thus rendering it doubtful that entry into the euro would enable the government to resolve the difficulties posed by Britain's continued relative economic decline, while the persistently high level of domestic antipathy to any notion of 'scrapping the pound' seems certain to preclude any moves by the government to call, let alone win, a referendum on the subject. Despite clear parallels with the governing strategies of the gold standard and the ERM then, New Labour's euro-strategy is unlikely to be realised.

*

The structure of this book is therefore as follows: In chapter 2 existing theoretical approaches to exchange rate policy-making are outlined, and an alternative approach based on an open Marxist methodology is developed. From chapters 3 to 6 this is then applied to an extensive analysis of Britain's interwar gold standard policy. Chapter 3 establishes the theoretical and empirical context for the return to the gold standard, presenting a critique of conventional approaches to this policy decision, outlining an alternative interpretation, and detailing the background to the policy in terms of growing economic and political difficulties in the British state from the last third of the nineteenth century. In chapter 4 the events leading up to the return to gold itself from 1923 to 1925 are examined, in chapter 5 the success or otherwise of this policy from 1925 to 1929 is analysed, while chapter 6 explores the collapse of the strategy and the construction of a new policy regime during the 1930s. This analysis of Britain's return to gold is then followed in chapter 7 by an examination of Britain's membership of the Exchange Rate Mechanism from 1990 to 1992, and by an analysis of the current situation regarding Britain's possible membership of the single European currency in chapter 8. Finally, a concluding chapter summarises these analyses and considers their implications for the future study of exchange rate policy-making.

2
The Political Economy of Exchange Rate Policy-Making

Introduction

This chapter establishes a theoretical framework for the analysis of exchange rate policy-making. Existing theoretical perspectives on this subject are shown to be problematic, and an alternative means of analysis based on an 'open Marxist' methodology is proposed and developed. In essence, this argues that exchange rate policy-making should be seen as a key component of a wider governing strategy that is designed by state managers with a view to containing class struggle, securing favourable conditions for capital accumulation, and providing a sufficient degree of governing autonomy for the pursuit of high political aims. On this basis, the chapter also examines some of the various ways in which alternative exchange rate regimes can be used to achieve these objectives, and explores their relative benefits and disadvantages.

Theories of exchange rate policy-making

A precise delineation of the existing literature on exchange rate policy-making is elusive. The boundary lines that distinguish one theoretical approach from another are frequently blurred and overlap, with no consensus as to what the demarcation lines themselves should be, and much work remains of an overly technical and normative, rather than an analytical character, such as that concerned with the question of 'optimal currency areas', or with prescribing 'appropriate' exchange rate regimes for differing types of economy. Nevertheless, despite these difficulties it remains broadly possible to identify three main theoretical perspectives on exchange rate policy-making within the existing literature. These are defined here as the 'rational choice', the 'country characteristics', and the 'interest group' approaches.[1]

The first of these perspectives, the 'rational choice' approach, is by far the most common. This presents an analytical model based on a series of interactions between equally rational, self-maximising groups of public and private actors, and views exchange rate policy-making as part of an attempt by the public authorities to establish a credible, anti-inflationary 'policy rule'. The need for this is believed to derive from the problems of discretionary economic management. Allowing the authorities to continually adjust policy in response to changing circumstances is seen to present them with an inherent temptation to use inflationary measures in order to stimulate economic growth and political popularity. As they do so, the inflationary expectations, and hence the price and wage setting behaviour of private actors is thought to rise, leading to growing instability, and to a decline in economic performance. In contrast, a regime which credibly binds the authorities to the pursuit of an anti-inflationary policy is thought to produce more optimal long-term outcomes in terms of political stability and economic performance, since this can effectively reduce the temptations open to policymakers, and can thereby help to constrain the expectations and behaviour of market actors.[2]

Translated into exchange rate policy-making, the rational choice approach primarily contends that the most credible, and hence the most optimal policy rule, is provided by a fixed exchange rate regime. A public commitment to maintain a pre-specified value for the national currency is believed to impose a clearly visible constraint on the economic policy-making behaviour of the authorities, since this will now need to be subordinated to achieving this end, while the high costs of reneging on the commitment in terms of international recriminations and a loss of trustworthiness are thought to significantly reduce the chances of it being abandoned for short-term political or economic gain. At the same time however, other rational choice theorists have arrived at exactly the opposite conclusion, and have argued that a floating rather than a fixed exchange rate regime will provide the most optimal policy rule. Since this will allow the value of the national currency to be determined directly by the market, it is argued that movements in the exchange rate will now provide a quick, clear, and forceful signal to private actors as to whenever inflation is emerging, and that the threat of a large fall in the rate will thereby also serve as an effective constraint on the policy-making behaviour of the authorities, and force them to maintain a sound anti-inflationary stance. This dichotomy however leaves the rational choice approach open to the charge of being ambiguous and inconclusive, since both floating and fixed exchange rate regimes are variously regarded as being able to provide the most optimal policy rule. With apparently no *a priori* grounds for choosing between them purely on the basis of rational choice then, the utility of this approach for an analysis of exchange rate policy-making is therefore diminished.

In contrast to the rational choice approach, the second perspective, known as the 'country characteristics' approach, argues that exchange rate policy is not made with a view to avoiding the inherent problems of discretionary economic management, but that it is a technocratic decision based on a cost-benefit analysis of all the options that are available at any one time. As such, the idea of a single 'optimal' policy is replaced by the notion that policy-makers will shift between exchange rate regimes in response to changing circumstances.[3] In particular, the key variables involved in this choice are considered to be the structural features of the country in question. Relevant factors for example are thought to include the size and openness of a country's economy, its degree of economic flexibility, and the pattern of its international trade. One commonly held view which emerges from this is that countries with small and open economies, rigid economic structures, and/or who possess extensive links with a large trading partner will prefer a fixed or tightly managed exchange rate regime as a defence against economic uncertainty and currency instability, while in contrast, countries with large and relatively closed economies, who have more flexible economic structures, and/or who have no suitable trading partner with whom to stabilise their exchange rate will prefer a floating regime, since this will provide them with a greater degree of domestic freedom with which to pursue their policy goals.

In addition to such economic factors, the political structure of a country is also believed to have an important influence. The key variables here are believed to be the relative strength and stability of the government in comparison to its main opposition party. As a general rule, weak and unstable governments facing strong political opposition are thought to prefer a floating rather than a fixed exchange rate regime, since the latter will not only allow the opposition to bolster their economic policy credibility by committing themselves to continuing with the same system, but will also prove to be electorally damaging should the government be forced to abandon it. Fixed exchange rate regimes then, are considered more likely to be adopted by stronger governments, since these will be better placed to defend it and to weather any political storms that may arise as a consequence.

A key problem with the country characteristics approach however, is that there is no consensus between its proponents as to which particular characteristics, or combination of characteristics, are the most important in the policy-making process. In direct opposition to the general views outlined above, it has also been argued for instance that countries with open economies or rigid economic structures will prefer a floating rather than a fixed exchange rate regime, since the flexibility this offers will provide the domestic economy with a degree of insulation from the constraints of the world economy; and that weak governments will prefer fixed rather than floating exchange rate regimes, since this, in common with the rational choice approach, is believed to provide a useful means of strengthening their economic policy credibility. Against this backdrop then, the country characteristics approach must also be regarded as having limited explanatory value.

In contrast to these approaches, the third theoretical perspective contained within the existing literature on exchange rate policy-making argues that the key factors involved are the relative balance of power between various socio-economic interest groups, and their respective degree of political organisation and interaction with the policy-making process. This 'interest group' approach is based on the notion that different groups will possess differing exchange rate preferences according to the nature of their business and the degree to which they are exposed to global competition. It is commonly argued for example that groups which are strongly oriented towards the global market will favour a fixed exchange rate regime in order to reduce the risks involved during the course of their business, while groups whose activities are more heavily weighted towards the domestic market will favour a floating regime since this will allow the authorities to adjust economic policy according to changing circumstances. In addition to this, it is also generally argued that groups whose business involves a high level of foreign purchases will prefer a relatively high exchange rate, since this will reduce the cost of such acquisitions, while groups engaged in domestic competition with foreign producers will favour a depreciated exchange rate, since this will raise the price of imported goods and will thereby increase their own relative competitiveness.[4]

Like the rational choice and the country characteristics approaches however, the interest group approach is also problematic. One problem for example is that there is no consensus as to which economic sectors are the most influential, and to which will be best positioned to realise their demands in the policy-making process. In relation to this, it is also unclear precisely how competing preferences are reconciled by the political system, and it is insufficiently recognised that policy-makers themselves may have interests that are in opposition to those of the dominant interest group. Further still, the assumption that exchange rate policy will simply reflect the preferences of the strongest group is also problematic, since it is extremely unlikely that policy-makers will be willing, or even able to overlook the wider political and economic ramifications of their policy, especially if its consequences prove to be socially unpopular.[5]

While existing theoretical approaches to exchange rate policy-making are not without merit, especially insofar as they draw attention to the anti-inflationary desires of the governing authorities, and to the constraints that are imposed on the policy-making process by wider political and economic pressures, their explanatory utility nonetheless remains circumscribed. Moreover, in addition to their individual difficulties, existing approaches are also open to criticism on broader methodological grounds. In particular, this concerns their failure to address the question of 'social form', namely that of why society itself should assume the specific pattern of organisation that it does. Instead, existing approaches treat the present form of society and its associated 'components', such as its division into separate public and private spheres, political and economic structures, and sectoral interest groups, in an unquestioned, ahistorical, and taken-for-granted manner, as *prima facie* given facts of social life. While this enables systematised accounts of exchange rate policy-making to be constructed by examining the interactions between these various components for causal influence, this approach ultimately lacks any substantial analytical depth, since it provides no means of explaining why these components themselves should exist, and therefore offers no means of examining the influence that the causal factors behind their emergence and reproduction may have on the policy-making process. In short, existing approaches to exchange rate policy-making are unable to conceptualise the fundamental constraints that are imposed upon this process by the wider composition and development of society itself.

A more illuminating analytical approach however can be derived from a Marxist, or more specifically, from an 'open Marxist' methodology. In contrast to more traditional interpretations of Marx, an open Marxist approach is based on a rejection of all forms of determinism, and seeks to replace the popular notion of social 'structures' with a conception of society as an organic process of development constituted by the centrality of class, and by the indeterminacy of class struggle. In contrast to existing approaches to exchange rate policy-making, the key advantage offered by this perspective is that it begins precisely by considering the question of 'social form'. Instead of taking the starting point of analysis to be the separate components of society and the interactions between them, an open Marxist approach begins with society itself as an integral whole, and seeks to understand how and in what way its various constituent parts are derived from, and related to its organisational composition. This provides a basis for analysis that is grounded in a wider social theory than is offered by existing approaches.[6]

Social form and capitalist production

An open Marxist analysis begins by drawing a distinction between the appearance and the essence of social reality. In contrast to its immediate appearance in the form of separate, autonomous, and independently existing components, be they 'spheres' of activity, 'structures', or sectorally defined groups of actors, the essence of social reality is believed to derive from the specific way in which human labour power is organised in the course of social production. The various components of which social reality is comprised are seen instead as the multifarious reflections, or 'theoretical expressions' of relations between people that are established during the process of production, and are simply understood to be the diverse and variegated 'forms' that this process assumes.[7] According to Marx, the most fundamental characteristic of social production has, since the most primitive days of human history, been its division along class lines. Through gaining and retaining control over the means of production, one class (or alliance of classes) has been able to exploit another class (or classes) for its own material gain through the forced and unremunerated extraction of surplus labour. The concept of 'class', which is therefore central to an understanding of social form, is thus not seen as something that is defined in sociological terms (such as a classification by income or social background), and nor is it seen to relate simply to the existence of class consciousness or political struggle, neither of which are necessary for classes as-such to exist. Rather, it is considered to be a fundamentally exploitative relationship arising from the process of social production, as 'the way in which exploitation is embodied in a social structure.'[8]

A subordinate class however does not simply accept its position in the social order. Instead, the existence of class exploitation also generates resistance to this exploitation, and hence gives birth to 'class struggle'. In contrast to more traditional understandings of the term, from an open Marxist perspective 'class struggle' is also not something which is seen simply in terms of consciously directed political action, and nor is it conceived as the occasional and one-sided outburst of direct and open resistance by workers. Instead, class struggle refers to a two-way process, comprising the ongoing resistance to exploitation by the labouring class on the one hand, and the ongoing efforts of the dominant class to impose and maintain it on the other. While not all members of a class will act according to their 'objective' class interests, the centrality of class to the process of social production therefore means that the nature and development of the social forms that this assumes are nevertheless conditioned as a whole by their class character, and by the struggle that this entails. As Marx explains:

> The specific economic form in which unpaid surplus labour is pumped out of the direct producers determines ... its specific political cal form. It is in each case the direct relationship of the owners of the conditions of production to the immediate producers ... in which we find the innermost secret, the hidden basis of the entire social edifice.[9]

The outcome of class struggle however is by no means certain. In contrast to more deterministic interpretations of Marx in which this is postulated in terms of the inevitable overthrow of capitalism by the proletariat, on a more open reading it is seen as a process which is inherently fluid and indeterminate. From an open Marxist perspective then, the most important aspect of a class society is not the way in which human labour is organised in a technical sense (in terms of its specific division of labour and the kind of work that is undertaken), but the way in which class struggle is contained and class exploitation reproduced.[10]

In capitalist society this takes place through the mechanism of the 'value form'. This inheres in the fact that the ordering principle of the capitalist mode of production, and the key feature distinguishing it from other forms of social organisation, is the production of commodities for the sole purpose of exchange. Capitalist production is undertaken in a private context by isolated, independent, and autonomous producers, and takes place in an uncoordinated manner without reference to any social plan or design. The concept of the value form then, refers to the fact that the social connection between producers in a capitalist economy is therefore not felt directly, but is only revealed in an indirect manner through the exchange of commodities on the basis of their value. For Marx, this is determined by the productivity of labour, and is expressed in terms of the average amount of socially necessary labour time that a commodity takes to produce, as opposed to the time that each individual commodity takes to produce *per se*. 'Value' then, is not seen to be a specific property of commodities themselves (although it appears as such), but is the product of a social framework based on commodity exchange.[11]

The basic content of this framework is one of class exploitation. While the mass of the population are separated from the direct means of producing their subsistence and must therefore sell their labour power on an ongoing basis in order to survive, the minority of the population who own the means of production are able to exploit the labour of this propertyless mass for their own material benefit. The specific means by which this exploitation takes place is through the extraction of 'surplus value'. This process is described by Marx in the form of the 'circuit of capital', which is expressed in its general formula as: M–C...P(lp-mp)...C'–M'. In the first phase, M–C, the owner of money capital (M), buys the commodities (C) of labour-power (lp) and means of production (mp) on the open market. In the second phase, these are put together to function as productive capital (P). Here, through the unequal provisions of the labour contract, the capitalist is able to compel the worker to provide their labour power for a greater length of time than that represented by the amount of wages received in remuneration, thereby enabling them to extract a volume of unpaid labour time which is embodied in the commodities produced (C') as surplus value. In the final phase, C'–M', this expanded mass of value in the form of commodities is thrown onto the market for sale in order to be converted into a sum of money greater than that with which the capitalist initially started (M'). Following this, the whole process is then repeated, ideally on a larger scale so as to facilitate ever greater levels of capital accumulation.[12]

This desire for a continual expansion of capital is not merely subjective, but is also driven by the competitive pressures of capitalist production itself. By such means as reducing wages, lengthening the working day, and adopting improved productive techniques and technologies, it is possible for an individual capital to increase its exploitation of labour, and to thereby obtain a higher rate of profit and a greater level of capital expansion. By raising the social productivity of labour however, such actions also impinge upon all other capitals connected to this sphere of production by reducing the amount of labour-time embodied in their commodities, and hence by reducing their value. In so doing, this forces other capitals to seek a similar increase in productivity, leading to the eventual generalisation of more efficient methods and practices. Those capitals who fail to keep apace with such developments will come under growing pressure in the form of declining productivity and a falling rate of profit, eventually leading to bankruptcy and a loss of jobs. Through this process, by pressurising capital to continually increase its exploitation of labour, and by eliminating those capitals that fail to do so, the mechanism of the value form (namely the organisation of society on the basis of 'value') transmits the competitive dynamic of capitalist production to all individual capitals, thereby helping to ensure the continued profitability of capital as a whole, and helping to maintain its continued class domination over labour.

The circuit of capital though cannot be understood as a single circuit, but as an expression of the movement of capitalist production in general presupposes the existence of a vast array of interrelated circuits throughout society. Considered in its entirety, the circuit consists of a unity of all the particular capitals in existence, each at various points of the production process, and each forming but 'partial movements of the reproduction process of the total social capital.'[13] This process however does not proceed smoothly but is vulnerable to various disturbances and crises. Primarily, these derive from the dependency of the circuit of capital on labour power and money. If sufficient quantities and qualities of labour power are not found to be available for exploitation then capitalist production will be inhibited or even prevented, while monetary fluctuations in the form of inflation and deflation can also destabilise the operation of the circuit due to the central role played by money in the mediation of commodity exchange and in the measurement of value in the form of price.[14]

On a more fundamental level, such disturbances are derived from the unstable class composition of capitalist society itself. The availability of labour power for example depends on the ability of capital to impose the daily yoke of work, and can be diminished or withdrawn through various forms of industrial action, while distortions to the price mechanism resulting from changes in the supply and demand for money and commodities are themselves subject to the forces of class struggle. The volume of goods (or rather the amount of value) that is produced is determined for instance by the volume of capital entering into the circuit and by the degree to which it is able to exploit labour (the increasing levels of which lead to periodic crises of overproduction), while the volume of money in circulation is determined, *inter alia*, by the general level of wages, which depends on the relative strength of capital and labour; by the amount of credit extended by the banking system, which is conditioned by the expected levels of future profitability; and by the economic policies of the state, which are also conditioned by perceptions of future economic performance.[15]

The specific effects of monetary disturbances on the circuit of capital however need to be examined according to their particular circumstances, since both rising and falling prices can at different times prove to be beneficial and detrimental to capitalist production. While a moderate level of inflation can help the accumulation of capital and can assist the flow of the circuit by stimulating profitability and by eroding real wages and debts, excessive inflation can deter capital from engaging with the circuit by creating instability and uncertainty over future economic conditions. Undermining the ability of money to measure the value of commodities can distort the operation of the price mechanism on which capitalist production depends, leading to speculation at the expense of productive activity and investment; rising costs can prompt an intensification of class struggle as workers seek higher wages and as capitalists seek to reduce their outgoings; the international competitiveness of the national economy may be reduced; and if taken to its extreme, inflation can even lead to the destruction of the currency and to social collapse. In a similar fashion, a period of deflation can also prove to be beneficial or harmful to the circuit of capital. On the one hand, this can serve to check the damage inflicted by a prior bout of inflation and can help to restore sound conditions for capital accumulation by re-enforcing competitive discipline, though on the other hand deflation can also impede the circuit of capital by creating instability and uncertainty, by reducing prices and profits and by raising the real value of debts, by intensifying class conflict as capitalists seek to reduce costs and wages, and by reducing productive activity and investment.

In order for the circuit of capital to flow normally then, certain conditions must therefore be met. A ready supply of skilled, appropriately priced, and disciplined wage-labour for exploitation is essential in order for capitalist accumulation to take place at all, while a relatively stable currency is necessary to ensure the mediation of commodity exchange and to provide a means of expressing value in the form of price. However, while such factors are clearly crucial to the capitalist mode of production, they themselves are not naturally occurring or self-reproducing, but instead need to be actively and continually created. The means by which this is achieved involves the capitalist state.

The capitalist state

At first glance the capitalist state appears as a neutral 'public' sphere of human activity that is distinct and autonomous from the 'private' sphere of capitalist relations contained within civil society. Conventionally understood as an impartial arbiter whose role it is to discriminate between competing particular interests in order to act in the 'national' or 'general' interest' for the benefit of all its citizens, from an open Marxist perspective such appearances are deemed to be illusory. Instead, the state is not seen as a dispassionate force that is separate from society, and as something which intervenes in it 'from outside', but is regarded as an integral part of the capitalist mode of production itself and is seen to play an essential role in maintaining capitalist class relations.

The origins of the capitalist state are to be found in the long drawn-out social changes and class struggles that led to the decline of feudalism and to the rise of capitalism. The desire of the landed nobility to impose ever greater levels of exploitation on the one hand, and the resistance of serfs to exploitation on the other, drove the lordly class to search for more efficient and profitable ways of extracting surplus labour from the peasant population. Starting in Western Europe, this led to the development of commercial agriculture and to the emergence of industrialisation, accompanied by an expansion of trade and an increasing monetisation of feudal society. These developments also led to the recomposition of class relations, as the direct and openly coercive character of feudalism was gradually supplanted by the emergence of a society based on formally free and equal individuals meeting as buyers and sellers of commodities in the open market. This veneer of apparent equality though, merely concealed the fact that the class relationship had not been abolished, but that it had simply assumed a new form. Control of the means of production was now concentrated in the hands of a small minority on the legal basis of the 'rights' of private property, while the mass of the population were now forced by the hidden and indirectly coercive pressures of the market to continually sell their labour power for wages in order to survive.[16]

An inherent and fundamental feature of these social changes was the emergence of the capitalist state. As the rising economic power of the bourgeoisie facilitated an expansion of their political influence, this enabled a restructuring of the old feudal institutional arrangements along lines that were considered to be more conducive to the maintenance of capital accumulation. In particular, this entailed an institutional separation of the state from civil society. In contrast to the feudal system in which the political and the economic realms of social life were effectively fused such that a person's political position determined their economic position in the social hierarchy and vice versa, a key characteristic of capitalist society was its delineation into distinct and apparently autonomous 'political' and 'economic', or 'public' and 'private' spheres. By giving political form to the newly constituted relations of production in this way, the capitalist state thus materialised as an institutional agency designed to uphold and legitimise the formal rights of private property and to reproduce the inherent class divide this contains.

Such a view of the state stands in direct contrast both to conventional and to more orthodox Marxist perspectives. While such approaches conceptualise the state as an institutional structure that either acts in the national interest or that is capable of being appropriated and wielded by various social groups, classes, or 'fractions' of capital for their own ends, these views ultimately lead to a conception of it as something that is essentially separate from capitalist society. The key problem with this is that such an impression leaves no room for conceptualising the general constraints on state behaviour that emerge from the process of capitalist production itself. This provides no means of explaining for example why it is that the state persistently acts in the interests of capital despite variations in the political complexion of the governing authorities over time, and is similarly unable to account for similarities in the behaviour of states with different social and political structures, such as the widespread adoption of 'social democracy' by Western capitalist nations after the Second World War, and the widespread adoption of 'monetarist' policies by the same states during the 1980s.[17] From an open Marxist perspective however the capitalist state is not understood as an institutional structure or apparatus that is outside economic relations, but is instead conceived as a particular historical form of social organisation, as the 'political' counterpart to the 'economic' process of capitalist production. The necessity for the state to act in the interests of capital is therefore not derived in an arbitrary or contingent fashion, but inheres through its existence as an integral aspect of capitalist relations themselves. Conventional notions of the capitalist state and the economy as two separate-but-connected 'things' that impinge upon each other in an external manner are thus replaced by one in which they are seen as different aspects of a single social system.[18]

The maintenance and reproduction of capitalist relations then, is not something that is automatically ensured, but involves continual action by the state in order to regulate class struggle and to address the various crises that emerge as a result of the instability of the capitalist social form. This does not mean however that the state acts in the interests of all specific capitals, or that it acts in the interests of any particular fraction of capital at the expense of another. Since the circuit of capital exists only as a unity of innumerable competing circuits, and since capital itself needs to transmute through all three of its money, productive, and commodity forms in order to expand, the state can only seek to provide the broad and necessary conditions within which capital expansion as a whole can take place, and hence can act only in the interest of 'capital-in-general'.[19] The limits on state behaviour though cannot be fully determined from an analysis of the state in isolation, since 'the state' itself does not exist in the singular, but can only be properly conceived as part of an international collection of states.[20] Indeed, for Marx, capitalism is a fundamentally and inherently global form of society. The tendency to create the world market is considered to be 'directly given in the concept of capital itself', and international competition is seen as 'the very basis and living atmosphere of the capitalist mode of production.'[21] From this viewpoint, each individual state is therefore considered to be but one part of a unified global system whose defining characteristic is the constitution of political authority on a national basis and the accumulation of capital on an international level. The global capitalist system then, is not seen as a mere sum of its parts, as an aggregation of compartmentalised units, but is 'a single system in which state power is allocated between territorial entities.'[22] In other words, national states are the 'political nodes' in the global flow of capital.[23]

As an integral part of global capitalist relations, the power and legitimacy of the national state is crucially dependent upon the continually expanding accumulation of surplus value within its borders. Since a policy of autarky is only viable for providing the most basic standards of living, such accumulation is itself fundamentally dependent upon an expansion of international trade and commerce. National prosperity and stability therefore rest not only upon the successful integration of the domestic economy, or the 'national' circuit of capital, into the international circuit, but also rest upon the prosperity and stability of the international circuit itself. Conditions within national states are thus subject to global pressures that lie beyond their individual power to control, such that the behaviour of each state is conditioned not only by a need to attract and retain globally mobile capital in order to secure domestic social reproduction, but also by the need to ensure the well-being of international capitalist relations as a whole.[24]

This dependency upon global conditions places certain fundamental pressures and restrictions upon national economic policy-making. The limits to the form, development, and management of each individual state is subject both to the level and development of domestic class struggle, and to global conditions of capital accumulation in general, which are themselves the result of class struggle on a global scale. In overarching terms, this means that each state must provide internationally favourable conditions for surplus value accumulation within its territory lest capital will seek more profitable avenues elsewhere, leading to mounting national economic and political crises. However, because such crises are an inherent feature of capitalist relations themselves, states cannot hope to achieve their resolution, but can only seek to mitigate their effects and strive to gain a better position for themselves within the global system.[25]

For national states, a key element in the achievement of these aims is to ensure the international convertibility of their currencies. This is needed in order to integrate the various territorial components of the global circuit itself, and to enable the continuous flow of international trade and payments. The means by which this convertibility takes place is determined by the exchange rate regime, the particular form of which therefore conditions the means through which the various dynamics and pressures of the global economy are transmitted to the domestic circuit, and conversely, through which the international influence of the domestic circuit itself is felt. In order for convertibility to be successful however, a national state must ensure global confidence in its currency, since if this is not forthcoming, due for example to a decline in national competitiveness or because of domestic instability, then the integration of the national circuit into the global circuit will be threatened, and the prospects for economic and political crises will rise. In this way then, just as the value form transmits the competitive discipline of capitalist relations to individual capitals through the role of money, it also transmits global capitalist discipline to national states through the international system of exchange rates. [26]

State managers and governing strategies

An analysis of state behaviour cannot be complete without an examination of the way in which key policy-makers themselves are influenced by the constraints of the capitalist social form. In economic policy-making terms the most important set of actors within the state are those of the 'core executive'. Although its precise composition may vary according to the specific policy issue at hand, the core executive can be usefully taken as a shorthand term for referring to the leading figures within the government, and for the senior officials at the state finance department and the national central bank. For these key state managers, national economic policy-making is driven by the need to regulate class struggle and to create conditions that are conducive to domestic stability and a more favourable integration for the state into the world system. Within this broad-based remit however, more subjective aims and ambitions also emerge. In particular, these are centred around the achievement of 'high political' goals such as the gaining and retaining of office, and the augmenting of factors such as status, authority, prestige, influence and the like. More specifically, high politics refers to those matters that are of central importance in the management of the state, and contrasts sharply with 'low politics', which can be taken as those matters which are of relatively minor importance, and which are simply 'too dull, time consuming or awkward to deal with'.[27]

The achievement of these various goals however is no simple task. In the first instance the ability of the state to secure the accumulation of capital is circumscribed by the need to contain class struggle and by the dependency of the state upon global conditions. In addition, the core executive are also subject to a wide array of other pressures and constraints deriving from membership of international bodies and organisations, from departmental or party political matters, and from the demands of social interest groups and public opinion generally. The formulation and development of economic policy therefore takes place not only within the limits of the capitalist social form, but also within the constraints of what is actually viable given the various political, economic, cultural, and ideological attributes of the particular state in question.

To help them achieve their aims, key state managers can be said to devise a 'governing strategy'. This will help them to identify the key problems that are faced, and will provide a plan for their resolution based on the particular context within which they are operating. While the development of such a strategy may at times be a fractious process, and while not all members of the core executive may be in complete agreement as to its content (indeed not all may even be involved in its formulation), the construction of a governing strategy will provide state officials with a broad guide to the political and economic terrain in which they are operating, and will offer some means of charting a safe course across it. In general terms, a particularly useful strategy for state managers is to seek to establish and maintain a degree of 'governing autonomy' from the various pressures with which they are faced. The more space and freedom that officials have to implement their key policy tasks, the higher is the likelihood that these will be implemented in a competent fashion, and hence the greater is the prospect that their high political aims will be achieved. The main challenge for the core executive therefore is to develop a governing strategy that will enable them to contain class struggle, to ensure favourable conditions for capital accumulation, and to attain a sufficient degree of autonomy with which to engage in high political activity.[28]

While members of the core executive may at times find it desirable or even necessary to pursue a governing strategy based on the directly visible involvement of the state in economic affairs, such as that associated with 'Keynesian' social democracy, such an approach contains inherent dangers. One major risk for example is that openly visible state intervention can lead to the politicisation of issues which have hitherto been regarded as being of a purely 'economic' character (such as wage levels and working conditions), and can thus lead to growing demands and pressures over these issues being directed at the state itself. In turn, such politicisation also contains the risk that a crisis in the 'economic' sphere will necessitate overt state action in order to secure the continued accumulation of capital, and that this will expose the class character of the state by openly contravening its claim to act in the general interest. A key danger of a governing strategy based on a politicised mode of economic policy-making then, is that in such circumstances this can aggravate class unrest, and can even lead to a wholesale crisis of political authority itself.[29]

Given these risks, a more useful approach for the core executive is to therefore try and remove key areas of economic policy-making from the realm of political accountability through a governing strategy of 'depoliticisation'. The central feature of such a strategy is that this seeks to relocate core aspects of economic policy-making away from the discretionary control of the state, and to place them instead under the control of 'independent' and ostensibly 'non-political' bodies and/or policy rules. By 'placing at one remove the political character of decision-making', a successful governing strategy of depoliticisation can enable the core executive to retain a degree of 'arms-length' control over key economic policy issues, while simultaneously allowing them to disclaim responsibility and hence accountability for such matters. [30]

A key advantage of a depoliticisation strategy is that this can therefore ease pressure on the governing authorities by fragmenting and redirecting class dissatisfaction over economic conditions and policy-making away from the state and into less threatening channels concerned with purely 'economic' or 'political' issues (such as wage levels, democratic representation, human and civil rights and so on), that do not provide enough room for questioning the organisation of society as a whole. Moreover, by 'locking-in' the future direction of economic policy through a credible relinquishing of discretionary control, a strategy of depoliticisation can also serve to condition the expectations, and hence the behaviour of both capital and labour, confining them within the limits set by the policy regime. This ability to constrain expectations is further increased if the set of rules and bodies to which economic policy-making tasks are reassigned are themselves constituted 'externally' as part of an international system, since this will not only enable the authorities to present the regime as being bound up with wider political and economic issues, but will also increase the costs of regime change, thereby enhancing both its credibility and its depoliticising effects. In this way, by imposing an effective discipline on national economic relations, and by furnishing the core executive with a means of insulating themselves from the adverse political and social effects of this process, a governing strategy of depoliticisation can leave key state managers better placed to enforce policies designed to contain class struggle, facilitate the accumulation of capital, and secure a greater degree of freedom for the pursuit of high political goals.[31]

Exchange rate policy-making

It is against this background of economic policy-making in general that exchange rate policy-making therefore needs to be examined. The specific exchange rate regime that will be adopted or maintained at any one time is dependent upon the particular context and aims of the governing strategy that is being pursued by the core executive. Of the various exchange rate regimes that are available for example, a floating regime in which the value of the national currency is free to fluctuate according to the market level of supply and demand can prove to be useful should the authorities wish to pursue a governing strategy of depoliticisation based on domestic policy rules or non-political bodies such as an inflation target and/or central bank independence. One major attraction of this is that a floating regime provides officials with a degree of flexibility and freedom that is not available under more restrictive systems. This can allow them to alter or abandon their strategy should the policy rule prove to be unsuccessful, with less risk of incurring the kind of repercussions that may follow the breaking of international commitments. In addition, this flexibility can also provide officials with a useful 'safety valve', helping to insulate the national circuit of capital from the competitive pressures of the global economy by permitting adverse developments such as rising inflation or declining productivity to be offset through a movement in the exchange rate. A decline in exports due to a loss of competitiveness for example will, *ceteris paribus*, lead to a fall in the value of the national currency which will itself help to redress the economic balance by reducing export prices. Conversely, while movements in the exchange rate can help to protect officials from the failure of a domestic policy rule, they can also help to support such a strategy. A rise in the exchange rate for instance can help to buttress an anti-inflationary commitment by imposing additional deflationary pressure on the economy through higher export prices, while in certain circumstances a fall in the rate can also have a similar effect since higher import prices, a rise in the external debt burden, and the threat of rising inflation can lead to an increase in production costs and justify the imposition of tighter fiscal and monetary measures.[32] Moreover, the mere possibility of a decline in the exchange rate can itself also help to strengthen the credibility of a domestic policy rule by providing a clear signal to the market as to whenever the rule is being broken and to whenever inflationary economic policies are being pursued.[33]

A floating exchange rate regime however is not without its disadvantages. A domestically based policy rule may lack credibility, and may therefore prove to be ineffectual due to the relative ease with which it can be broken or revoked compared to an international commitment. This problem may be compounded by the fact that the depoliticising effects of a domestic rule may also wear thin should economic conditions deteriorate. In the event that the rule itself should come to be seen as a key source of difficulties, then this may not only leave officials with no means of defence against criticism but can even pave the way for a re-politicisation of economic conditions and policy-making, thus putting the governing authorities under even greater pressure. Furthermore, while the ability to change or abandon the rule will still remain an option, there can be no guarantee that the adoption of a new rule will prove to be a success, and in fact the reverse may even be the case, since in reneging on their original policy commitment state managers may now have acquired a reputation for being manipulative, deceitful, and opportunistic.

Further still, while a floating exchange rate can help to ensure macroeconomic stability by offsetting changes in national economic performance through changes in the value of the currency, in other circumstances it can prove to be destabilising. Fluctuations in the exchange rate that are unwarranted by national economic 'fundamentals' (such as levels of economic competitiveness and productivity), but that are the result of factors such as changes in market sentiment or shifting economic conditions elsewhere, may run counter to, and may even undermine domestic policy commitments. Exchange rate uncertainty and instability may adversely affect the integration of the national economy into the international circuit of capital; an excessive rise in the exchange rate may impose an excessive deflationary strain on the economy; while the inflationary pressures resulting from an undue decline in the rate can also erode the effectiveness of an anti-inflationary rule.

To an extent, some of these problems can be overcome by utilising a 'managed' exchange rate regime in which the authorities undertake to limit any excessively large or rapid fluctuations in the rate. This practice, known as 'leaning against the wind', can offer greater stability than a floating regime, and can also enable the authorities to retain many of the benefits of policy flexibility, as well as the advantages of a domestic policy rule, by allowing the rate to adjust to any medium- to long-term changes in underlying fundamentals. Should the pursuit of a domestic policy rule prove to be impractical or undesirable however, another possible strategy for officials is to utilise a floating or a managed exchange rate regime as part of a directly politicised mode of economic policy management. A key advantage of this is that the absence of any firm exchange rate commitment can provide the authorities with the discretionary freedom with which to pursue objectives such as high employment and economic growth, since any rise in inflation and loss of competitiveness can be accommodated by a decline in the value of the currency. This flexibility may be a particularly attractive feature should the authorities wish to ease any economic or political difficulties (especially those closely associated with the breakdown of a policy rule), by allowing the core executive to introduce measures designed to stimulate an economic recovery such as the adoption of a looser fiscal and monetary policy. In relation to this, such a regime also affords the authorities with an opportunity to obtain an economic advantage over competitor nations by deliberately driving down the level of the exchange rate in order to encourage export-led growth, and provides the further advantage in that a politicised governing strategy will make it easier for officials to directly claim the plaudits and hence the political rewards for any success, since no credit need be given to international parties or to non-political domestic organisations.

However, though promising much, these advantages of a floating or managed exchange rate regime may in fact prove to be more apparent than real. Despite the lure of freedom and flexibility, state managers are in reality unable to ignore or even avoid large or rapid movements in the exchange rate since the volume of funds available to the foreign exchange markets is far in excess of that which can be mustered by any national state, and since such developments will have a direct and potentially severe impact on the national economy. In contrast to a floating or a managed exchange rate regime however, a fixed or 'pegged' regime in which the authorities undertake to hold the value of the national currency at or around a specific value can also be consistent with the pursuit of a politicised governing strategy. Although this will require certain provisions in order to ensure that the national economy is afforded a degree of insulation from global capital flows, and in order to enable a periodic alteration in the exchange rate in response to changing national economic and social conditions (features incorporated for example by the postwar Bretton Woods system), a steadier rate can nonetheless help to deliver the benefits of even greater economic certainty and stability, and can therefore help to secure the political advantages associated with a rise in national prosperity.

Despite this however, utilising a 'fixed-but-adjustable' regime as part of a politicised governing strategy also faces several problems. Since the level of the exchange rate will now be determined by the authorities themselves, one possibility is that the chosen value may be too high or too low in relation to national economic conditions, and that the commitment to maintain the rate may therefore lack credibility and/or prove to be difficult to uphold. Indeed, since a politicised strategy is likely to be adopted precisely because the authorities wish to be free to respond to domestic pressures, then the emergence of any political or economic difficulties are themselves likely to generate speculative pressures that may destabilise the regime or even force a change in the rate. On a more general level though, while the pursuit of a politicised mode of economic policy management can allow the authorities to take all the credit for policy successes, such an approach will also subject them to growing social pressures and will make them directly and visibly responsible for economic conditions, thereby curtailing their freedom of high political manoeuvre. Given the unstable and inherently crisis-ridden nature of capitalist society then, this therefore remains a high risk strategy.

Faced with these various difficulties, a more useful approach for the governing authorities can be the pursuit of a governing strategy of depoliticisation based on a fixed exchange rate regime. A key benefit of this is that by committing themselves to maintain a fixed rate with provision for realignment only in exceptional circumstances, the authorities can impose a more credible constraint on their discretionary freedom than by using either a fixed-but-adjustable regime or a domestically based policy rule. Not only will reneging on this commitment now prove to be more costly in terms of international as well as domestic repercussions, but the adoption of a fixed regime will also serve to 'lock-in' the future direction of economic policy in general, since this will now need to be geared towards ensuring the maintenance of the chosen exchange rate. A particular advantage of this, is that such a constraint can help to ensure that national economic conditions remain internationally competitive, since a decline in competitiveness will now require a tightening of economic policy in order to prevent a fall in the value of the currency. While it still remains possible for the authorities to set the exchange rate at a relatively undervalued level in order to gain a competitive advantage or to offset a competitive deficiency, such an approach will now run the risk of producing rising levels of inflation that may eventually destabilise and undermine the regime. In the opposite fashion, although it contains deflationary dangers, a fixed regime also offers state managers the ability to strengthen the competitive discipline on the national economy by establishing a relatively high level for the exchange rate, since even tighter and tougher economic policies will now be required to maintain it.

In political terms, a fixed exchange rate regime can also offer useful benefits. Among these is the ability to shield state managers from the unpalatable social and political effects that may result from the economic constraints of the regime. By enabling the effects and the responsibility for tough economic policies to be presented as having derived from the regime itself rather than from the discretionary behaviour of the core executive, a fixed regime can thereby make it easier for officials to disclaim accountability for key economic policy decisions, and can even help to remove such issues themselves from the political agenda. Moreover, these economic and political advantages are both likely to be enhanced if the regime itself is embedded in a wider set of international commitments and obligations (such as European integration), since this will further legitimise the maintenance of the regime, and will enable its constraints to be further presented as emanating 'from outside'.

Despite these benefits however, a fixed exchange rate regime is also not without its difficulties. The ability to gain a competitive advantage through an undervalued exchange rate, or to enforce greater economic discipline through the use of a relatively high exchange rate cannot be available to all nations at the same time and will thus depend on the various strategies that are being pursued by other countries. Furthermore, such moves may themselves create or exacerbate instability in the national and international circuits of capital, and may therefore prove, in the event, to be counterproductive. A more general problem associated with the use of a fixed regime though, is its lack of flexibility. By committing themselves to maintain a specific value for the national currency, state managers leave themselves open to the danger that a change in economic circumstances, either domestically or in the country to which the currency itself has been fixed, can lead to the development of a 'internal–external' conflict between the aims of maintaining the exchange rate and the aims of ameliorating social and political pressures through a more relaxed economic policy stance. The main risk here is that if such a conflict is allowed to go unchecked, then this can eventually lead to the growth of speculative pressures against the currency as questions about the will or the ability of the authorities to continue defending the rate begin to rise, and can in some circumstances ultimately lead to the collapse of the regime itself.

One way of overcoming some of these problems is through a process of monetary union. This can strengthen both the credibility and the discipline of a fixed exchange rate regime by completely removing the possibility of any future change in the value of the national currency, and can further strengthen its depoliticising properties, since key economic policy issues will now be even further removed from the sphere of democratic control and accountability. Despite these benefits however, a strategy of monetary union also contains its own dangers. The complete lack of flexibility now means that any deterioration in national economic conditions cannot be alleviated through a change in the exchange rate or through the adoption of a more relaxed economic policy stance, with the result that should the national economy fail to adapt to the constraints of the regime then the risk of social and political tensions will increase, raising the ultimate danger that the legitimacy of the union itself could be undermined.

Concluding remarks

This chapter has argued that existing theoretical approaches to exchange rate policy-making are problematic. In particular, their failure to consider the question of social form is thought to prevent such approaches from adequately conceptualising the constraints that are imposed on the policy-making process by the organisational composition and development of capitalist society itself. In contrast, an approach based on an 'open Marxist' methodology is able to offer a more useful framework of analysis. By conceptualising the apparently separate and autonomous components of capitalist society as aspects of a unified social process that is conditioned by the development of an indeterminate class struggle, an open Marxist approach facilitates an analysis of exchange rate policy-making from within a wider social context. This leads to a view of exchange rate policy-making as a component part of a wider governing strategy that is made by the core executive with a view to containing class struggle, providing favourable conditions for capital accumulation, and ensuring a sufficient degree of governing autonomy for the pursuit of high political aims. However, while this alternative analytical approach provides a means of surmounting the methodological difficulties posed by conventional theoretical perspectives, its claims nevertheless need to be substantiated empirically. The attempt to do so begins in the following chapters with an extensive analysis of Britain's return to the gold standard in 1925.

3
Contextualising the Return to Gold

Introduction

Britain's return to the gold standard in 1925 at the prewar parity of $4.86 is one of the key and defining moments in its political and economic history. This policy episode has been the subject of intense scholarly attention, and is one that is widely regarded as a classic case study into the process of exchange rate policy-making. The purpose of this chapter however is to provide the contextual background for a new analysis of this policy decision. Traditional explanations for the return to gold are shown to contain a number of shortcomings, and an alternative account based on the theoretical framework developed during the previous chapter is presented. This theoretical analysis is followed by an examination of the empirical backdrop to the return, which charts the development of a growing political and economic crisis in the British state from the last third of the nineteenth century. This shows that the return to gold at $4.86 was the key component of a governing strategy designed to address these difficulties through the imposition of financial discipline and the depoliticisation of economic conditions and policy-making. The chapter begins however, with a brief summary of the 'gold standard' itself.

The gold standard

The 'gold standard' was a monetary system in which national currencies and gold were inter-convertible at legally defined ratios, and in which gold could be freely imported or exported to and from participating nations without restraint. Gold provided the medium (or 'standard') through which the value of all participating currencies could be measured and compared with each other, with the ratio between any two currencies (known as the 'parity', or the 'par value') being determined by their relative gold content. During the nineteenth century for example, one pound sterling could be converted at the Bank of England into 113 grains of fine gold, which in turn could be exchanged in the United States for $4.86, thereby establishing a parity between the two currencies of £1 = $4.86 or $1 = £0.205.

The gold standard was first introduced in England during the eighteenth century (although it was not placed on a *de jure* footing until 1821) and by the 1880s had been adopted by most of the world's major trading nations, effectively establishing the first truly global exchange rate system. By allowing the inter-convertibility of their currencies in this manner, nations participating in the gold standard effectively became part of an international mechanism for constraining exchange rates, national price levels, and discretionary economic policy-making within tightly defined limits. The operation of this mechanism can be clearly illustrated through the interaction between two gold standard countries. If the price of goods produced by one country (for example Britain) rose above those of another gold standard country (for example the United States) due to factors such as a decline in competitiveness or the pursuit of inflationary economic policies, then all other things being equal, Britain would experience a decline in the demand for its exports and a subsequent fall in its exchange rate with the dollar. If this reached the point at which it became profitable for traders to convert sterling into gold and use this to purchase goods from the United States (accounting for variables such as the cost of transport and insurance), then gold would duly flow out of Britain and into America.

This would now indicate to the Bank of England that a rise in interest rates was required in order to reverse the outflow, since Britain could not remain on the gold standard if its reserves of gold became exhausted. The result therefore, would be a contraction of credit, a curtailment of demand, and downward pressure on prices and wages. In converse fashion, the inflow of gold to America would now indicate the need for a reduction in US interest rates, leading to an expansion of credit, a rise in demand, and upward pressure on prices and wages. As this process continued, the price levels of the two countries would once again come to approximate each other, their respective exchange rates would move back towards parity, and economic equilibrium would be restored. In this way, the gold standard therefore provided participants with an effective and ostensibly automatic means of ensuring the pursuit of non-inflationary economic policies, and with a valuable safeguard against political interference with the economy.

In practice however the gold standard did not operate in such a clean and precise manner as this. Central banks frequently sought to neutralise the effects of gold flows through measures designed to manipulate the supply of money (such as the buying and selling of securities), while many countries, especially those on the 'periphery' of the world system, frequently opted for a temporary departure from the regime in times of severe pressure rather than endure the scale of deflation that would be required to remain on it. Moreover, the operation of the gold standard during its 'classical' nineteenth century era was also underpinned by several fortuitous factors. An unparalleled expansion of the world economy provided a continuous supply of new markets as outlets for surplus value; a general absence of major war combined with the relative weakness of the international working class ensured political and economic stability; and a steady rise in the global supply of gold enabled the increasing demand for its use to be met without destabilising its utility as a monetary measure. In addition, the system was also supported by a substantial degree of central bank co-operation between the major gold standard countries (namely Britain, America, France, and Germany), and by the centrally orchestrating agency of the Bank of England, a role deriving from Britain's global economic dominance, which helped to ensure that the regime continued to function in a relatively smooth and harmonious manner.

Despite the success of the gold standard however, by 1914 these factors were starting to break down, and with the outbreak of the First World War the system itself collapsed amidst a haemorrhaging of global financial confidence. Attempts to reconstruct the gold standard as an international regime after the war were hampered by a series of seemingly intractable economic and political difficulties, and by the time this was finally achieved in 1928, these pressures were now leading to the emergence of a new global crisis. As the world economy descended into the worst depression in its history, gold standard nations were increasingly compelled to abandon the regime, and instead turned to protective measures in an attempt to shield themselves from the full force of the downturn. By the time the world once again descended into war at the end of the 1930s, any hopes that the regime could be restored for a second time had long been extinguished. The gold standard was now extinct.[1]

The conventional narrative

In Britain the attempt to return to the gold standard after the First World War was finally accomplished in 1925 with the pound sterling being restored to its old prewar parity of $4.86. The 'conventional narrative' that has developed to account for this policy decision is based on an eclectic mix of overlapping motives and themes. One of the most common of these is that the return was driven by long-held values and ideational factors. The longevity of Britain's commitment to the gold standard is thought to have given rise to deeply ingrained 'sentiments', 'habits', and 'governing traditions', such that an adherence to the regime at $4.86 came to be viewed by the vast majority of people as the normal and natural way of life. This is also thought to have been reinforced by considerations of 'national pride' and 'prestige' deriving from the international supremacy of the pound, and by a belief that Britain even had a 'moral obligation' to ensure sterling's convertibility into gold at the age-old parity. From this perspective, domestic opinion in Britain is thus believed to have regarded the departure from the regime during the First World War as a purely temporary affair, and the return to gold at the prewar par is considered to have simply been the accepted thing to do.[2]

A second prominent theme within traditional accounts of this policy decision is that the restoration of the gold standard at $4.86 was also largely driven by economic factors. According to this view, Britain's governing authorities attributed the high level of prosperity enjoyed during the nineteenth century to the operation of the international gold standard, which was seen to have provided stability and certainty to world finance and trade, and to have established an effective bulwark against inflation. On this basis, it is thought that the reconstruction of this regime was seen to offer the best means of enabling Britain to overcome its postwar economic difficulties of rising inflation and high unemployment by ensuring a stable international environment for free trade and commerce. This would help the world economy to recover from the trauma of war, would facilitate renewed growth in British exports, and would restore global confidence in sterling. From this perspective then, the decision to return to gold is therefore considered to have been an 'employment policy', and to have essentially been motivated by a desire to return to a prewar 'golden age'.[3]

In contrast, another common theme in the conventional narrative is that the return to gold was not designed in the interests of Britain's economy as a whole, but was instead made to benefit the particular financial interests of the City of London. According to this line of argument, the City held a return to gold at $4.86 as being crucial for the restoration of its financial earnings and for its position as the world's leading financial centre, while the government were imbued with the notion that the interests of the financial sector were of paramount importance. This is thought to have derived from the 'exceptional' character of Britain's economic structure, with the predating of industrial development by that of finance and commerce being thought to have produced a divergence of interests between the manufacturing and financial sectors, and to have given the latter an unequal influence over the policy-making process through extensive socio-cultural links with the Bank of England and the Treasury. As a result of this, it is therefore claimed that the interests of the City were granted a privileged status by Britain's state managers, while those of British industry were subsequently left marginalised.[4]

In addition to economic considerations, the final theme offered by conventional accounts of Britain's return to gold is that it was chiefly motivated by political factors. In particular, it is argued that the policy was largely driven by departmental self-interest, and that it was designed to further the concerns of senior officials within the Bank of England, the Treasury, and the Cabinet. On the one hand, the Bank and the Treasury are thought to have wanted a return to gold in order to restore their institutional power and status that had been lost to politicians during the war. A proliferation of new ministries and a vast expansion of wartime spending had dramatically curtailed the Treasury's ability to control public expenditure, while the Bank had lost their traditional control over monetary policy and were now also facing the prospect of nationalisation. On the other hand, Cabinet ministers are believed to have seen a return to gold as an effective means of insulating themselves from the social pressures of postwar reconstruction. Handing control of interest rates back to the Bank of England and re-establishing the economic policy-making constraints of the gold standard, it is thought, would enable ministers to resist demands for large-scale social reform and at the same time evade the responsibility for the unpopular effects of a return to financial orthodoxy.[5]

Based on these conventional explanations for Britain's return to the gold standard at $4.86, traditional assessments of the decision tend to fall into two camps. The first of these is the classical 'Keynesian' view that the return to gold was one of Britain's major policy disasters of the twentieth century. In restoring the gold standard at the old exchange rate, the governing authorities are believed to have mistakenly overvalued the pound by around 10% given Britain's prevailing structure of costs and prices, and are thus considered to have miscalculated the extent of the adjustment that this would impose upon the British economy. As a result, the authorities are thought to have markedly reduced the competitiveness of British exports, to have forced the maintenance of high levels of tax and interest rates in order to defend the par value of the pound, and to have inadvertently produced industrial stagnation, chronically high levels of unemployment, and outbreaks of severe industrial unrest, the apogee of which was a general strike in 1926. Furthermore, the persistence of these difficulties is also believed to have contributed to the emergence of a financial crisis, culminating in a huge speculative attack against the pound and the enforced abandonment of the gold standard in September 1931. On this basis, proponents of the Keynesian view therefore argue that insofar as a managed money policy was not yet considered to be feasible, Britain should instead have returned to gold at a lower exchange rate, since this would have reduced the pressure on the old export industries, thereby helping to ensure a higher level of economic growth, lower unemployment, and industrial peace.[6]

In contrast, a second 'revisionist' assessment of the return to gold argues that the difficulties experienced by Britain after 1925 were primarily due to factors other than the par value of the pound. Although acknowledging that the return to $4.86 added to the problems of British exporters, proponents of this view claim that factors such as a fall in American prices, competitive devaluations by France and Belgium, and the rigidity of domestic prices and wages (buoyed by relatively high unemployment benefits, excessive trade union power, and labour immobility) exerted a much greater influence. From this perspective, while the decision to return to gold at $4.86 is still generally regarded as having been a policy failure, it is therefore not seen as a grievous policy error, but is regarded as having been a sound and justifiable decision given the known conditions of the time. Revisionists claim that in 1925 it was not unreasonable to have expected the British economy to have withstood an exchange rate of $4.86, and point out that there was no real support for any alternative to a return to the gold standard at this level. As such, in contrast to the Keynesian analysis, it is argued that returning to gold at a lower exchange rate would not only have failed to avoid the difficulties that were subsequently encountered, but may even have exacerbated them by easing the pressure on Britain's economy to remain internationally competitive.[7]

An alternative view

While the conventional narrative concerning Britain's return to gold is not without merit, especially insofar as it draws attention to the desire of the governing authorities to establish an effective anti-inflationary mechanism and to protect themselves from unpopular policies after the war, it is also subject to a number of shortcomings. The emphasis on the role of values and ideational factors for example, not only fails to sufficiently explain how and why such factors came into existence, and how they managed to endure in the face of opposing values and ideas, but also reveals little about the actual development of the gold standard policy itself, since 'tradition', 'prestige', 'financial morality' and the like remained just as prevalent following the loss of the gold standard after 1931 as they were before 1925. The emphasis on the institutional dominance of the City too, is similarly problematic. This both fails to sufficiently demonstrate in empirical terms precisely how and in what way causal influence was exerted by the City during the development of the gold standard policy, and overemphasises the divergence between Britain's financial and industrial sectors. In empirical terms the strength and international predominance of the pound, deemed crucial to the interests of the City, was itself dependent on the global strength of British manufacturing industry, while in theoretical terms no single 'fraction' of capital can have substantially different interests from those of capital as a whole, since capital itself must transmute through all three of its money, commodity, and productive forms in order to expand. As such, the interests of finance, industry, and commerce must therefore be seen as interwoven rather than separate, while state managers, as politically responsible for conditions in the domestic circuit of capital generally, must also therefore be seen as concerned with the total pattern of domestic economic activity rather than with the interests of any particular sector.

Another problem with traditional explanations of Britain's return to gold is that these also tend to overstate either the 'economic' or the 'political' aspects of the policy rather than attempting to conceptualise the inter-relationship between its political and economic aims. Explanations which view the policy as having been designed to resolve Britain's postwar economic difficulties for instance, fail to recognise fully the political advantages that it would provide for the governing authorities, while conversely, explanations which emphasise the political benefits of the return for state officials similarly underplay its economic advantages. Although it is a well-established maxim that the return to gold would enable the authorities to avoid responsibility for unpopular policies and to thereby increase their autonomy from social pressures, explanations focusing on such political benefits do not sufficiently acknowledge that these 'unpopular policies' themselves may have been deliberately designed to provide the economic advantages of greater competitive discipline upon capital and labour.

These difficulties are further compounded by the fact that many of the material benefits that are believed to have motivated the decision are derived from an excessively narrow timeframe of analysis in that they are seen to have emerged from events during and immediately after the First World War. Such a periodisation crucially overlooks the influence of prewar developments upon the decision making context, and is thus only able to offer a partial understanding of the aims and motivations informing the gold standard policy. Although the war undoubtedly exacerbated the various problems that Britain faced during the 1920s, given that their roots are to be found in the period prior to 1914, the implication that the conflict was solely or even primarily responsible for them must therefore be seen as erroneous.

In contrast, an analysis based on the alternative view of exchange rate policy-making developed in the previous chapter offers a markedly different way of understanding and assessing the return to gold. From this perspective the policy is not thought to have been primarily driven by long-held values and ideational factors, but by more immediate economic and political considerations; it is not thought to have been motivated by a desire to return to a prewar golden age, but to resolve difficulties that had their origins in the prewar period; it is not considered as having been an attempt to serve the particular interests of the City, but to have been directed at the British economy as a whole; and it is not understood to have been primarily driven by either economic or political ambitions, but to have been designed to provide both economic and political benefits. From this alternative view, the return to the gold standard is instead seen to have been the central component of a wider governing strategy designed to contain class struggle, to provide favourable conditions for capital accumulation, and to secure a greater freedom of high political manoeuvre for the governing authorities. More specifically, the policy was designed to address long term political and economic difficulties within the British state through the imposition of financial discipline on capital and labour, and through the depoliticisation of monetary and economic policy-making.

On this basis it is also possible to reach an alternative assessment of the policy. Although in economic terms the return to gold cannot be regarded as having been a great success, producing no significant change in Britain's pattern of economic activity and no substantial breakthrough in competitiveness, in political terms the strategy was largely successful in establishing a credible and a depoliticised framework for economic policy management. This enabled the governing authorities to effectively disclaim responsibility for economic conditions and policy-making, effectively reduced the pressure on state officials, and ensured a greater degree of high political freedom for key state managers than that prevailing since the abandonment of the gold standard during the First World War. The rest of this chapter then, outlines the empirical background to the return to gold from this alternative perspective, charting the emergence of an economic and political crisis in the British state during the last third of the nineteenth century, and examining the difficulties encountered by the authorities in their initial attempts to resolve it.

The crisis of the British state

For much of the nineteenth century Britain was the world's leading economic power. It produced almost a third of the world's manufacturing output, provided well over a third of its industrial exports, supplied much of its capital, and accounted for a fifth of all international trade. Industrially, Britain's strength derived from its old staple exports of textiles, heavy metals, and shipbuilding (to which were later added engineering equipment and coal), and though ever-rising imports of foodstuffs and raw materials led to a progressively worsening deficit in its balance of trade, this gap was more than filled by Britain's invisible earnings, which derived primarily from the City of London as the world's foremost financial centre. This pattern of economic activity was underpinned by a policy regime designed to ensure a minimal involvement of the state in economic affairs. An adherence to the gold standard was buttressed by a firm commitment to the principles of *laissez faire* and to the maintenance of a Gladstonian balanced budget, while political stability was ensured through the fragmentation and marginalisation of the working class, a theme resonating from the violent suppression of Chartism during the 1830s through to the judicial suppression of trade unionism in the Osborne and Taff Vale cases of the early 1900s.[8]

From the 1870s however this halcyon era began to disintegrate. As competitor nations began to develop with increasing vigour, Britain's global economic dominance was progressively undermined. By 1914 its share of world manufacturing output had fallen by more than half from its peak during the mid-nineteenth century, its global share of industrial exports had declined by more than a quarter, and the City's international position was under increasing pressure from rival financial centres in Berlin, Paris, and New York. At the same time, Britain's industrial structure was also becoming increasingly misaligned in relation to the changing demands of the global market as world trade began to shift towards newer and more advanced industries such as motor vehicles, electrical engineering, chemicals, and consumer durables. Nevertheless, despite this onset of relative economic decline, domestic awareness of the need for adaptation remained limited. By 1914 Britain was still the world's leading economy, demand for British goods and capital remained strong, and the availability of captive markets within the Empire was helping to shield industry and finance from the growing need for organisational and productive changes.[9]

Accompanying these economic difficulties, the latter years of the nineteenth century were also a time of growing political difficulties in Britain. Efforts to contain mounting social tensions were leading to a seemingly inexorable rise in public expenditure, undermining the commitments to *laissez faire* and a balanced budget, while the growth of working class dissatisfaction with their position in British society was giving a strong impulse to their industrial and political organisation. In 1873 the Trades Union Congress (TUC) was established in an attempt to increase the influence of labour in industrial affairs, and in 1900 the Labour Representation Committee (later becoming the Labour Party) was formed in order to further working class interests through Parliament. In the years immediately preceding the First World War however, the problem of labour discontent became particularly acute. From 1910 to 1914 rising disillusion with the pursuit of social reform through constitutional means produced a wave of unparalleled labour unrest, leading to a doubling in the average number of new industrial disputes compared to the previous decade, and to a five-fold increase in the average number of working days lost.[10]

The character of this 'Great Unrest' was also gravely disconcerting to Britain's governing authorities. A marked increase in the popularity of radical ideas, even among traditionally moderate elements of the labour movement, was accompanied by increasing discontent from other sections of society such as the Irish Nationalists and the

Suffragettes, creating an impression that the old order itself was now falling apart. In response, the government sought to implement a strategy of containment. Fearing that direct intervention would merely exacerbate the problem, though equally fearful that to do nothing at all would have the same effect, officials turned to a mixture of coercion and concessions, combining the use of force with palliatives such as the introduction of a residual minimum wage for the most vulnerable workers, and the establishment of a National Industrial Council to help settle disputes. While this approach proved to be relatively successful in stalling the spread of radicalism, in 1914 the unrest began to intensify still further as Britain's most powerful and militant trade unions, the Miners' Federation of Great Britain (MFGB), the Transport Workers Federation, and the National Union of Railwaymen joined forces to establish the 'Triple Alliance'. This raised the prospect that a huge strike could soon be used for political ends, and seemed to portend a new and even more dangerous wave of working class discontent.[11]

These economic and political difficulties were exacerbated by the First World War. Britain's international position was further undermined by the intense strain placed on its industrial and financial resources, by high levels of inflation (which caused wages to double and wholesale prices to rise by two-and-a-half times), and by the effects of the conflict on the global economy. Many countries cut off from international markets by the hostilities were forced to develop their own industrial capacities, especially in staple goods; many of Britain's old export markets were severely damaged; and the United States now superseded Britain as the world's leading economic power. Moreover, Britain's ability to cope with these pressures was also diminished. The national debt rose from £650 million in 1914 to an enormous £7800 million in 1918 as politicians chose to finance the war through borrowing rather than higher taxation, while the management of economic policy was further complicated by an enforced suspension of the gold standard due to the rising cost of maintaining the exchange rate. Although sterling remained technically convertible into gold throughout the conflict (albeit at a slightly devalued rate of $4.76) in order to provide a stable conduit for the vital flow of war supplies and finance from abroad, a combination of moral suasion against the withdrawal of gold and an inability to insure gold shipments meant that the regime was now effectively inoperative.[12]

The war also propelled the governing authorities into an unprecedented expansion of state control over the economy. The necessity for this was starkly illustrated in 1915 as revelations of military shortages led to the collapse of the Liberal government and to the establishment of a wartime coalition. This was followed by a systematic application of state management, leading to the suspension of restrictive trade union practices, the abolition of the right to strike, the imposition of tight regulations on prices, wages, profits, and production, and the introduction of strict controls on the movement of goods and labour. The supply of money and credit was also taken over by the state, with the Treasury issuing their own currency notes, and with the Bank of England coming under extreme pressure (including the threat of nationalisation) to defer to the government's wishes on interest rate decisions.[13]

While these measures successfully raised the efficiency of wartime production however, they also had the effect of transforming economic conditions and policy-making into overtly political issues. This made the governing authorities directly responsible for such matters, and put them under growing pressure from representatives of capital and labour as both now began to direct their grievances towards the state rather than at each other. A continuation of labour unrest throughout the war for example, driven by rising prices and the draconian nature of the government's controls, forced officials to continually intervene in order to resolve disputes, while the growing popularity of radical ideas combined with a large rise in trade union membership (from 3.4 million in 1913 to 5.5 million by 1918) compelled the introduction of wide-ranging measures designed to secure working class support for the war effort. These included higher wages, more extensive price controls, the entry of the Labour Party into the wartime coalition, and promises of great postwar social reforms in areas such as health, education, industrial relations, and the franchise. In addition to this, the war also increased the political organisation of capital. Many senior businessmen were drawn into the state's machinery for wartime management, and the number of employer organisations grew rapidly in response to the heightened strength and status of the labour movement. The largest of these was the Federation of British Industries (FBI), which was established in 1916, and which by 1919 was widely considered to be the most senior channel through which the views of British industry could be represented to the state.

A further problem for Britain's governing authorities as a result of the politicisation of economic conditions and policy-making during the war, was that this also raised the level of expectations from capital and labour as to what could be expected from the state in the postwar period. Many industrialists for example now pressed state officials for the introduction of protectionist measures in order to help Britain win an expected postwar trade battle with Germany, while the majority of industrialists, traders, and financiers called for closer consultation with the government, and pressed officials for a rapid dissolution of all state controls after the war and for cuts in tax and public spending in order to raise profits by reducing production costs. The labour movement however, harboured quite different designs for the postwar state. Though many on the left were looking forward to a re-emergence of the prewar sharpening of class conflict and to the destruction of capitalism (though with little consideration of what to replace it with), the majority of labour opinion held the view that the best way to further working class aims was to work within the existing system, and in line with public opinion generally were now looking forward to an era of great social reform. To consolidate this, moderate labour opinion not only pressed for the retention of many of the state's wartime controls, but also sought to buttress this with the introduction of a Capital Levy on wartime profits, and with a programme of widespread nationalisation.[14]

Anarchy and revolution

The main aims of Britain's governing authorities as they emerged from the war were to withdraw from their direct involvement with the economy, to reduce and contain labour unrest and inflation, and to secure a rapid economic recovery and an adjustment to changing global conditions. The most influential official body on postwar reconstruction for example, the Committee on the Currency and Foreign Exchanges After the War (better known as the Cunliffe committee after its Chairman, Sir Walter Cunliffe, the former Governor of the Bank of England), warned that high inflation and labour unrest posed the main dangers to Britain's postwar competitiveness and social stability. Similar sentiments too were expressed by the less prestigious Committee on Financial Facilities After the War, which warned that continuing inflation would lead to a 'grave disaster', and by the Governor of the Bank of England, Brien Cokayne, who observed that 'the most disquieting feature' of the present situation was 'the prevalence of the "Strike" habit and the pace with which the vicious circle of rising wages and rising prices is revolving.'[15] Officials were also keen to assert the need for an adjustment in Britain's pattern of economic activity, with the Balfour Committee on Commercial and Industrial Policy emphasising the necessity for Britain to keep up with advances in productive methods and technology, and with Sir Otto Niemeyer (one of the key figures in the return to gold, though at this time still an undersecretary at the Treasury) later remarking that it was now imperative for Britain to face up to the 'brute facts' of the postwar world.[16]

Such views were prevalent throughout official circles. While some sections, such as the Ministry of Reconstruction and the Haldane Committee on the postwar machinery of British government, were now calling for greater state intervention in order to help support postwar economic growth, reconstruction, and social reform, the dominant view of the governing authorities at this time was that state intervention had produced wholly deleterious economic and political effects, and that it was now therefore essential that this be reduced to a minimum. As Austen Chamberlain, the Chancellor in the postwar coalition explained, state control was not only prolonging industrial unrest, since neither capital or labour 'would say the last word as to what they were prepared to concede', but it had now eliminated 'all the usual motives which induced economic production', and had placed 'the whole burden of making things move ... upon the Controller'.[17]

The central component of the governing strategy that was adopted to deal with these difficulties was a return to the gold standard at the prewar parity of $4.86. This, it was thought, would re-establish an 'automatic machinery' for helping to force prices and wages to conform to internationally prevailing standards, would re-expose the British economy to the competitive pressures of the world market, and at the same time would also ease the pressure on the governing authorities by ostensibly precluding discretionary control over economic affairs. Returning control of interest rates to the Bank of England would rule out any political interference in monetary policy, and would also displace questions about the general direction of economic policy as a whole from the political realm of democratic accountability, since this would now be subordinated to the need to maintain the value of the pound. Furthermore, placing the Bank within the confines of an international regime constituted by the need to defend an exchange rate set by the government would also neutralise the accountability of Bank officials, thus enabling Britain's authorities as a whole to disclaim responsibility for economic conditions and policy-making. As the Cunliffe report explained, a return to gold would ensure that monetary policy was 'permitted a freedom from State interference' not possible 'under a less rigid currency system'. Or as Ralph Hawtrey (the Treasury's Director of Financial Enquiries) later put it:

> The principal ground for entrusting credit regulation to an independent Central Bank is to place it outside political criticism. If the

intervention of the Government is to be a normal part of credit regulation, the way is opened to political criticism.[18]

These advantages of a depoliticised mode of economic policy management were also echoed in the deliberations of the Cunliffe committee. The notion of establishing a state controlled central bank after the war for example was forcefully rejected by Cunliffe himself, who argued that those in charge would have to be 'super-human' in order to handle the responsibility, while as Sir John Bradbury, a Joint Permanent Secretary to the Treasury and another key figure in the return to gold remarked:

We are just about to sail on uncharted seas and to enter into a new world. It is quite possible, human nature being fallible, that those directors might make an error which would be disastrous to the country. Do you not think it would be difficult to find people to act as directors with an absolutely unfettered discretion on a matter of such vital importance as that?[19]

While establishing an automatic regime for economic policy management would therefore provide the governing authorities with an effective means of avoiding responsibility for such issues, it would not however preclude any official control. Rather, this would be retained, but placed at 'arms-length'. As Niemeyer later explained, although an independent central bank was essential in order to avoid 'short-sighted and dangerous political influence' over monetary policy, such an arrangement would not signal the abolition of state control, but would mean simply that this was now 'farmed out', leaving 'expert economic problems to be solved by an independent authority acting on economic grounds only'.[20] In addition to this, a return to gold would also reduce the pressure on state officials by providing a clear framework for economic policy decisions, thereby helping to discipline the postwar expectations of capital and labour. As Hawtrey again put it, while continuing with a discretionary monetary policy would depend:

purely on the judgement of the Bank [of England] which may be fallible, and is far less clearly understood by traders etc. concerned. With a gold standard the dangers of excessive prices are apparent to everyone and the movement in the Bank reserves is at once a warning which everyone understands.[21]

Despite these benefits however, state officials were aware that given the rise in prices and wages during the war, a process of rapidly withdrawing from the economy and returning to a gold standard at $4.86 would impose harsh deflationary pressures and would therefore contain great social and political dangers. Cokayne for instance warned that deflation would be 'a very painful process', Bradbury pointed out that a return to gold would be incompatible with the government's 'very large and very costly schemes of social reform', and that there would be 'considerable difficulty' in reducing wages given the imminent extension of the franchise, while Cabinet ministers were becoming increasingly concerned that the shock of rapidly removing the state's wartime controls would lead to severe economic dislocation and social disorder.[22]

The reality of these dangers became clearly apparent during the early months of 1919, as discontent with the slow pace of social reform triggered a new wave of labour unrest on a scale which surpassed even that of the prewar turmoil. The number of new strikes in the first year after the war was more than twice the annual average for the previous decade, and the number of working days lost was more than double the annual average of the Great Unrest.[23] To make matters worse, a resumption of Triple Alliance activity following a wartime interlude and the spread of unrest to sections of the police and the armed forces were raising ministerial doubts about the security of the state itself, while to compound this, the international situation was also becoming increasingly turbulent, with revolution in Hungary, and with the threat of revolution in Austria, Germany, and parts of the British Empire. Not surprisingly, this rise in labour radicalism was extremely disconcerting to state officials. The Ministry of Labour warned of 'a large mass of discontent' within Britain, and called on the government to encourage 'responsible' trade unionism in order to strengthen the position of labour moderates, a view that was also shared by Bonar Law (the leader of the Conservative Party), who warned that moderate trade unionism was now the only thing standing 'between us and anarchy'. Even the Prime Minister himself, Lloyd George, was now of the view that it was imperative to secure 'a certain contentment in the labour world', warning Cabinet colleagues that failure to do so 'may end in a revolution.'[24]

The failure of deflation

In response to the unrest a ministerial committee of enquiry was established to examine means of bringing about a rapid improvement in economic conditions. In contrast to the Bank of England and the Cunliffe committee, which were now calling for an immediate return to gold,[25] the inquiry concluded that introducing the level of deflation that would now be required to reverse the wartime rise in prices would be too dangerous in the present social climate, and argued that inflation therefore now needed to be maintained in order to stimulate economic growth. Accepting these findings, ministers decided that interest rates needed to be held at their present level of 5%, and in March formally terminated Britain's adherence to the gold standard by indefinitely prohibiting the export of gold. In addition, the government also sought to deal with the situation through a mixture of coercion and concessions. Major industrial disturbances were met with the use of troops and a barrage of propaganda, while a series of palliative measures were introduced in order to regain the confidence of both capital and labour. Many of the promised social reforms were quickly implemented, many of the wartime controls were temporarily retained, industry was granted a degree of temporary protection from foreign competition, and a raft of industrial policy devices were introduced in an attempt to placate labour discontent, including the restoration of restrictive trade union practices, reductions in working hours, and a freezing of wages at their inflated wartime levels. Unrest in the coal industry, a potential trigger for Triple Alliance action, was also successfully forestalled by the government with the establishment of a Royal Commission to examine conditions in the trade, and another National Industrial Council was created in order to consolidate moderate labour opinion by holding out the promise of more extensive reforms.[26]

From spring 1919 these various measures, combined with the stimulus of global postwar reconstruction, facilitated the fiercest economic expansion ever seen in Britain. However, while this enabled the authorities to avoid the dangers of a recession, and allowed them to begin the process of dismantling the state's wartime controls, the boom also brought with it many disadvantages. The continuing rise in inflation led to a sharp fall in the pound to $3.20 by February 1920 and helped to sustain class unrest over prices and wages (which rose by 22% and 131% respectively from 1918 to 1921), while the high level of demand insulated both capital and labour from the need for economic adjustment, leading to a reconstruction of industry along old and safe, rather than newer and more advanced lines, further augmenting the maladjustment in Britain's pattern of economic activity in relation to the changing composition of world trade.[27]

As these problems mounted during the latter half of the year, official frustrations also began to grow. Lloyd George warned Cabinet colleagues that the main problems facing Britain were the high level of labour unrest, declining productivity, and rising inflation (which was now considered to be 'at the bottom of the trouble in this country'), Chamberlain too now derided inflation as 'a danger to the stability of the country', and senior Bank and Treasury officials began to vigorously press the government for a sharp reduction in public spending, a retrenchment of state activity, and a rise in interest rates in order to clear the way for a return to gold. As Cokayne remarked, the risks of deflation were now 'as dust in the balance compared with the restoration of free trade and the removal of social unrest and political discontent.'[28]

By the end of the summer the dangers of labour radicalism were thought to have peaked, prompting the governing authorities to adopt a tougher approach. The Industrial Council was now allowed to fall into desuetude (though was not formally abolished until 1921), the programme of social reform was severely cut back, and in August the government announced that there would be no nationalisation of the coal mines, a central plank of labour's plans for postwar reconstruction. This prompted a retaliatory strike declaration from the MFGB and was followed by the threat of a general strike from the Triple Alliance, though this rapidly collapsed as the Alliance leadership proved to be sharply divided over who should be in control of any action. In turn, this was followed by a further hardening of the government's position. A permanent anti-strike organisation (the Supply and Transport Committee) was established in November, and early in 1920 the introduction of an Emergency Powers Act provided state officials with wide-ranging capacities to deal with the threat of any future large-scale disruption. In December 1919 the government also publicly declared its desire to return to the gold standard, and to this end began to implement a series of deflationary measures, imposing restrictions on the growth of the money supply and raising interest rates to 6%. These measures were increased the following April with a rise in interest rates to 7% and with the introduction of a deflationary budget of tax rises and cuts in public spending.[29]

This tightening of deflation also coincided with the ending of the postwar boom, plunging Britain into its worst recession for fifty years. From 1920 to 1922, industrial production dropped by almost a fifth, GDP fell by a quarter, and unemployment increased five-fold, reaching the unprecedented height of more than two million. Despite this however, the slump was not entirely disadvantageous for the authorities. Retail prices fell by 10%, wholesale prices fell by 25%, sterling recovered to $4.70 by March 1922, and the pressure of unemployment gradually undermined the strength and radicalism of the labour movement, enabling the dissolution of the state's wartime economic controls to be completed by the end of 1922. This weakening of labour was demonstrated most clearly in April 1921, when the Triple Alliance itself collapsed amidst another dispute over control of a national strike. This event, known in labour annals as 'Black Friday', was followed by the onset of a capitalist counterattack as employers sought to rein back the gains made by the working class during the war. By 1922 real wages had fallen by 13%, trade union membership had declined by 16%, the number of working days lost had reached their lowest point since 1918, and the number of new stoppages were now at their lowest since 1916.[30]

For all these benefits however, the effects of the slump proved to be largely negative. An initial rise in trade union membership during the first twelve months of the recession was accompanied by a resurgence of labour radicalism and by another explosion of unrest. Despite a resounding vote by the TUC against calling a general strike in an attempt to force the nationalisation of the coal mines in early 1920, politically motivated industrial action resurfaced during the summer when the government's decision to extend support to Poland in its war with Russia provoked a vitriolic backlash, raising the prospect that a general strike could now become a reality. While this threat was subdued by a swift Polish victory, the number of new stoppages during 1920 now rose to its highest level for the entire interwar period, and though this had more than halved by the following year, 1921 saw more working days lost than in the entire years of the Great Unrest combined. As Montagu Norman, the new Governor of the Bank of England (and one of the central figures in the return to gold) warned, the industrial situation was now 'most serious'.[31]

Of further concern to the governing authorities was that the extent of the deflation achieved during the slump proved to be insufficient to raise sterling back to its old parity of $4.86. In part, this was due to the continued resistance of capital and labour to lower prices and wages, with the Bank of England and the Treasury complaining in particular about the slow fall in retail prices (as the basis for wage negotiations), and in part this was due to the simultaneous pursuit of deflation by the United States, which helped to maintain the strength of the dollar against the pound. Compounding this, the prospects for a return to gold at any time soon were also undermined by the persistence of international instability, with widespread economic deterioration being accompanied by rising tensions over war debts, reparations, tariffs, and exchange rate fluctuations, as well as by the onset of severe monetary disorder throughout Eastern Central Europe.[32]

To make matters worse, as the slump progressed the governing authorities also came under growing pressure from capital and labour. While the labour movement considered the primary cause of the downturn to be the poor state of the world economy, with the destruction of export markets, exchange rate instability, and the continuing uncertainty in Europe all seen to be key factors in Britain's difficulties, state officials themselves were also considered to be largely responsible. In particular, the government were criticised for their foreign policy stance, with the economic blockade of Germany, the imposition of harsh reparations conditions, and the isolation of Russia all thought to be exacerbating the situation, and officials were also attacked for the high level of interest rates, with the TUC and the Labour Party both calling for an enquiry into the effects of monetary policy. While the majority of labour opinion now believed that the only means of ensuring a national economic revival was through concerted international co-operation to revitalise the world economy, the government were also urged to adopt an expansionary domestic policy, including increased state intervention and higher spending on public works in order to ameliorate the impact of unemployment.[33]

For representatives of capital on the other hand, the remedy for the slump was seen to lay with domestic rather than international measures. While many industrialists were reluctant to seek government assistance for fear that this could lead, as the FBI put it, to a renewal of 'cumbersome, expensive, and irritating' interference, many were now increasingly critical of the government for their lack of direct help. Industrial, commercial, and financial opinion all argued that the key to overcoming the recession was to improve competitiveness, and claimed that this could be best achieved through a reduction of wages, taxation, and public spending. The high level of interest rates though were also criticised as a central factor in the poor state of the economy, with the FBI too calling for an enquiry into the effects of monetary policy.[34]

The waiting strategy

As dissatisfaction over economic conditions mounted, officials recognised that the use of deflation would not secure a quick return to gold at the prewar par. As early as the summer of 1920 Chamberlain was warning that the level of interest rates that would be required to raise sterling back to $4.86 would now be 'politically impossible', while Norman bemoaned that any resolution of 'the everlasting difficulties about increasing wages' was 'sadly remote', since interest rates had now become 'a political as well as a financial question'. In November the recognition that there would be no quick return to gold was formalised when the prohibition on the export of gold in place since April 1919 was put on a statutory footing, with the Gold and Silver (Export Control) Act extending the embargo until the end of 1925,[35] and by 1921 pressure over the deterioration in the economy was also leading the governing authorities into a relaxation of their deflationary policy stance. Warnings by Norman that high interest rates were now being 'bitterly attacked' were soon followed by their reduction to 5% and by a further series of cuts to 3% by July 1922. This easing of the government's economic policy was also supported by cuts in taxation, and by a reduction in planned cuts in public spending.[36]

The loosening of the deflationary pressure however did not signify a change in the long-term objectives of the governing authorities. Calls for an enquiry into the effects of monetary policy were rejected by Lloyd George on the grounds that this would merely increase economic uncertainty; criticism of high interest rates was rejected by ministers, who asserted that the responsibility for such decisions had now been returned to the Bank of England (although in practice interest rates remained under political control); and pressure for a substantial increase in state intervention was also firmly resisted by officials. Norman for example decried such measures as 'impossible remedies for unavoidable unemployment', and as one Treasury report put it, while immediate action to ameliorate unemployment was now needed in order to avert 'a serious state of unrest and a probable cause of social disaster', increased state intervention would only serve to 'check the fall in prices ... and so delay the recovery of productive enterprise.' Moreover, the political dangers of renewed state intervention also remained a cause for concern, with Niemeyer pointing out that this would lead people to regard the economic involvement of the state as a panacea for Britain's difficulties, and would thus produce 'great exasperation' when it inevitably failed.[37]

In addition to this, while several officials such as Hawtrey and Robert Horne (the Chancellor from April 1921 to October 1922) were now calling for a period of low interest rates in order to stimulate the economy, and for monetary policy to be managed with a view to ensuring stable prices, the majority of official opinion remained firmly committed to securing a return to gold, and viewed the easing of deflation as but a temporary and strategic response to economic and political pressures. Sir Basil Blackett (the Treasury's Controller of Finance) for example, warned that lower interest rates would now initiate 'a new cycle of rising prices and rising wages', Niemeyer maintained that it was now 'generally admitted' that the price of British goods and wages needed to be reduced if Britain was to compete in the world market, while Norman was harshly critical of Hawtrey's views, slamming them as being unrepresentative of opinion within both the Bank and the Treasury.[38]

Nevertheless, given their inability to secure a return to gold through the imposition of deflation, Britain's governing authorities now turned to a 'waiting strategy'. With deflation in the United States having attracted a huge amount of the world's gold since 1920, officials believed that American prices would soon be forced to rise, and that the subsequent weakening of the dollar would facilitate a rise in the pound back to $4.86 with minimal economic and political disruption. The way forward then, was to hold domestic conditions relatively stable until external conditions had brought about the required adjustment.[39] In conjunction with this, Norman also began to redirect his efforts towards achieving the stabilisation of the international environment in order to secure the conditions for a reconstruction of the gold standard on a global basis. Along with the Governor of the Federal Reserve Bank of New York (FRBNY), Benjamin Strong, Norman was now convinced that the sound and healthy world economy upon which Britain's prosperity depended could only be revived through the removal of 'economic' issues (such as tariffs, war debts, and reparations) from the 'political' sphere, and that this itself could only be achieved through a restoration of the international gold standard operating through a network of politically independent central banks.[40]

The two Governors were assisted in this objective by the high level of support for a return to gold. International conferences held in Brussels during 1920 and in Genoa during 1922 both called for nations to return to the gold standard at parities appropriate to postwar conditions, and this aim was also supported by the vast majority of British public opinion, and by representatives of both capital and labour, for whom the recent and dramatic experiences of boom and slump (as well as the sight of emerging hyperinflation in Eastern Central Europe) had heightened the appetite for economic stability. Both the Labour Party and the TUC were becoming increasingly concerned with the damaging effects of exchange rate instability and with the low value of the pound, which was seen to be a key factor in generating rising inflation and in thereby undermining working class living standards through higher import costs, and both were increasingly of the view that the only remedy was a general return to gold by the world's main trading nations at 'appropriate' parities.[41] From the ranks of capital, similar conclusions were also in evidence. The City were almost universally in favour of a return to gold (despite some isolated dissent, mainly from Reginald McKenna, a former Chancellor and the Chairman of the Midland Bank), while the FBI maintained that it was 'highly desirable that an arbitrary control of the currency in all European countries should, if possible, be replaced by some automatic means of regulation'. A national conference of British business, including representatives from the FBI, the National Confederation of Employers' Organisations (NCEO), and the Association of British Chambers of Commerce (ABCC) also held a similar view, declaring that the re-establishment of exchange rate stability and a rise in the value of the pound were now 'of the utmost importance'. While the process of deflation had stalled, a return to gold remained very much on the agenda.[42]

Concluding remarks

While conventional explanations for Britain's return to the gold standard at the prewar parity of $4.86 are problematic, a markedly different way of understanding this policy can be derived from an open Marxist approach to the analysis of exchange rate policy-making. This argues that the return to gold should be understood as the key component of a wider governing strategy designed to contain class struggle, to provide favourable conditions for capital accumulation, and to improve the high political freedom of the governing authorities. More specifically, this policy was developed against the backdrop of long-term economic and political difficulties in the British state. These were manifest as the onset of relative economic decline, a sharp increase in labour unrest and radicalism, and a politicisation of economic conditions and policy-making during the First World War. In this context, a return to the gold standard at the prewar parity was designed to address these difficulties through the imposition of anti-inflationary pressure and through the depoliticisation of monetary and economic policy-making. This would help to contain class unrest by disciplining the expectations of capital and labour, would re-expose the British economy to the competitive pressures of the global market, and would displace pressure over economic conditions and policy-making away from the state.

The initial attempt to implement this strategy however, was unsuccessful. The introduction of deflationary measures was delayed after the war for fear of acute social unrest, allowing the development of a fierce economic boom which further exacerbated the problems of inflation, class unrest, and economic maladjustment. In 1920, with the risk of potentially revolutionary labour unrest thought to be diminishing, deflationary measures were finally implemented. At the same time however, the boom also began to collapse, and while the ensuing slump led to a reduction of inflation and to an eventual reduction in unrest, the pressure on state officials over economic conditions and policy-making continued to grow. By the end of 1922, this had forced the authorities to withdraw from their attempt at securing a return to gold at $4.86 through deflation, and had led to the adoption of a 'waiting strategy' in the hope that a rise in US prices would enable this to be achieved with minimal disruption. The success or otherwise of this strategy is the subject of the following chapter.

4
The Return to the Gold Standard

Introduction

This chapter examines the events leading up to the return to the gold standard from the beginning of 1923 to May 1925. The central theme of this period was the abandonment of the waiting strategy as US prices failed to rise, and the subsequent re-adoption of a more active approach towards securing the return to gold. At the same time, official views on this policy itself also underwent a strategic shift in emphasis. While a return to gold at $4.86 was still seen as a key means of preventing inflation and of depoliticising economic conditions and policy-making, Britain's core executive were now also of the view that the move itself could be used as a means of forcing an adjustment in Britain's economy through the deliberate imposition of a relatively high exchange rate. This would impress financial discipline upon capital and labour, help to condition expectations, and encourage a shift in Britain's pattern of economic activity away from old and declining sectors, while at the same time the depoliticising effects of the regime would provide officials with an effective shield from the unpalatable social and political effects of this process.

Hopes abandoned

For Britain's governing authorities 1923 began with much promise. The collapse of the coalition government in October 1922 and a general election victory for the Conservatives the following month had presaged a return to political normality, a rise in US prices had lifted sterling to $4.76 by February, and a recovery from the slump was well underway. Unemployment was in decline, industrial production was expanding, and there were increasing signs that Britain was finally starting to adapt to the changing demands of the global economy, as prices continued to fall and as newer and more advanced branches of production began to grow more forcefully. The position of the labour movement also continued to weaken, with trade union membership falling to its lowest level for five years, and employers continued to press home their advantage. Real wages were forced below their prewar levels, and though a rise in the number of industrial disputes led the government to take the precautionary step of further strengthening its anti-strike machinery, the actual number of working days lost in stoppages was almost half that of the previous year.[1]

Increasingly optimistic that their difficulties were at last starting to recede and that the continuance of US inflation would soon enable a return to the gold standard at the prewar par, Treasury and Bank officials now set about devising more specific plans for this eventuality, and an informal committee was set up at the Bank to examine the matter.[2] This optimism however proved to be misplaced. Despite the recovery Britain's general economic performance remained sluggish, unemployment remained chronically high at around 1.6 million, and the growth of more advanced industries remained limited. Moreover, while the Cabinet were becoming ever more anxious to encourage 'the development of trade and industry in all their branches', both capital and labour continued to resist pressure for economic adaptation.[3] Trade unionists were increasingly concerned that economic modernisation would lead to even higher unemployment, many industrialists were still able to take advantage of captive Empire markets and to make a satisfactory profit from old production methods and practices, while the invisible earnings of the City remained relatively weak as Britain's financial sector also struggled to adjust to the growth of international competition. These impediments were further compounded by the structural remnants of the postwar boom. Many industries were now burdened with excess capacity and large debts, thus reducing the amount of capital available for new investment and restructuring, while Britain's banking system was left greatly overexposed, thus reducing the incentive to make the new advances necessary for a shift in production, or to put financial pressure on firms to modernise lest this increase the risk of default.[4]

Despite having formally relinquished their wartime economic controls, Britain's authorities also remained under pressure over economic conditions and policy-making. The overwhelming majority of the labour movement continued to regard the government's foreign policy as a major factor in Britain's difficulties, and though a revival of domestic prosperity was still believed to depend on a wider international recovery, the government remained under fire for its indifference to the effects of deflation. In relation to this, the question of monetary policy was also now a subject of growing debate within the labour movement. While the predominant view was still that a general return to gold at appropriate parities was essential for global economic stability, calls for an enquiry into the effects of monetary policy continued to gain strength. Moreover, the notion that Britain should remain off the gold standard and adopt a deliberately managed monetary policy with the aim of maintaining domestic price stability, a view that was also being publicly promoted by the economist John Maynard Keynes and his associates such as Hugh Henderson, was now becoming ever more popular.[5]

Representatives of capital also continued to regard economic conditions as a political issue, though disquiet over monetary policy came almost wholly from industrial manufacturing. The ABCC for instance were of the view that the time was now ripe for taking steps to return to gold, while the only real opposition from within the City continued to come from McKenna, who was now also calling for a managed money policy.[6] The FBI however continued to argue that the remedy for Britain's economic difficulties lay with improving the competitiveness of industry through a reduction of production costs, and as such continued to press for lower levels of wages, taxation, and public spending. In addition, the Federation also continued to call for a re-examination of monetary policy, and though acknowledging that 'a further period of deflation' might prove to be 'necessary in the broader interests of the national welfare', were now opposed to the idea of moving sterling back to its prewar parity. Such a step they warned, would not only be detrimental to trade (especially exports), but would result in higher taxes, rising unemployment, and falling prices and wages, thus risking 'the most serious social and political consequences'. Instead, the FBI now added to the growing calls for a policy of price stability, though also added the qualification that this should be preceded by a mild dose of inflation in order to raise prices and profits.[7]

'Nothing but troubles'

These domestic concerns were accompanied by growing international difficulties. In January the seemingly intractable crisis over reparations plunged to a new low and further disrupted global economic confidence as France and Belgium re-occupied Germany's industrial heartland in the Ruhr, while at the same time the gap between British and US prices which had been recently narrowing was now also start-ing to widen. In February the FRBNY raised interest rates to 4.5% in a bid to arrest the inflationary pressure resulting from the continuing flow of gold to America, although the Bank of England were forced by political pressures to hold their rates at 3%. This widening differential now led to a fall in US prices, a renewed rise in British prices, and a slow but sustained depreciation of sterling throughout the rest of the year.[8]

By May the informal Bank of England committee established to examine the return to gold had also reached some provisional conclu-sions. Among these was a recommendation that Britain should return to the gold standard once it was clear that this could be maintained without any great difficulty, namely when the Bank had held a gold reserve of £150 million under favourable conditions for two consecut-ive years, or by 1930 at the latest.[9] Official opinions on monetary policy however, were now divided. Though it was clear that higher interest rates could still not be actively pursued, differences continued to persist over whether or not to engage in some measure of inflation in order to ease the political and economic pressure. Hawtrey for example was continuing to advocate the pursuit of a managed money policy, adding that this should be preceded by a period of low interest rates in order to raise British prices to a level conducive to stimulating economic growth, while a similar view was held by Stanley Baldwin, the latest Chancellor of the Exchequer and also the Prime Minister from May. Though insistent that the responsibility for interest rate decisions lay with the Bank of England, there was, as he told the House of Commons 'no greater necessity for this country ... than cheap money', and for keeping prices 'steady and on a level'.[10]

Others however took a different view. Niemeyer for example (now the Treasury's Controller of Finance and the chief adviser to the Chancellor) regarded any reconsideration of the deflationary policy as 'premature', and while Norman recognised that the gold standard was not now 'a question of practical politics', a key benefit of a return to gold was seen to be precisely that this would put an end to such calls for higher prices.[11] Antipathy to inflation was also shared by Bradbury, (now the principal British delegate to the Reparations Commission) who con-curred with the Governor that it was essential to establish 'a strong bulwark' against political interference with the money supply, and who claimed that it was imperative that the Bank should not allow themselves to be manoeuvred into bearing the responsibility for any inflationary policy that the government might foist upon it. As he put it:

> if the Chancellor of the Exchequer designate continues to develop on the lines of his recent speeches, I should, if I had any responsibility for the Bank, much prefer to leave him with the entire responsibility for his own experiments.[12]

With any prospect of being able to bridge the gap with US prices through a further dose of deflation now looking increasingly bleak, and with the Federal Reserve making it abundantly clear that they were aiming to prevent any domestic inflation, Britain's authorities turned their attention towards the possibility of forcing American prices to rise through a strategic export of gold. In May another Bank of England committee was established to examine whether this could be achieved, and by the end of the year two variants of the 'gold export scheme' (a Treasury and a Bank version) were under consideration.[13] In July however, the prevailing uncertainty over monetary policy within official circles was publicly revealed when Norman raised interest rates to 4% in a bid to arrest the fall in sterling. By directly contradicting the stated view of the Chancellor (who nonetheless did not oppose the measure), the rise further increased public interest in monetary policy and added greater impetus to calls for an enquiry and a managed money.[14] As the pressure mounted, Britain's governing authorities began to grow increasingly concerned. Baldwin warned Cabinet colleagues that failure to address the high level of unemployment 'might wreck the government', while at the Bank of England Norman was becoming increasingly keen to get back to the gold standard. As he explained to Strong: 'We can have and perhaps deserve nothing but troubles until we are again anchored to Gold. How and when can we do it?'[15]

In October these difficulties were compounded still further when the Minister of Labour, Sir Montagu Barlow, declared that the government were considering the pursuit of an expansionary economic policy in order to alleviate the effects of unemployment. Coming at a time of heightened nervousness in the world economy, with the recent ending of the Ruhr occupation having been followed by the onset of hyperinflation and acute social disorder in Germany, the announcement triggered a large flight of capital and a run on the pound. Despite an attempt by Baldwin to calm the markets by restating the government's commitment to price stability, the calling of a surprise general election in an attempt to gain a mandate for protectionism merely inflamed the situation, and with fears rising that the 'socialist' Labour Party might possibly win, sterling weakened even further. Such tensions were heightened still more by the outcome of the election itself. With the Conservatives being returned as the largest single party in Parliament but failing to secure an overall majority, the government were unable to introduce the very policy on which they had called the election, and the future direction of Britain's economic management thus remained unsettled.[16]

These difficulties and uncertainties grew persistently worse during the early months of 1924. Sterling remained under pressure, the gap between British and US prices continued to widen, unemployment remained chronically high, and the competitiveness of the old export industries continued to deteriorate. Political troubles too, refused to abate. Officials were forced to abandon the gold export scheme on the grounds that this was now likely to exacerbate public interest in monetary policy and further undermine confidence in the pound, while a rapid collapse of the Conservative government following a vote of no confidence led to their replacement by the first minority Labour government. To add to these pressures, the first six months of the year were also characterised by a new wave of labour unrest as workers sought, often successfully, to reverse the capitalist attack on wages. The number of new stoppages now rose to its highest level for three years, Philip Snowden (the new Labour Chancellor) described the outbreak as an 'epidemic', and the government were now prompted to seriously consider invoking the Emergency Powers Act in order to deal with the situation.[17]

The issue of monetary policy also remained a politically sensitive matter. Concerns were now growing within official circles that Britain might soon be left isolated as the rest of the world began to return to the gold standard, and at the Bank of England Norman was becoming increasingly anxious about the rising popularity of the view that a managed money policy could form 'a permanent alternative' to the regime.[18] Many on the labour left such as Oswald Mosley, John Strachey, J. A. Hobson, and the Independent Labour Party (ILP) were also becoming increasingly vocal in their calls for an enquiry into monetary policy, while despite staunch opposition from its leadership, the Labour Party conference passed a resolution calling for the banking system to be publicly controlled. Moreover, many within the labour movement (including the TUC and the Labour Party) were now also opposed to the idea of using deflation to secure a return to gold at the prewar par, claiming that this would lead to higher unemployment and would fail to deliver economic stability in the absence of a general return to gold, and many on the labour left were instead now calling for the pursuit of expansionary measures in order to revive economic growth.[19] Such concerns over deflation were also shared by prominent figures in the City, such as McKenna, F. C. Goodenough (the Chairman of Barclays bank), and Harold Goschen (the Chairman of the National Westminster bank), and were harboured too by the FBI, who continued to call for an enquiry into monetary policy, and who warned that the scale of deflation that would be required to return to gold at $4.86 would damage trade, lead to rising unemployment, and provoke 'serious industrial friction'.[20]

Hurrying slowly

Despite these difficulties however by 1924 conditions were now improving for Britain's state authorities. The world political and economic situation was at last beginning to look more stable, with Germany on the way to recovery and with plans now underway to facilitate the reconstruction of the global economy through the 'Dawes scheme'. Based on an expansion of American credit to debilitated countries, the scheme was designed to stimulate a renewal of world economic growth by recycling the excessive amounts of capital gravitating towards the United States in order to provide funds for economic redevelopment and to facilitate the payment of reparations and war debts. Almost immediately the success of the plan seemed to be evident, and as the year progressed the global economy began to enjoy another upswing centred upon reconstruction in Europe and an economic boom in America.[21]

Domestically, the worst of the slump was also now over. Industrial production surpassed prewar levels for the first time, and though the staple export trades continued to struggle, Britain's new and more advanced industries continued to grow. The uncertainty over economic policy and the decline in sterling were also dispelled as the new Labour government declared its commitment to avoid inflation and its desire to secure a return to gold 'as soon as possible', while state intervention to deal with unemployment remained minimal, with the government claiming that the problem could only be resolved by greater economic flexibility and an adjustment to changing global conditions. Furthermore, despite the rise in industrial unrest the position of the labour movement also remained relatively weak compared to recent years. Despite the rise in the number of new stoppages, the actual number of working days lost now fell to its lowest level for six years, and trade union membership fell to its lowest point of the entire inter-war period. By the middle of the year the resurgent unrest itself was now also subsiding, and as the Labour Research Department (LRD) observed, by August the 'forward move' had almost disappeared.[22]

Also beneficial for the authorities was the fact that while support for a managed monetary policy was now growing, discontent over monetary policy itself was paradoxically now diminishing. In contrast to the labour left, the bulk of the labour movement for example were generally indifferent towards the subject, and were now primarily concerned with more tangible issues such as wages, working conditions, and unemployment. As the Labour Party would ruefully acknowledge, while the process of deflation had produced 'serious industrial and social consequences', monetary policy issues were now 'the subject of surprisingly little political discussion'.[23] Similar views were also evident from representatives of capital. The ABCC were now hopeful that a return to gold could be achieved within a 'comparatively short period', and while opinion within the City was now divided over the use of deflation to force the issue, the financial sector was also overwhelmingly in favour of an eventual return. Even the FBI, despite their misgivings, were not opposed to a return to gold *per se*, nor necessarily to the use of deflation, but were rather concerned with the use of excessively rapid deflation in order to return at the prewar par. Indeed, the Federation now considered a general return to gold to be essential for a revival of both international and domestic prosperity, and did not regard a managed money scheme as being practicable for anything other than a temporary interim measure. As such, while the FBI favoured continuing with the policy of waiting for US inflation, they also continued to maintain that 'other considerations' such as the need to encourage a general return to gold could make deflation necessary.[24]

With conditions for a return to gold thus becoming more favourable, Britain's governing authorities were now able to engage in a more detailed consideration of how this could be achieved. Nevertheless, political sensitivities over the issue were still prevalent. Baldwin for example was fearful that renewed deflation could lead to a resurgence of labour unrest and radicalism, and state officials in general remained keen to avoid re-igniting public interest in the subject.[25] As Niemeyer maintained, renewed public debate on monetary policy would raise hopes of a managed money and inflation, the loose talk of which had 'already done us an infinitude of harm', while as Norman pointed out, raising interest in the issue by publicly announcing a specific date for a return to gold would be 'difficult and perhaps dangerous.' Summarising the events so far, as he explained:

> There have always been some here for whom the idea of gold was repugnant because they favoured, or pretended to favour, some new-fangled scheme: there have been public speakers ... who were liable to torpedo confidence at any time: there have been many who feared a crisis if prices were deliberately forced down and margins on loans eliminated ... Therefore, on the whole, my feeling is that however wearisome the pace has been, we have been wise so far to hurry slowly.[26]

From the summer the prospects for a return to gold became even more propitious as the FRBNY embarked on an easing of monetary policy (lowering interest rates to 3% by August) in a bid to allay domestic fears of a recession and to encourage a return to gold by Britain and Europe. As the interest rate differential between London and New York widened, growing expectations that Britain would soon re-establish sterling at the old parity now led to a speculative rise in the pound.[27] At the same time, an official committee known as the Committee on the Currency and Bank of England Note Issues (though better known as the Chamberlain-Bradbury committee after its two chairmen) was also established by the government. Ostensibly, this was designed to consider the technical question of amalgamating the Bank of England and Treasury note issues that had remained in circulation since the war, though in reality the committee was set up to examine means by which a return to gold could now be brought about.[28] In particular, the committee were concerned with the question of whether deflation should now be re-imposed in order to raise sterling to par quickly, or whether Britain should continue to wait for US inflation in the hope that this could be achieved with less friction. For key state officials however, neither option offered an ideal solution. On the one hand, deflation was thought to be difficult to achieve and would entail a long period of high interest rates and economic dislocation. As Hawtrey explained:

> no method of returning to the gold standard at pre-war par (apart from a rise in prices in America) can avoid the depression and unemployment incidental to a fall in prices.[29]

On the other hand, continuing to wait for US inflation was now thought to be a futile venture. The increasingly predominant view was that American prices would not now rise by any substantial amount despite the pursuit of low interest rates by the FRBNY, and that British prices would therefore have to fall in order to raise the value of the pound back to $4.86. Norman for example warned that while it would be 'much easier' to return to gold with US inflation, this was now an unlikely prospect and Britain would instead have to endure a 'big fall in price.' For both Norman and his co-representative to the committee, Sir Charles Addis (a senior Bank of England director) however, such a fall was nonetheless considered to be worth the 'sacrifice'. Deflation, they argued, would not only force Britain to become globally competitive, but by enabling a return to gold at the prewar parity would also help to ensure economic stability, restore international confidence in sterling, and prevent a future resurgence of inflation and hence 'further social disturbances, further strikes and discontent.' Moreover, adherence to such an 'automatic' regime with its clear economic signals was also seen as a useful means of enhancing the Bank's freedom of manoeuvre. The Governor for example complained of the Bank's present organisation that 'I certainly am not blessed with a "machine" which so far runs itself that I am free to be away from London as much as I would like', while Addis, arguing that the government should announce its definite intention to return to the gold standard, claimed that this would provide the Bank with 'the reason, and if necessary the excuse' for its actions.[30]

Aware of the potential dangers of deflation however (not least the possibility that this could lead to political pressures for the nationalisation of the Bank itself), both Norman and Addis were also keen to ensure that responsibility for the operation of monetary policy would rest entirely with the government. As Norman again explained, while it was 'difficult not to have political views', it was nonetheless 'dangerous to express them', and as he told Niemeyer, while the Bank was willing in principle 'to lend its services for the re-establishment of a free gold market in this country ... [it] would not desire to participate in the result of Exchange operations.' Moreover, although a return to gold would once more imbue the Bank with formal authority for the management of sterling, the Governor was also insistent that the Chancellor would nonetheless remain 'the ultimate authority for the maintenance of the Currency, and therefore of the Exchanges.'[31]

A shift in strategy

Despite the assertions of Norman and Addis, Britain's state authorities were however still undecided as to their course of action. Hawtrey for example favoured continuing to wait for US inflation, arguing that a return to deflation would create 'another acute and serious unemployment crisis', Bradbury now purported to have 'no settled conclusions' on the matter, and the Bank of England as a whole were also uncertain. As Cecil Lubbock (the Deputy Governor) explained to Strong:

> The question of the gold standard will no doubt be prominent before very long ... something will have to be done soon: but are we to force our prices down, or will you allow yours to rise?[32]

Though undecided about the timing of the return, state officials were nonetheless resolutely agreed on the par value, with the rate of $4.86 now so ingrained that the Chamberlain-Bradbury committee did not even consider it to be worth discussing. This did not mean however that $4.86 was decided upon merely out of precedent, or that the lack of discussion signified negligence on the part of the authorities.[33] Rather, a return to gold at the prewar par was seen by state officials to be of fundamental importance for Britain's entire pattern of economic organisation and for its integration into the global circuit of capital. Returning at a rate less than $4.86 would, it was thought, not only damage international confidence in sterling and diminish Britain's invisible earnings capacity (with dangerous implications for the balance of payments), but would also lead to higher import costs and renewed inflationary pressures. Moreover, a return at $4.86 itself would not only encourage other countries to return to the gold standard, thereby increasing global economic stability, but as Hawtrey later explained, this was also considered to be the only credible rate available since a lower parity would send out a signal that further devaluations might follow should similar difficulties arise in the future. Thus:

> The advantage of the old parity was that, once the country had returned to it by a great effort, people would expect great efforts to be made to retain it. For that reason it would command a greater degree of confidence than a new rate chosen to suit the circumstances of a particular moment.[34]

The need for Britain's return to gold to be credible was therefore considered by officials to be of vital importance, not least for helping to shape the expectations and hence the behaviour of capital and labour by convincing them that there would be no future change in monetary policy. As Norman put it, the situation was 'much more a question of … the psychology of the announcement than of the facts'.[35] Indeed, with uncertainty over monetary policy still a potential source of political difficulty, the need for a credible commitment was even considered to be in many ways more important than the actual date of the return itself. As the Governor, who did not now expect sterling to go to par for 'months or years', told Strong:

> There is no need for great hurry in our reaching gold parity, but there is great need for hurry in having a policy which is clear to everybody and which is definite and final.[36]

The question of when Britain should return to gold thus hinged upon which date was thought to be the most credible, or as Bradbury put it, which date people were 'most likely to believe.' Officials though, remained in disagreement as to when this should be. Neither Chamberlain or Hawtrey suggested any particular date, Bradbury thought an eighteen month period to be the most credible, while Addis and the Bank of England's executive body, the Committee of Treasury, favoured a period of twelve months. For Norman though, the best date was thought to be in three years time. As he explained, returning to gold at $4.86 in a shorter period would entail a more rapid rise in the pound and would be an unreasonable proposition 'to put before the man in the street', thus running the risk of antagonising public opinion and losing credibility.[37] Announcing that Britain would return to gold in three years however would not mean that the authorities would have to wait that long for the benefits to accrue. On the contrary, the Governor argued that the speculative inflow of capital that would follow a credible announcement to return at the prewar parity would quickly lift sterling back to $4.86 well in advance of the date set, thereby providing the authorities with 'extremely valuable camouflage', giving the public time to get used to the 'new' exchange rate, and drawing the political sting out of the move. As he again explained,

> if you can … draw up a façade which impressed everybody with its certainty as to its date, I believe long before that date arrives you

will have reached gold and the agitation will have died away; people will have forgotten about it.[38]

In September the Chamberlain-Bradbury committee produced its first draft report, advocating a continued wait for US inflation but arguing that Britain should return to gold regardless within a maximum period of twelve months. Following criticism from officials that the draft was too vague, with Norman for example claiming that it was too ambivalent over the date for a return, and with Chamberlain arguing that it should be more explicit in pointing out that sterling would now be managed by the Bank of England and not the government, a second more robust version was produced the following month, though this too proposed continuing to wait for a rise in US prices.[39] By this time however the emphasis in official thinking was beginning to shift more decisively towards favouring an active policy of deflation. Key authorities were now increasingly of the view that Britain could no longer afford to wait for American inflation, and were coming to recognise that in conjunction with its depoliticising properties, a return to gold at $4.86 could itself be used as an effective means of forcing down British prices, and of thereby putting pressure on capital and labour to become more competitive, to modernise, and to adjust to the changing demands of the world economy. As Strong pointed out for example, it was now 'illusory to expect price adjustments of themselves to effect a recovery of sterling', and the only way in which Britain could return to gold was through an act of 'force majeure'. This view was also now shared by Niemeyer, who maintained that a successful return no longer required British and American prices to be level beforehand, but could now only be achieved by actually putting the pound at par. 'When you get within a certain distance of par', he later explained, 'there is one thing ... which will carry the last fence, and that is to put your rate at par, to say it is there.'[40] On this assessment Norman too was now in full agreement. Indeed in his view, US inflation would now not only fail to reduce the price difference between Britain and America, but would itself trigger a renewal of domestic inflation. As he told Strong,

it would not be sufficient to wait for exchange parity to be reached merely through the price levels coming together. Indeed, if while we were waiting your prices were to rise ... I do not believe we could ever prevent ours from following.[41]

As this change in strategy was developing however, the domestic political situation was facing renewed uncertainty. Following allegations that the Prime Minister, Ramsay MacDonald, had intervened in the trial of a communist editor for sedition, the minority Labour government collapsed, precipitating yet another general election. Moreover, as it became increasingly clear that the Conservatives were likely to win, the prospects for using a return to gold as a means of imposing deflation began to diminish. As Norman bemoaned, the Conservatives were,

> apt to listen to the traders and manufacturers, who, while they profess a remote affection for gold and a real affection for stability, always want a tot of brandy (in the shape of inflation) before the level is fixed![42]

Unfortunately for the Governor however, the Conservatives were now re-elected, and discussions on the return to gold were paralysed. The political upheaval, Norman complained, had 'side-tracked all thoughts on gold policy', had left no political desire to take the 'drastic steps' necessary to bring about a return to par, and no decision was now expected until possibly as late as 1927.[43]

'Not a word...'

By October 1924, all attempts to return to the gold standard since the end of the war had been thwarted. A quick return in 1919 had been ruled out for fear of the social and political consequences, the deflationary policy adopted in December 1919 had been forcibly reversed by the end of 1922 for similar reasons, hopes for US inflation had proved fruitless, and now the renewed optimism of 1924 had apparently collapsed along with the Labour government. On top of this, interest in the subject of monetary policy was once again starting to increase. Keynes and Henderson were now joined in their continued attacks on the prospect of a return to gold by several sections of the press, while many on the labour left also remained critical of the policy, arguing that this was being dictated by the financial sector and that it would mean higher interest rates, rising unemployment, and lower wages.[44] On the side of capital, the FBI too maintained a critical line. The Federation asserted that a return by Britain alone would fail to provide economic stability, and expressed concerns that a return at $4.86 would lead to 'restrictive measures' and impose 'serious strains' on industry. As such, the view of the FBI was that they 'would naturally be inclined to prefer a policy directed to the maintenance of the present stability in prices', rather than one in which 'the restoration of our full competitive power requires the forcing down of our prices and costs until they are in adjustment with the value of the exchange as fixed by our monetary authorities'.[45] In addition, similar concerns were now evident within commercial circles, where the prospect of higher interest rates and lower prices was also causing increasing unease. As one major commercial group, the Manchester Association of Importers and Exporters (MAIE) warned for example, a return to gold at $4.86 under the present circumstances risked producing 'disastrous consequences'.[46]

Despite these criticisms however, conditions were nevertheless continuing to improve for Britain's governing authorities, and those explicitly opposed to the gold standard policy were still in a minority. The overwhelming majority of press and public opinion remained either uninterested in, or unconcerned about the prospect of a return to gold, the Labour Party leadership remained fully committed to a return (with Snowden concurring in the view that there now needed to be no prior convergence of British and US prices), and the labour movement in general continued to focus on more traditional matters such as wages and working conditions.[47] Representatives of capital too, for all their concerns, were increasingly positive about a return to gold. The City were now universally in favour of the policy (with even McKenna describing it as having 'great and striking advantages'), while many within industry and commerce were now looking forward to an era of lower prices in the expectation that this would lead to a rise in sales.[48] Despite their anxieties, the FBI were also now increasingly optimistic about the future economic situation, and were of the view that continuing to wait for a rise in US prices would merely lead to renewed inflation and would thus be damaging to Britain's long-term prosperity. Although the governing authorities were presently believed to be holding sterling at an artificially high rate, the rise in sterling was also thought to reflect growing confidence in the British economy, and any attempt to question the discretion of the Bank of England on interest rate matters was regarded as being 'highly improper and undesirable'.[49]

While the political will needed to engineer a return to the gold standard was still deemed to be lacking, at the Bank of England Norman remained anxious to get back to gold as soon as possible. Though now hopeful that sterling would rise to par 'naturally' by the end of 1925, the Governor was also increasingly concerned about a possible re-emergence of inflation, telling one colleague that 'the tendency of our price level to rise is discomforting'.[50] Equally sensitive to the dangers of public debate on the issue of a return to gold however, Norman also remained keen to keep it out of the spotlight. As he told Strong:

> you know how controversial a subject it is – how it is everybody's business – and how secretly it must be treated … not a word can be breathed until some decision has been reached.[51]

In an attempt to force the pace of events, towards the end of the year the Governor travelled to New York to draw up a plan of action with senior figures at the FRBNY. During these discussions it was agreed that Britain's embargo on the export of gold should be allowed to expire at the end of 1925, and that all official considerations of the issue should be delayed until March in order to keep it out of Parliament until the last minute. Assurances of US co-operation were also obtained, with the FRBNY agreeing to provide a credit facility of $500 million (later reduced to $300 million) as an insurance against speculation, and guaranteeing that they would not engage in any destabilising activities while Britain implemented its return to gold. Norman was also warned however that higher interest rates might be needed in New York in the near future for domestic purposes, and that the deflationary pressure on the British economy following a return might therefore be greater than anticipated.[52]

By early 1925 conditions were looking increasingly propitious for a return to gold. The basic outlines of a plan were in place, sterling was close to par, the political and economic situations were increasingly stable, and as Norman put it only 'certain politicians and cranks' were now opposed to the policy.[53] The new Chancellor, Winston Churchill, was of the view that while a return to gold would require high levels of tax and interest rates in order to defend the pound, the decision would nonetheless be 'almost impossible to avoid', and in January the Chamberlain-Bradbury committee produced its third draft report, which also recommended that the gold export embargo be allowed to expire at the end of the year. Moreover, the report added that while a lack of US inflation would require a 6% fall in British prices in order to maintain the pound at $4.86, this would only be 1.5% greater than that required to hold sterling at its present rate of $4.79, and as such the actual degree of adjustment imposed by the return to gold would therefore be 'comparatively small.'[54]

Despite the promising outlook however, official opinion on the New York plan was divided. In particular, senior Bank and Treasury figures were concerned about the dangers posed by the provision of US credits. As Niemeyer explained, the use of such credits would not only fail to halt a determined speculative attack on sterling, but their very existence would now complicate the situation by making the state directly responsible for the regulation of the currency, something which, as he reminded the Governor, 'we hoped to have got away from'. In the event that Britain should encounter any difficulty following the return, Niemeyer warned that public opinion would therefore call for sterling to be defended with the use of the credits rather than with a rise in interest rates, thus serving to prolong a lack of economic competitiveness. In addition to this, a number of senior directors at the Bank were also nervous about implementing a return to gold before British and US prices had converged, warning that the risk 'would be too great and the consequences of failure too grave for us to commend it.'[55] For Norman though, such concerns were now a mere bagatelle. As he triumphantly remarked, while the Bank had a 'general approval in principle but a strange opposition in detail', its opposition to the newly formed gold standard strategy would soon 'be worn down'.[56]

On the seas of history

With the key components of a plan now all but settled, the centre stage in the discussions was now assumed by the Chancellor of the Exchequer. Self-confessedly ignorant about economic matters and highly dependent on his advisors, Hawtrey, Niemeyer, Bradbury, and Norman, Churchill's primary interests lay not with the technical details of a return to gold, but with its political implications.[57] More specifically, the Chancellor was anxious to assemble sufficient arguments for use as a defence against any criticisms that a decision to return might attract, and as such dispatched a memo to his advisors at the end of January outlining his concerns. In particular, these focused on whether a return to gold would lead to higher interest rates, lower economic activity, and rising unemployment, and if so, whether this would leave the government (and especially himself) open to attack. In contrast, Churchill wondered whether it would be possible to justify higher interest rates more effectively under a managed money regime, since this would leave room for claiming that even higher rates would be required under the gold standard, and would therefore ensure that no-one could attribute them 'to the action of the British Government'.

At the same time however, with the political and economic momentum now clearly in favour of a return to gold, Churchill was also 'ready and anxious to be convinced' of its merits, although he warned that 'only very plain and solid advantages' could 'justify the running of such a risk'.[58]

In response, all of Churchill's advisors with the exception of Hawtrey (who continued to urge waiting for US inflation), now emphasised the importance of a quick return to the gold standard at the prewar parity. The general consensus was that a decision on the subject could no longer be avoided, that the Chancellor would be exposed to criticism whatever course of action was taken, and that a return to gold offered distinct political and economic advantages. Churchill was reminded for example that the overwhelming majority of public opinion was in favour of the policy, and was warned that failing to return would lead to economic instability and a loss of confidence in sterling, which would require even higher interest rates in order to prevent its collapse than would be needed to maintain the pound on gold. For this, as Norman maintained, 'the ignorant would doubtless blame the Chancellor'. In addition, Churchill's advisors also emphasised that a return to gold would ensure less economic fluctuations than a managed money, and would provide an effective defence against political pressure for inflation, with all its negative consequences in terms of rising wage demands, lost competitiveness, and social unrest. As Norman warned, 'no sane man anywhere … could recommend or even tolerate another boom', and while merchants, manufacturers, and workers should all be considered in the design of economic policy, they should not be any more consulted than they should 'about the design of battleships'. Furthermore, Churchill's advisors also emphasised that a return to gold would provide officials with an easier means of managing economic policy, with Niemeyer pointing out that should the move require a large fall in prices then this would be no bad thing since the fall would have been inevitable in any case, and since the gold standard would therefore 'have shown its use as an instrument of danger'. In sum, Niemeyer thus maintained that a return to gold was now imperative. A managed money policy, he claimed, would not produce an easing of the political pressure, but on the contrary would lead to 'great disappointment and considerable opposition', while as Norman put it, the gold standard was still 'the best "Governor" that can be devised for a world that is still human, rather than divine.'[59]

These views were also mirrored by the final report of the Chamberlain-Bradbury committee. This maintained that conditions were now uniquely favourable for a return to gold, and re-iterated that in the absence of US inflation British prices would only have to fall by a 'significant, though not very large amount' in order to hold the prewar par without difficulty. The report also argued that this adjustment process would be aided by the credibility that a return to gold would provide, claiming that a 'courageous policy' would surmount 'apparently formidable obstacles with surprising ease', and re-emphasised the warning given by Churchill's advisors that continuing with a managed money policy would require higher levels of interest rates in order to avoid a sharp loss of confidence in the pound.[60]

Despite maintaining that these various points offered 'a solid foundation both of argument and authority justifying the actions proposed', Churchill however was not entirely convinced and had yet to make any recommendation on the subject to the Cabinet.[61] With the high level of unemployment still a politically sensitive issue, and with officials acknowledging that a return to gold at the prewar par would require a tightening of the government's economic policy stance in order to defend the exchange rate, the Chancellor remained acutely anxious about the potential for criticism. Nonetheless, though sharply rebuking senior Treasury and Bank officials for their apparent lack of concern over the issue of unemployment, Churchill was in the end forced to admit that the gold standard was 'a great policy', and that there was simply no alternative. As he explained:

> I do not pretend to see even 'through a glass darkly' how the financial and credit policy of the country could be handled so as to bridge the gap between a dearth of goods and a surplus of labour; and well I realise the danger of experiment to that end. The seas of history are full of famous wrecks.[62]

In February however the forewarned rise in New York interest rates took place with an increase to 3.5%, prompting the Bank of England to raise their interest rates to 5% in March, and heightening official anxieties about a renewal of public interest in monetary policy. Cabinet ministers, aware of, but not participating directly in the discussions on the return to gold, were keen to keep quiet on the issue in order to avoid attracting public attention, while Niemeyer, concerned that the rise would elicit a temperamental outburst from Churchill (who had not been informed of the move beforehand), sought to head off any adverse reaction by dispatching a memo to the Chancellor pointing out that the responsibility for such decisions now lay squarely with the Bank, and that any political interference would be extremely damaging for confidence in the pound. As he put it:

> It is not either necessary nor the practice for the Bank to consult the Government of the day ... We have neither claim to be consulted nor power to enforce our views; and I think it would be generally recognised that in order to avoid political interference on these matters it is not desirable that we should have any such claim.[63]

In the event however the rise in interest rates attracted no great criticism, and though privately indignant, Churchill nevertheless followed the line presented by Niemeyer, telling the House of Commons that the Bank were acting independently, and asserting that it would be an 'inconvenient practice' if the Chancellor were to state his opinions on such matters.[64] With the end now in sight, Churchill also invited prominent figures from both sides of the monetary policy debate to a dinner party for one final deliberation. Representing the case for a managed money, Keynes (as the chief advocate of this policy) argued forcefully that a return to gold at the prewar par would overvalue the pound, damage Britain's export industries, and lead to downward pressure on wages, rising unemployment, and increased industrial unrest. In contrast however, Bradbury extolled the virtues of the gold standard. It was, he said, a 'knave proof' mechanism that could not be rigged for political or 'even more unworthy reasons', and he maintained that adherence to the regime would ensure that Britain's exports remained competitive by forcing inefficient industries to reduce their costs and to adopt more productive practices. Britain's staple trades, he argued, were likely to contract whatever policy was adopted due to increasing foreign competition, and the best future for Britain was now seen to lay with developing its means of invisible earnings and in adjusting its industrial structure towards the production of higher quality goods. Once the arguments were in, Churchill asked McKenna, as an ex-Chancellor, what he would do. In a stark reply, McKenna stated bluntly that there was no alternative to a return to gold, but that it would be 'hell'.[65]

Three days later on the 20th March the official decision to return to the gold standard at $4.86 was formally taken at a meeting between Norman, Churchill, Chamberlain, Bradbury, Niemeyer, and Baldwin. It was agreed that the embargo on the export of gold would be allowed to expire at the end of December, that there would be an official announcement to this effect in the budget speech in April, and that licenses for the export of gold would be available from the Bank of England in the interim. It was also agreed that the US credits would be used only in the event of a substantial outflow of gold, and that any rise in interest rates to bolster the pound would be delayed until a week after the return in order to diminish any criticism of the decision. Following this, the Cabinet were now informed, and the authorities began to prepare themselves for what would be a momentous and potentially dangerous move.[66]

Concluding remarks

This chapter has charted the collapse of the waiting policy and the accompanying shift in the governing strategy of Britain's state managers between 1923 and 1925. It has shown that Britain's economy continued to struggle despite a recovery from the recession, that political conditions remained unstable, and that official hopes for securing a smooth return to gold at $4.86 through a rise in US prices proved to be ill-founded. Against this background, by mid-1924 Britain's authorities were increasingly of the view that more active steps would now need to be taken. As such, officials turned to a governing strategy in which a return to the gold standard at a deliberately overvalued exchange rate would itself be used as a means of imposing deflationary financial discipline. The relatively high value of the pound accompanied by a tightening in the government's economic policy stance would put pressure on capital and labour to reduce prices and wages, to modernise, and to adjust to the changing demands of the world economy, while at the same time the depoliticising properties of the regime would displace any pressure resulting from the unpalatable consequences of this process away from the state, thereby improving the high political freedom of the authorities. The success or otherwise of this strategy is discussed in the following chapter.

5
The Golden Shield

Introduction

While traditional assessments of Britain's return to the gold standard view this policy episode as having been a major disaster, this chapter demonstrates that it can instead be interpreted as having been a relative success for Britain's governing authorities. Although the strategy did not lead to any significant adjustment in Britain's pattern of economic organisation or to any substantial breakthrough in competitiveness from capital and labour, and although the subsequent continuation of economic difficulties worked to constrain the high political freedom of Britain's state managers, the return to gold was nevertheless largely successful in establishing a credible and a depoliticised means of managing the circuit of capital. While the authorities were not completely immune from criticism and pressure, especially over the persistence of high unemployment, monetary and economic policy matters were for the most part no longer seen to be key political issues, and officials were effectively protected from rising social disquiet over economic conditions. Dissatisfaction from capital and labour was largely displaced away from the state, and on the whole the governing authorities now enjoyed a greater freedom of manoeuvre than they had under the politicised mode of economic policy regulation that had preceded the return to gold.

Shackled to reality

In May 1925 Britain returned to the gold standard at the prewar parity of $4.86. The Bank of England, already obliged under the 1844 Bank Act to purchase any gold offered to it at the rate of £3 17s 9d per standard ounce, were now legally obliged to sell gold at the rate of £3 17s 10$^1/_2$d per standard ounce, and were legally responsible for regulating interest rates within the remit of maintaining an adequate gold reserve. To increase the flexibility of the system however, a minimum purchase level of 400 ounces was introduced in order to restrict the availability of gold for export purposes only, and no minimum level was stipulated for either the gold reserve or the fiduciary issue.[1]

More fundamentally, the return to gold at $4.86 was the key component of a governing strategy designed to address the long-term economic and political difficulties of the British state. As such, the policy had several interrelated objectives. Chief among these were to contain class unrest, and to secure favourable conditions for capital accumulation by addressing the problem of Britain's relative economic decline. By stabilising the pound on gold, officials hoped to signal that the future direction of Britain's economic policy would now be subordinated to maintaining the exchange rate, and by fixing this at the prewar par, aimed to impose deflationary pressure on the British economy. Since the rise in the pound from mid-1924 had been driven largely by speculation rather than by any real improvement in Britain's economic performance, an exchange rate of $4.86 was now too high to accommodate the level of domestic economic activity at its prevailing structure of prices. By deliberately raising the price of Britain's exports, officials thus sought to put pressure on capital and labour engaged in the staple trades to reduce wage costs, adopt more efficient methods of production, and to move into newer and higher quality lines of production more attuned to the changing demands of the world market. As Baldwin astutely noted, the high pound would impose a 'necessary and salutory' discipline for this purpose.[2]

The economic pressure of a return to gold at $4.86 however would not simply affect the old export trades, but would also enable and encourage those producing for the domestic market to reduce costs and re-organise. This process would be enhanced by the general tightening of economic policy required to maintain the parity, and as the high value of the pound lowered the price of essential imports, thus helping to reduce production and living costs. As Hawtrey explained, the measures required to maintain par would 'depress all industries, including those which produce for export'.[3] Indeed, even the financial sector would now face pressure for adaptation, since the high level of interest rates necessitated by the return would constrain any tendency towards excessive lending and force the adoption of more prudent financial practices. Describing the situation in the City shortly after the return for example, as Norman put it:

> I think it is true to say that many of the financial community do not realise the importance and even the possible dangers of the step which has been taken. They have lived for ten years in a dream: they have not had to use their wits: they have not been able to help making money and they have not yet had time to shake off the habits of thought of these ten years.[4]

The discipline imposed by reintegrating Britain into the global circuit of capital on the basis of a fixed exchange rate would also be augmented by the fact that this would now directly expose the British economy to the competitive pressure of the world market, itself compounded by falling prices in America. Through the operation of the gold standard mechanism, this would force economic conditions in Britain to conform to those pertaining globally, and would therefore not only ensure that Britain became economically competitive, but that it remained so. It would, as Churchill explained, 'shackle us to reality'.[5]

Alongside these economic benefits the gold standard strategy was also designed to provide political advantages for Britain's governing authorities. The first of these was that placing legal control of interest rates in the hands of the 'independent' Bank of England would apparently rule out any political interference in such matters, thus removing questions of monetary and economic policy from the realm of democratic control and accountability. In addition, by placing the Bank within the confines of an international regime constituted by the need to defend a parity set by the government, the return to gold would also neutralise the accountability of Bank officials themselves, thereby enhancing the high political freedom of the core executive as a whole by enabling them to disclaim responsibility for economic conditions and policy-making. In turn, this would enable officials to shield themselves from the unpalatable effects of their tight economic policy stance by helping to condition the expectations of capital and labour, thereby confining class struggle within the limits prescribed by the regime and by displacing pressure over economic conditions and policy-making away from the state. As Baldwin again put it, the gold standard would provide officials with a 'coping stone' for aiding the reinvigoration of Britain's economy and for helping to keep an enlarged and 'untrained' electorate away from socialism.[6] Finally, the return would also simplify the management of the national circuit of capital by providing state managers with a clear signal, in the form of changes to the level of the gold reserves, as to whenever economic conditions in Britain were diverging from those elsewhere. In sum, as Churchill again explained, the return would provide the authorities with a 'warning of every economic danger':

> If wages are, or hours of labour are, out of economic relation to our competitors, if employers become slack or unenterprising, if the plant of our industries becomes obsolete, if the organisation is anti-quated, if we consume too much or borrow too much or lend too much, all the alarm bells begin to ring immediately.[7]

The mountain and the mouse

The initial reaction to the return to gold was favourable. Britain's commitment to maintain the par value was deemed to be credible, the majority of press and Parliamentary opinion was largely welcoming, and there was no substantial criticism from either capital or labour. The City were strongly approving of the decision, the FBI, though concerned about the immediate impact on competitiveness, believed it would bring long-term economic benefits, and while many on the labour left argued that the high pound would damage exports, increase unemployment, and put pressure on wages, the labour movement as a whole were largely unmoved by the return, with the Labour Party and the TUC censuring the government merely for having acted with 'undue precipitancy'.[8]

For the authorities, although the return was also accompanied by a degree of trepidation, with interest rates now being held at 5% and with Norman remarking that 'we must hope now that the "gamble" is as promising of success as even the doubters seem to believe,' the absence of any significant controversy was nonetheless viewed with some satisfaction. Niemeyer for example observed that fears over the return had been shown to be unjustified, and the Governor commented that the decision had been 'well received' and that the general position was one of 'unexpected tranquillity.' As he put it:

> the transition to free gold has been easier and has caused not only less alarm but even less interest than could have been expected. We rather prepared for a mountain and have (so far) brought forth a mouse![9]

This initial calm however was short-lived. Although industrial production continued to rise and although wholesale and retail prices both fell, the balance of payments began to deteriorate as the effects of the high pound started to assert themselves through a rise in imports and a decline in exports. In response, employers in the old export industries now began to try and overcome the pressure of the rise in the pound by laying off workers and reducing wages rather than by engaging in any modernisation or shift in production. This augured a new confrontation with labour, and unleashed a new wave of unrest during the summer. The epicentre of the unrest was located in the coal mines. Highly dependent on exports, though long in decline and operating with outdated technology and production methods, Britain's coal industry was not only under pressure from the rise in the pound, but was now also hit by a fall in the world price of coal following a dramatic increase in global supply as a result of the war. While the solution to this problem according to the owners of the coal mines, the Mining Association of Great Britain (MAGB), was to sustain profits by introducing substantial cuts in wages and by lengthening working hours, the MFGB instead called for a minimum wage, nationalisation of the mines, and extensive industrial restructuring.[10]

Though anxious to avoid becoming involved in the dispute due to the political dangers of state intervention, ministerial opinion was nonetheless on the side of the mine owners. As Baldwin explained, the government's view was that British wage levels now needed to be reduced across the board in order to 'help put industry on its feet'.[11] Fearing that the attack on the miners was therefore the prelude to an attack on working class living standards as a whole, the TUC declared their full support for the MFGB, threatening a severe escalation in the conflict. In response, the government set-up a fast-track Court of Inquiry into conditions in the coal industry, although the subsequent report satisfied no-one. With a stoppage looming, officials were now forced to take more substantive measures to avoid industrial action. A Royal Commission was established to examine the coal industry in more detail, and the government agreed to provide a six month subsidy to enable present rates of wages and profits to be maintained in the meantime. This event, known as 'Red Friday', was heralded as a great victory by the labour movement and as signalling the end of the capitalist attack on working class conditions. In reality though, it would prove to be a mere interregnum.[12]

The intensification of Britain's economic difficulties during the summer also fuelled criticism of the return to the gold standard. In a well-publicised addendum to the Court of Inquiry's report, the economist Josiah Stamp cited the high pound as a key factor in the problems of the coal industry, a view that was also present within the leadership circles of the MAGB and the MFGB, and which was held by many on the labour left, with the ILP, the LRD, and prominent figures such as Oswald Mosley and John Strachey all harshly criticising the return to gold. From the ranks of capital, McKenna too had now rejoined those remonstrating against the policy, and the FBI were also expressing their dissatisfaction with the course of events. As they put it, the return had been 'somewhat precipitate', and a combination of the high pound, an absence of US inflation, and resistance to wage cuts were thought to be driving Britain into recession. The most infamous and widely publicised attack on the gold standard however came from Keynes, who argued that senior officials at the Bank of England and the Treasury had miscalculated the discrepancy between British and US prices, and as a result had mistakenly overvalued sterling by around 10%. Churchill, he claimed, had been 'gravely mislead by his experts', and Britain, he warned, would now have to endure a much greater level of deflation than had been anticipated, leading to greater pressure on wages and employment, and to a higher risk of serious industrial unrest.[13]

Britain's governing authorities however were unmoved by these criticisms. Although Hawtrey decried the current level of interest rates as 'disastrous', Keynes' claim that industrial unrest could be avoided with a managed money policy was viewed with derision by officials at the Bank of England and the Treasury. Niemeyer insisted that Britain's economic problems were due to 'many causes' and that the effects of monetary policy were being 'very greatly exaggerated', and Sir Warren Fisher (the Permanent Secretary to the Treasury) warned Baldwin that any attempt to ease the competitive pressure through a relaxation of economic policy would lead to rising inflation, higher interest rates, and would render the maintenance of the gold standard 'impossible'. Such a view was also now held by Churchill, who described the notion that the gold standard was responsible for the problems of the coal industry as 'strange' and 'ill-founded', and who maintained that it was essential to encourage economic adaptation, and 'to get the cost of production down and to get the efficiency of production up'.[14] Similar points too were made by Baldwin, who told TUC delegates that it was essential for the coal industry to improve its own competitiveness, and by Bradbury, who remonstrated against Keynes' criticism by claiming that while the pressure on Britain's economy could theoretically have been reduced with a managed money policy or by a return to gold at a lower exchange rate, in practice either move would have entailed even higher interest rates in order to prevent a rise in inflation and a loss of confidence in the pound.[15]

The golden shield

Though dismissing criticism of the gold standard, the Bank of England were unable to completely ignore public opinion for fear of the potential political repercussions, and in August interest rates were cut to 4.5% in a bid to ease the strain on the economy. The move however failed to quell the dissenters, and calls for a further reduction quickly grew. These were also now strengthened by pressure from Churchill, who was becoming increasingly anxious about the political consequences of high unemployment. As Norman observed, the picture was now a mixed one:

> We seem to have slipped back to Gold with fewer pains and penalties than was generally expected – but we are not out of the wood yet. London still has to re-start as a free lender to all and sundry, while the industrial position in general and the coal position in particular are deplorable : they might jeopardise stability anywhere.[16]

Despite the inflationary dangers of lower interest rates, as the pressure continued to rise the Governor was forced to introduce a further cut to 4% in October, explaining to Strong that nothing else would have done more 'to silence criticism of the gold standard.'[17] This however offered only a temporary respite, and the situation soon deteriorated again as pressure on the pound combined with renewed speculation in New York led to an outflow of gold. In December this compelled Norman to put interest rates back up to 5% in order to defend the exchange rate, inciting further protests against monetary policy. The FBI were sharply critical of the decision, the labour left continued to attack the gold standard for its effects on trade, wages, and employment, Churchill's displeasure deepened further still, and Hawtrey declared the rise to be nothing short of a 'national disaster'.[18]

For all these difficulties however, the return to gold was nonetheless proving to be a successful political strategy, providing the governing authorities with a credible and a largely depoliticised framework for economic policy, and with an effective shield against disquiet over economic conditions. The commitment to maintain the par value of sterling had not been challenged, the troubles of the export industries had not led to a wider resurgence of unrest, organised labour remained numerically weak, and industrial action as a whole was now relatively low in comparison to recent years. The number of new stoppages during 1925 was 15% lower than in 1924, while the number of working days lost was now at its lowest point since the war. Moreover, for all the apparent furore over interest rates, monetary policy was no longer a major political issue for capital or labour. The majority of domestic opinion remained either uninterested in, or unconcerned about the subject, and only a minority attributed Britain's economic problems to the return to gold and to the actions of the governing authorities. While state officials remained sensitive to criticism, they were therefore now under less pressure than they had been in the period preceding the return to gold.[19]

Despite the attacks on monetary policy by the left, the majority of the labour movement for example remained primarily concerned with more traditional issues. Though voting for nationalisation of the banking system, the Labour Party conference rejected calls to establish a specific programme for doing so; a special trade union conference on unemployment emphasised the long-term nature of the problem and did not apportion any blame to the return to gold; and TUC representations to government ministers, including the President of the Board of Trade (Sir Cunliffe-Lister), the Prime Minister, and the Chancellor, all failed to broach the issue of monetary policy. Indeed, as one observer wryly remarked, the working classes were about as interested in the subject 'as they were in the nebular hypothesis.'[20]

Instead, the majority of the labour movement attributed Britain's problems primarily to a range of non-monetary factors including the still uncertain state of the global economy, and the 'natural' process of structural change. Though citing the return to gold as a contributory factor in the coal dispute for example, both the MFGB and the TUC regarded it as of relatively minor importance, and considered the primary cause of the crisis to be the poor industrial organisation and management of the mine owners, while the more general failure of employers to modernise British industry was also regarded by the wider labour movement as being the key element in Britain's economic difficulties. As such, the only real solution was considered to be a process of industrial restructuring in order to reduce production costs and to improve economic competitiveness. Even Keynes, the arch critic of the return to gold, was now arguing the need to work within its confines, and was describing the policy as a potential 'blessing in disguise' should it lead to a significant shift in Britain's pattern of economic organisation away from the old export trades, and as one joint TUC–Labour Party report put it, the 'real remedy' was 'the adoption of better appliances and equipment, and improved organisation'. Another joint report argued that a managed money policy

> would not of itself directly promote the comprehensive and scientific development of resources and economic possibilities which are essential for the absorption into employment of a growing population and for a progressive improvement in the standard of life of the workers.[21]

In addition to the labour movement, representatives of capital were also of the view that the return to gold was not the principal source of Britain's difficulties. Though Lord Weir, the President of the NCEO argued that the return had been a 'severe strain', T. B. Johnston, one of the few industrialists actively campaigning against the gold standard, bemoaned that protests from employers against the policy were 'practically non-existent'.[22] Moreover, despite McKenna's criticisms the overwhelming majority of City opinion remained in favour of the regime, the MAGB also regarded the gold standard to be but one of several factors contributing to the coal crisis, and the FBI admitted that it was impossible to determine the extent to which the return had added to the problems of British industry. For the majority of industrial opinion, the key factor in Britain's difficulties was instead considered to be the excessively high costs of production compared to those of competitor nations, and the main solution was seen to be cuts in wages, and reductions in tax and public spending rather than any change in monetary policy.[23] Indeed, as Roland Nugent (a chief FBI economic advisor) explained, the view of British industry was that they should no longer challenge but 'put up with the position' that the government had created, and as Charles Tennyson (the FBI's Deputy Director) observed, any open discussion of alternative monetary policies 'would be tantamount to recommending that we should relinquish the gold standard', something which was now regarded by the majority of the Federation as 'unthinkable'.[24]

The trial of the strikes

In spring 1926 the Royal Commission on the coal industry published its report. Rejecting both longer working hours and nationalisation, though advocating limited wage cuts and an end to the subsidy, the report satisfied neither the MAGB or the MFGB, and with the TUC still threatening a sympathetic strike in support of the miners, industrial action once more seemed unavoidable. The government too remained unwilling to extend their involvement for fear that this would turn them into a scapegoat for all the problems of the industry, and that it would reduce the pressure for higher productivity and greater competitiveness. Following the rejection of the report the MAGB announced sharp reductions in wages, provoking another strike declaration from the MFGB, who were subsequently locked out. At the end of April the subsidy expired, and with the government refusing to grant any further concessions the TUC decided to carry out their strike threat in support of the miners. The so-called 'general' strike (although only the 'first line' of key workers were ever called out) lasted for nine days and was strikingly unsuccessful. As the realisation dawned that the government would not alter their position, the TUC General Council (TUCGC) unilaterally decided to withdraw their support, leaving the miners to struggle alone to their inevitable defeat six months later.[25]

The conventional view of the general strike is that this was primarily caused by the return to the gold standard at the prewar parity, and that it therefore provides clear evidence that the policy was an abject failure. With the high pound making exports of coal more expensive, the government are thought to have forced the mine owners into a direct confrontation with the MFGB and, given fears that this would lead to a wider compression of working class living standards, to have antagonised the labour movement as a whole.[26] The truth of the matter however, is less clear cut. Indeed, while the rise in coal prices associated with the return to gold was undoubtedly a causal factor in the unrest, other factors played a more important role. Chief among these was the fact that Britain's old export industries (especially coal) were already facing huge long-term difficulties due to their continued failure to modernise and adjust to the changing demands of the global economy, a state of affairs that would have continued regardless of the direction of monetary policy. Given their refusal to modernise, the MAGB would certainly have attempted to overcome the continued decline in profits by a reduction of wages and longer hours, the MFGB and the TUC would have undoubtedly sought to resist such measures given their determination to avoid any further lowering of working class living standards (especially given the events of Black Friday in 1920), and the government would have remained equally unwilling to become involved given their previous experience of state intervention.

In fact, what is most striking about domestic opinion at this time is that for the most part the gold standard was not thought to be chiefly responsible for Britain's economic problems. Neither the MAGB nor the MFGB held monetary policy to be of primary importance in the general strike, with the Association continuing to blame excessively high wages, and with the Federation continuing to blame factors such as the global economic situation and the inefficient organisation of the coal industry, and despite later attributing the general strike to the return to gold, neither the FBI nor the TUC made any significant link between the two at this time. Though claiming that their warnings over the return had now been 'fully borne out by events', the Federation placed no great emphasis on the gold standard as being a key influence in the strikes, and though Walter Citrine (the General Secretary of the TUC) claimed that monetary policy was now proving to be 'damaging in every way', the labour movement as a whole failed to pay any real attention to the issue. Neither the TUC or Labour Party conferences made any mention of the return to gold, the TUCGC made no mention of monetary policy either in their internal discussions during the crisis or in their subsequent review of events, and the issue was even completely ignored by a TUC deputation sent to the Minister of Labour to discuss the unrest. The subject was also largely overlooked by the labour left in their interpretations of the strikes, and subsequent accounts by Snowden, Arthur Pugh (the TUC President), A. J. Cook (a radical MFGB leader), and H. Fyfe (editor of the labour paper the Daily Herald) also failed to yield any reference to the gold standard.[27]

Furthermore, the unrest also failed to provide the catalyst for any renewed criticism of monetary policy. The majority of the labour movement remained primarily concerned with traditional issues, and discontent over economic conditions was now directed mainly at employers rather than the state. Despite persistent attacks from the left and continued disquiet from mainstream labour over the high level of unemployment, calls for greater state intervention remained largely confined to the nationalisation of the coal mines, and the main remedy for Britain's economic ills was still considered to be industrial re-organisation and modernisation.[28] On the side of capital, monetary policy also remained an uncontentious issue. The City were still staunchly in favour of the gold standard, the FBI and the NCEO were not overly concerned with the subject, and although there was some dissatisfaction within the ABCC, an attempt to establish an internal enquiry into its effects was defeated. Neither the FBI, the NCEO, or the

ABCC made any calls for a revision in monetary policy, and instead maintained that the best means of improving Britain's productivity and competitiveness was through lower production costs.[29]

The unrest also failed to generate serious concerns within official circles of any threat to the gold standard strategy. Although the Bank of England were forced to refrain from any rise in interest rates during the general strike for fear of undermining confidence in sterling, there is no evidence to suggest that such concerns were anything but short-term anxieties, and though Churchill later spoke of the return to gold as having led to 'fierce labour disputes', Cabinet discussions also reveal no fears that the regime was under serious threat.[30] While remaining keen to avoid any public debate of monetary policy, the authorities did not therefore believe that the strategy was now unravelling. As Niemeyer put it, though open discussion of monetary policy was now 'ill-advised' and that 'the less said on it the better', recent experiences had shown that apprehensions over the return to gold 'were not well founded'. Furthermore, the unrest also failed to damage the credibility of Britain's commitment to the gold standard in the eyes of the world's financial markets, and just five days after the end of the general strike sterling reached a par with the dollar on New York for the first time since 1914. With state officials now convinced that the main danger to their position had passed, the US credits obtained for the return in 1925 were discontinued, and as J. P. Morgan (the government's financial agents in America) declared, this was the 'final proof' that the return to gold had been a success.[31]

'So much to be done'

Despite the disruption caused by the coal and general strikes, the return to gold can therefore still be seen to have successfully depoliticised the issues of monetary and economic policy, and to have effectively displaced responsibility over economic conditions and policy-making away from the governing authorities. In contrast to this political success however, the strikes also compounded Britain's lack of economic adjustment. Despite the persistence of high unemployment and a fall in trade union membership of more than 10% between 1926 and 1928, the unrest was not followed by any great moves from employers towards increasing the exploitation of labour by cutting wages or by lengthening working hours (except in the coal industry where such measures were ruthlessly imposed following the collapse of the strike), and only a minority of industrialists such as Sir Alfred

Mond and Sir Hugo Hirst (respectively establishing ICI and General Electric) were actively engaged in any serious restructuring. The growth of newer and more advanced industries thus remained insufficient to offset the stagnation of the staple trades, production costs remained comparatively high despite a fall in import prices, due to the persistence of inefficient practices and pre-1926 wage levels, and there were no signs of any significant modernisation or adjustment in Britain's economy. Though both wholesale and retail prices were now being gradually compressed, real wages for those in employment continued to rise (though remained substantially below the heights reached in 1920), and the relative decline in Britain's international economic position continued unabated as competitor nations pressed further ahead with technological and productive improvements. While the authorities had therefore survived the trial of the strikes, as Norman lamented, there remained '*so* much to be done.'[32]

The reasons for this lack of adjustment were varied. Migration of labour from contracting to expanding lines of production was hampered by the relative immobility of the British workforce, while the reluctance of industrialists themselves to switch from declining to expanding sectors was accentuated by the high costs involved, and by the continued availability of adequate returns from many old lines of production despite their economic troubles. The structure of Britain's old industries was also a strong impediment to change. Still rooted in the nineteenth century pattern of small family firms, pressure for raising productivity through mergers was strongly resisted, while those amalgamations that did take place were frequently designed as a means of sheltering from the need for economic adjustment rather than a means of pressing ahead with restructuring. Furthermore, industrial adjustment was also hampered by a lack of access to capital. Many firms were now unable to accumulate sufficient investment funds out of their own profits due to the high burden of tax and the continued servicing of debt accrued during the postwar boom, and with many of Britain's banks still heavily extended to British industry, many remained unwilling to make any significant new advances for the purposes of reconstruction, or to force adjustment through the pressure of bankruptcy for fear of endangering their investments.[33]

These factors alone however cannot fully account for the continuation of Britain's faltering economic performance. Labour immobility for example cannot be said to have impeded the growth of Britain's new industries, since at no point were these short of manpower, and there is no evidence to suggest that Britain's employers would have been more willing to engage in significant restructuring even had conditions for such an undertaking been more favourable. Instead, the key cause behind Britain's ongoing decline is to be found in the particular composition of its class relations. With the intense class struggle of the last sixteen years having exacted a heavy toll on both capital and labour, each side was now keen for a temporary cessation of hostilities, and was prepared, for the time being at least, to accept the entrenched position of their opponent. Employers, especially in the old export trades, remained firmly wedded to the extraction of surplus value with outmoded technology and production methods, while the labour movement remained firmly opposed to any further reduction of living standards, or to the introduction of any modernisation that may threaten employment. Both sides of Britain's class divide then, remained capable of resisting the pressure for painful economic change.

Following the failed attempt by industrialists to surmount the pressure of the return to gold through wage cuts and longer hours, the recognition that overt class struggle in Britain was now at a stalemate was formalised in the adoption of an 'industrial truce' by September 1926. With employers increasingly keen to return to orderly business and to avoid the high costs and dangers of industrial conflict, and with the labour movement now demoralised and weakened by the evident failure of direct action, a series of talks were established between representatives of the TUC, led by Ben Turner (the Chairman of the General Council), and a group of employers headed by Sir Alfred Mond. Although the FBI and the NCEO initially refused to participate in the talks, growing fears of a labour backlash also led to the establishment of a separate series of tripartite discussions with the TUC by 1927. As a result, industrial unrest declined markedly in the wake of the general strike. By 1928 the average number of new disputes had fallen to half the levels of 1925, while the average number of working days lost had fallen by more than four-fifths.[34]

Though ensuring industrial stability however, this class stalemate further impeded the process of economic adjustment. Despite this, the governing authorities remained unwilling to become more actively involved, and continued to insist that capital and labour had to adapt to the new economic environment. Direct state intervention remained limited to measures designed to encourage private enterprise, such as the establishment of the National Grid in 1926 (set up in part to facilitate the adoption of mass production techniques), and to curtail the disruptive ability of labour, such as the Trade Unions and Trade

Disputes Act of 1927, which imposed severe (though never used) restrictions on industrial action.[35] Nevertheless, with ministers acutely aware of the dangers of continued economic atrophy, the government turned to the Bank of England, whom it was felt would be better able to encourage the process of adjustment without incurring the political costs. For their part, the Bank were also keen to avoid a resumption of state intervention. As Niemeyer (now an executive director at the Bank) explained, it would be impossible to confine assistance to selected industries, and intervention would merely delay the 'more radical cure' of industrial restructuring and widen the clamour 'to get some of the Government dope'. At the same time however, Bank officials were also anxious to avoid any responsibility for economic conditions, and though reluctantly agreeing to help those parts of British industry in most difficulty, also remained emphatic that their assistance would be strictly limited. Although it rather defeated the object, the Bank were adamant that any provision of new capital would have to be preceded by industrial restructuring.[36]

The global crisis

To add to Britain's domestic problems, during the latter half of 1926 global economic conditions also began to deteriorate. Though on one level the world economy was now becoming increasingly stable, with Britain's return to gold in 1925 proving to be the trigger for a wider international movement that saw the gold standard restored to almost universal usage by 1928, various nodes of instability were now also starting to appear. The first of these lay in the structure of the restored gold standard itself. With most countries now seeking to economise on the use of gold by holding a large part of their official reserves in the form of sterling and dollars (the so called 'gold exchange standard'), this created the possibility that a crisis in one country could rapidly turn into a scramble for gold, thereby putting severe strain on the Federal Reserve and the Bank of England as the lynchpins of the international monetary system, and threatening to destabilise the regime as a whole. The second node of instability lay with developments in the world economy. The spread of industrialisation fostered by the war and driven by the search for ever greater levels of surplus value by capital had now led to an overproduction of key commodities such as coal, heavy metals, and agricultural goods, putting downward pressure on prices; while a widening geographical disparity between conditions for capital accumulation in most parts of the world and those prevailing in

America was leading to a rising expansion of global debt and to mounting speculation on the New York stock market. The roots of these problems were to be found in the provisions of the 1924 Dawes scheme, which sought to facilitate the reconstruction of the postwar global economy through a series of large foreign loans by the United States (amounting to some $6.4 billion between 1924 and 1929), but which provided no means of ensuring that these loans were used productively. In fact, for the most part the Dawes loans were not invested by recipient nations in ways that would ensure the smooth expansion of global capital accumulation, or that would enable them to raise productivity in order to repay the debt, but were instead spent on investments in already over-expanded economic sectors or on unproductive schemes such as public works and welfare provisions in an attempt to contain social tensions and shore up balance of payments weaknesses.[37]

Tensions within the world economy were exacerbated still further as gold continued to flow to the United States, sustaining its position as a net importer of capital despite the huge scale of its foreign lending, and as France and Belgium returned to the gold standard at undervalued exchange rates in order to secure a competitive advantage over other nations. In addition to this, the American economy itself was now starting to exhibit signs of overproduction due to a swathe of mergers and the development of mass production techniques since the war, leading to a large expansion of domestic credit in a bid to sustain levels of economic activity and stave off recession.[38] In turn, this growth in the US circuit of money capital led to the further growth of speculation on Wall Street as capitalists increasingly sought to bypass the productive exploitation of labour expressed in the formula M–C ... P(lp–mp)...C'–M', and instead sought to secure the expansion of capital on a purely financial basis (M–M'). Attempts by the FRBNY to address this with higher interest rates however merely served to compound the magnetism of the United States for international capital, and exacerbated the problems elsewhere in the world economy by forcing other central banks to raise interest rates in defence of their gold reserves. This put further pressure on world commodity prices (especially primary goods) and added to the burden of debtor nations, many of whom were now unable to respond to their growing balance of payments difficulties with a rise in interest rates due to economic weakness and domestic resistance to deflation. Instead, those in most trouble now turned to a further expansion in the production of primary goods, and to even greater levels of borrowing.[39]

By 1927 it was increasingly clear that the gold standard was not functioning in the way in which officials had originally envisaged. The Bank of England were losing gold (primarily for speculation in America), and as Norman complained, the extent to which central banks were now manipulating international gold flows meant that these were frequently 'irrelevant' to economic circumstances. Moreover, the regime itself was also coming under renewed domestic criticism. Hawtrey for example was arguing that the costs of the return had been 'much heavier than could have been foreseen' and that high interest rates had 'frightfully aggravated' Britain's difficulties, the FBI were also protesting against the 'abnormally high' level of interest rates, and the labour left continued to attack the gold standard and called for the Bank of England to be nationalised. In addition, rumours were also now circulating that Norman himself was 'extremely worried' about the situation, that he believed the return to gold to have been a mistake, and that he was considering its abandonment if matters did not soon improve.[40]

Though a brief respite in the pressure during April allowed another politically expedient cut in interest rates to 4.5%, problems resumed the following month when the Banque de France began converting its reserves of sterling into gold in a bid to ease upward pressure on the Franc by forcing a renewed rise in British rates. At the same time, political concerns over economic conditions also continued to grow, with Churchill resuming his attack on Norman and senior Treasury officials for the persistence of high unemployment. Though the Governor was insistent that this was the government's responsibility, the Chancellor was equally insistent that unemployment was 'an immense fault and shortcoming in our economic organisation' that could not be ignored. Although the gold standard policy had secured international confidence in the pound and had lowered the cost of living, Churchill also argued that it had produced labour unrest, had led to a huge increase in unemployment, and had raised the threat of a dangerous political backlash in the not too-distant future. In all, Britain's monetary policy since the war had, he warned, been 'entirely unsatisfactory'.[41]

Again however, such events do not signify the failure of the gold standard strategy. Despite his dissatisfaction Churchill could see no alternative to the regime, and for all its problems the Chancellor was nonetheless of the view that the gold standard had proved to be 'less disastrous' than a managed money policy with all its 'successive alterations and reversals'. Moreover, contrary to the rumours Norman did not now view the return to gold as having been a mistake, and nor was he remotely contemplating its abandonment, while the criticism from Hawtrey was also not considered to represent any significant body of official opinion. As the Governor later remarked:

> Except perhaps in the range of pure theory I have never heard anyone agree with him: and indeed it would have been true to say, for years past, that he represents neither opinion in the City, nor the official views of Whitehall, nor any deliberate and instructed views in political circles.[42]

Furthermore, the pressures of the global economic situation also soon subsided. French sales of sterling were halted once it was realised that continuing to damage the pound would also endanger the Franc, and international tensions were further eased in July as a conference of leading central bank Governors gathered in New York to discuss ways of improving global stability. A key outcome of the conference was a cut in US interest rates to 3.5%, providing a welcome relief for the global economy. This also diverted capital away from America, enabled the lowering of European interest rates, and aided the recovery of sterling throughout the rest of the year.[43]

From bad to worse

This apparent easing of the global economic crisis however proved to be a false dawn. By seeking to deal with the world's difficulties through a relaxation of credit instead of addressing its structural deficiencies, the New York conference merely cleared the way for continued commodity overproduction and further speculation on Wall Street. As global capital once more gravitated to the United States, New York interest rates were again increased, reaching 5% by July 1928. Once more though the rise failed to break the speculative boom, and acted only to increase the flow of gold to America and to force another tightening of rates elsewhere. Moreover, as speculation grew, much of the US foreign lending that had been helping to sustain the global economy through the Dawes scheme was now also redirected towards the more profitable domestic money circuit, intensifying the crisis for debtor nations and forcing many to draw on their reserves of sterling in order to service their repayments. At the same time, France, Germany, and Holland were also converting their holdings of sterling into gold in an attempt to establish a 'full' gold (as opposed to a 'gold exchange') standard, exacerbating the pressure on the pound and raising fears of a global gold shortage. As a finishing touch, the destabilising issue of reparations had again returned to the political agenda, with German pressure for a final settlement leading to the establishment of the Young Committee to re-examine the matter.[44]

As conditions in the global economy went from bad to worse, the pressure on economic conditions in Britain also mounted. Unemployment continued to rise inexorably, industrial production was now falling following a brief respite between 1926 and 1927, Britain's export industries were continuing to struggle, and monetary policy was attracting renewed criticism. The 'Mond-Turner' conference for example revived calls for an enquiry into the issue, complaining that the rigid determination of interest rate movements according to the level of the gold reserves at the Bank of England was proving to be detrimental to British industry; the TUCGC denounced the unemployment situation as a threat to 'the very stability of the nation' and declared that the actions of the Bank had been 'extremely injurious'; both the Labour Party conference and the labour left continued to call for the Bank to be taken into public ownership; and some on the more radical left were now even calling for the gold standard to be abandoned altogether.[45] From capital, although the vast majority of City opinion continued to support the gold standard, McKenna continued to criticise the regime, calling for lower interest rates and for an enquiry into monetary policy; the FBI were now claiming that their warnings over the return to gold had been proved 'right in every single particular'; while the Mond group of employers stated that the return had damaged trade and promoted industrial unrest. Along with the labour left, there was now also a growing feeling within industrial circles that monetary policy was biased in favour of the interests of finance, and as Vincent Vickers, a former Bank of England director asserted, an increasing number of 'influential industrialists' were now coming to realise this fact.[46]

In official circles too, anxieties were again growing. Hawtrey was continuing to press for lower interest rates in order to ease the pressure on the economy, the Treasury were becoming increasingly uneasy about the high and rising cost of unemployment benefits, while Churchill continued to berate senior figures at the Bank and the Treasury for their indifference to the problem. Moreover, Parliamentary calls led by the Liberal party for reducing unemployment through greater state intervention in the form of a large public works programme were now being vigorously promoted by Keynes and Henderson, and were starting to grow in popularity.[47]

Such political tensions continued to constrain the response of the Bank of England to these difficulties. The possibility of easing the pressure on the pound through even higher interest rates was rejected by Norman in November 1927 on the basis that this would be 'grossly unfair to industry' and would benefit no-one, and in mid-1928 by Cecil Lubbock, the Bank's Deputy Governor (in temporary control with Norman absent through illness) on the grounds that this would attract undue 'public attention' given the scale of unemployment. Instead, Norman's hopes now turned towards securing greater central bank co-operation as a means of addressing the international crisis. At the same time though, the Governor remained extremely keen to ensure that such co-operation would be kept strictly secret in order to avoid politicising the issue, warning that any publicity would 'make a public target' out of the decisions arrived at 'and would leave them much more difficult to achieve'. Similar fears concerning the extra responsibility that such measures would involve were also conveyed to Strong. As Norman wrote:

> I am sceptical as to how far it would be practicable and how far it would be wise for the Central Banks to admit in any way that they can regulate prices through their gold and credit policies: or, in other words, how far the power of fixing prices ... could or should come within the admitted purview of any Central Bank.[48]

Nevertheless, despite the growing concerns over monetary policy and the ongoing restrictions on state managerial freedom of manoeuvre, the gold standard was still continuing to provide officials with a credible and a largely depoliticised framework for economic policy-making. For all his dissatisfaction with the regime Churchill could still see no alternative to gold, and while Hawtrey continued to harangue the Bank, he also remained opposed to any political control over monetary policy, arguing that there was no real advantage in 'bringing in the Government'. Parliament, he maintained, should 'content itself with prescribing the end', and the responsibility for monetary policy should continue to rest with the Bank, even though they may not relish the prospect.[49] At the Bank itself, though Norman was now becoming increasingly anxious that the global crisis might soon force Britain off the gold standard, the Governor did not believe that there was any great desire in Britain for a change in the monetary system. As he put it, the number and influence of people wishing to significantly alter it was 'almost negligible', and consisted of:

> certain professors who no longer convince or even tickle the public: doubtless a number of manufacturers and exporters in the North whose attitude is more understandable than reasonable, and others, mainly cranks, who think in solitude more than they mix and argue with others.[50]

Indeed, Norman's assessment proved to be largely accurate. Despite the growing difficulties, for the most part monetary policy remained a non-political issue, and state officials managed to continue avoiding responsibility for the poor state of the British economy. Despite their criticisms the general view of the TUCGC was that the decline of the staple trades was still primarily due to 'natural and other causes beyond our control', and Britain's economic difficulties were still generally thought to derive from global circumstances and from the fact that 'so many British industries have failed to keep pace with the times'. In addition, debates on unemployment at the TUC and Labour Party conferences made no reference to the gold standard, and the TUC also did not regard the Bank to be responsible for domestic economic conditions, arguing instead that the reason for Britain's high level of interest rates was 'not because the Bank wishes to bring them about ... but because the rigid working of an automatic system leaves the financial authorities with no alternative.'[51]

Representatives of capital also directed their criticism at factors other than the behaviour of the governing authorities. The ABCC, the Mond group of employers, and the FBI emphasised that most of the responsibility for Britain's economic conditions lay with factors such as excessively high wages and the self-interested behaviour of foreign central banks (especially in the United States and France), while the FBI even considered the Bank of England to have had no choice but to maintain high interest rates due to external conditions, and claimed that they had done their best to help British industry even though they themselves were in a 'very difficult situation'. The Federation also maintained that most critics of Britain's monetary policy were 'cranks', and while generally having no strong views on the issue were now arguing against any enquiry into the matter on the basis that it would give credence to labour's calls for the nationalisation of the Bank.[52]

In addition, both capital and labour also continued to argue that Britain's problems could not be resolved with greater state intervention, and there were no significant calls for any great change in the direction of monetary policy. The main emphasis was still placed on the need for international co-operation and industrial re-organisation, and pressure concerning monetary policy was directed at the need for reform in order to make the gold standard work properly rather than at securing its abandonment. The Mond-Turner representatives for instance continued to highlight the need for global co-ordination and domestic industrial adjustment, while the Industrial Committee of the TUCGC also continued to emphasise the necessity for economic re-organisation and modernisation. As they put it, although monetary policy had 'undoubtedly affected the situation in a highly injurious way', it could not 'be held responsible for the post-war depression', and the only remedy was 'to produce more and to produce it more efficiently' in order to 'compete more effectively in foreign markets with our export goods.' On the subject of monetary policy the majority of the Labour Party also remained deferential to Snowden, who was still resolutely committed to the gold standard and of the view that monetary policy should be kept free from political control since Parliament was 'not a competent body to deal with such highly delicate and intricate matters.' Furthermore, both capital and labour also remained optimistic about Britain's future economic prospects. To the TUCGC and the FBI alike, Britain's difficulties were now thought to be coming to an end, the export industries were finally seen to be driving level with their major competitors, and the economic outlook was considered to be the brightest than at any time since the war.[53]

Concluding remarks

The return to the gold standard at the prewar par of $4.86 was designed to contain class struggle, to provide favourable conditions for capital accumulation by addressing Britain's long-term economic difficulties, and to increase the governing autonomy of state officials by imposing competitive discipline upon the expectations and behaviour of capital and labour, and by depoliticising the issues of economic conditions and policy-making. This strategy however was not entirely successful. The financial pressure imposed by the deliberately high exchange rate did not overcome the resistance of capital and labour to significant economic restructuring, and although prices fell, Britain's relative global competitiveness did not substantially improve. In part however this was also due to factors beyond the control of the core executive, such as the onset of an international economic crisis from

1926. Nonetheless, despite these difficulties, and despite the fact that the continuation of economic problems led to growing criticism of state officials and constrained their freedom of manoeuvre in response to the crisis, the gold standard still managed to provide distinct political benefits. The strategy was largely successful in establishing a credible and depoliticised framework for economic policy management, and was for the most part largely successful in insulating the core executive from political pressures. Class unrest subsided following the general strike of 1926, disquiet from capital and labour over economic conditions was now primarily displaced away from the state, and for all their problems Britain's governing authorities were now subject to less pressure and to fewer constraints than had been the case under the politicised mode of economic policy regulation prior to the return to gold.

6
The Collapse of the Strategy

Introduction

Although the gold standard strategy enabled Britain's governing authorities to successfully avoid responsibility for the deterioration in economic conditions during the latter half of the 1920s, a combination of growing international difficulties and a lack of domestic economic adjustment put increasing pressure on the British state, ultimately leading to the collapse of the regime in 1931. Throughout the development of this crisis however, the gold standard continued to provide a credible and largely depoliticised framework for economic policy management, and the high political freedom of the core executive still remained greater than it had been under the politicised regime preceding the return to gold. Moreover, following the enforced abandonment of the strategy, officials remained keen to retain the benefits provided by the gold standard. The new economic policy regime constructed after 1931 was designed to achieve similar objectives, and indeed state managers were anxious to secure another return to the gold standard at the old parity as soon as possible. Such a move however now proved to be impossible given the level of international instability and the extent of domestic antipathy to the regime.

Shifting the blame

From 1929 the crisis in the international circuit of capital began to intensify. Speculation on Wall Street grew, high interest rates at the FRBNY continued to draw in global capital, and world commodity prices fell sharply. These difficulties were also exacerbated as the growing crisis of overproduction in the United States tipped the

American economy into a steep depression during the latter half of the year, and as primary producers began trying to meet their growing debt burden through the introduction of protectionist measures and through a further expansion of production, thus swelling the oversupply of primary goods on the world market. By the end of the year the world depression was rapidly becoming the worst in the history of global capitalism.

The growing international crisis impacted directly upon Britain. The Bank of England continued to lose gold, unemployment remained high, and Britain's pattern of economic organisation continued to display little sign of any significant modernisation. This lack of adjustment was also compounded by the ongoing industrial truce, with the number of new disputes and working days lost both remaining low compared to the first half of the 1920s, and with employers still reluctant to try and impose a higher exploitation of labour through wage cuts or longer hours for fear of inciting a resurgence of unrest.[1]

The governing authorities however were still constrained in their response to the crisis by the political tensions surrounding the problems of the British economy. In February an attempt by the Bank of England to ease the pressure on its gold reserves with a rise in interest rates to 5.5% attracted fervent protests from the press, the Parliamentary opposition parties, and from representatives of both capital and labour. Though the City were unsurprised by the move, the FBI were sharply critical, both sides of the Mond-Turner talks reasserted their calls for an enquiry into monetary policy, and the ILP reissued their demands for an expansionary economic policy and for the nationalisation of the Bank of England. Several government ministers were also disconcerted by the rise, with the Minister of Labour (Sir Arthur Steel-Maitland) publicly voicing his concerns, and with Churchill warning the Cabinet that it would have a 'chilling effect' on the British economy.[2]

While monetary policy was now becoming an increasingly political issue however, the gold standard was still helping the governing authorities to displace criticism of Britain's economic difficulties. Cabinet ministers continued to insist that they had 'no responsibility' for interest rate movements, Blackett, Bradbury, and Niemeyer all emphatically maintained that the Treasury did not, and should not have any influence over the Bank of England, and on their advice Churchill responded to Parliamentary criticism with the assertion that interest rate decisions were the 'sole responsibility' of the Bank. Furthermore, although under intense pressure, the Chancellor was now staunchly defensive of the gold standard, arguing that the high level of interest rates was not due to the regime, that there was 'not a shadow of a doubt' that it had 'contributed materially to the national well-being', and that there was 'no remedy which would be more ill-judged than interference on political grounds with the working of our banking system.' Instead, Churchill attributed Britain's problems to the international situation and to the failure of both capital and labour to adapt to postwar economic conditions. Nevertheless, with a general election approaching the Chancellor was also anxious to minimise any open debate of monetary policy, warning colleagues that it would 'be inexpedient to open the door for fresh controversies', and was keen to resist pressure for dealing with Britain's economic problems with greater state intervention, claiming that this would lead to criticism of a 'devastating nature'. To strengthen this resistance, Churchill also instructed Treasury officials to draw up a systematic refutation of the case for public works. In the resulting document the Treasury vigorously argued that the only remedy for Britain's problems was higher competitiveness through lower production costs, improved efficiency, and industrial modernisation and restructuring in order to meet 'the changes that have taken place in world demands'. The introduction of public works, they claimed, would merely alleviate the pressure for economic adjustment, discourage private enterprise, dampen labour flexibility, and lead to pressure for higher wages and resurgent inflation.[3]

Such views also found resonance elsewhere within official circles. The final report of the long-running Balfour committee for instance stated that any difficulties experienced since the return to gold had now been overcome and that abandoning the regime was 'unthinkable', Blackett asserted that the only solution to Britain's economic difficulties was 'a ruthless scrapping of old plant, method, and directors', while Sir Cunliffe-Lister strenuously warned against state intervention to assist industry on the basis that this would encourage firms to sit and wait for government help, thereby enabling 'indifferent undertakings ... to maintain their industrial existence when they ought either to die or be absorbed in other and more efficient concerns'. At the Bank of England, Norman was also continuing to press ahead with efforts to minimise state intervention, establishing a Securities Management Trust to assist with the process of industrial reorganisation, and insisting that he wished 'to keep Government out of Industry in every way'.[4]

The Bank of England also forcefully rejected the growing criticism of monetary policy. The high level of interest rates, they claimed, had been forced on the Bank by the need to defend the par value of sterling on the gold standard, and the dire state of the economy was primarily considered to be due to the long-term failure of British industry to adapt to changes in the global economy, a problem which the return to gold had itself been designed to address. Though admitting that stabilisation at the prewar parity had created 'temporary difficulties', the Bank insisted that these had been more than offset by the provision of economic stability and cheaper imports, and that the main problem facing Britain was the failure of industrialists to recognise 'certain facts', and their continued adherence to outdated methods and practices. As Norman put it, the return to gold had 'directed attention to the need for the re-equipment, re-organisation etc. of productive industry necessary to enable it to compete with foreign industries'.[5]

Though providing state officials with a means of shifting the blame for economic conditions and policy-making, the gold standard was not however an automatic guarantor of political success. While the issue of monetary policy did not feature highly in the May general election, discontent over economic conditions (especially the high level of unemployment) led to the defeat of the Conservatives, and saw a second minority Labour government installed in their place. In economic policy terms though, the change again made little difference. The gold standard remained the cornerstone of the new government's political and economic strategy, and more proactive measures to address the economic situation remained limited to palliatives such as the introduction of some small-scale public works, and the establishment of the relatively ineffective Economic Advisory Council (EAC).

In spite of the electoral shift however the pressure over monetary policy continued unabated, and in August a sudden rise in interest rates at the FRBNY led to a renewed outflow of gold from the Bank of England. A corresponding rise in rates by the Bank though was now ruled out for fear of antagonising Snowden (the new Chancellor), who had publicly announced his opposition to higher rates in order to avoid unsettling public opinion.[6] As the Bank continued to lose gold, Snowden and Norman met to discuss means of protecting themselves from the political consequences of the crisis. With the Governor now increasingly anxious to furnish the Bank with an 'insurance against Labour snipers', and with the Chancellor keen to distance the government from the responsibility for monetary policy, both were now convinced as to the necessity for reasserting the formal distinction of duties and responsibilities enshrined in the gold standard. The result was an agreement that the Chancellor would now restrict his activities to fiscal and political matters, that the Bank would possess complete control over all technical and financial issues, and that Norman would not raise interest rates unless it was absolutely necessary.[7]

At the end of September however a financial crisis in the City provided the Governor with a sufficient reason to raise rates to 6.5% (their highest level since 1921) in order to arrest the outflow of gold. Though the move was welcomed by the City, the rise attracted a hostile response from the ABCC, the FBI, and the TUC, and led to increasing calls for an enquiry into the operation of the Bank of England. In response, while Snowden dismissed all responsibility for the increase and argued that the decision was made by the Bank alone, the Chancellor also sought to placate the criticism by adding that the move had been forced upon the Bank by international circumstances, and by announcing the establishment of an enquiry, headed by Lord Macmillan, into the effects of monetary policy. At the same time though, Snowden was also anxious to ensure that the enquiry would not lead to any significant change in monetary policy, and asserted that the government were still resolutely committed to maintaining the gold standard. Moreover, in conjunction with Treasury officials the Chancellor also sought to prevent the enquiry from examining the Bank of England too closely by ensuring that most of its members held 'sound, or at least not unsound' financial views, and by making its remit 'as vague and nebulous as possible'.[8]

'A very fine fight'

In October the speculative boom on Wall Street came to a spectacular end as the New York stock market collapsed. While this was disastrous for the United States, the crash temporarily eased the pressure on the global economy, enabling a worldwide relaxation of credit conditions and allowing the Bank of England to reduce interest rates to 5% by the end of the year. Despite this however the crisis in the international circuit of capital continued to intensify, and despite further reductions in interest rates to 3% by May 1930, economic conditions in Britain also continued to deteriorate. As they did so, the strain on the authorities grew further still. Parliamentary pressure continued to mount for state intervention in order to deal with the rising tide of unemployment (now edging towards two and a half million), the TUCGC were now directly criticising the return to gold at $4.86 for having forced employers to try and cut wages in order to maintain profits, while the labour left and the Labour Party conference both continued to press vigorously for increased state intervention and for public control of the Bank of England.[9] Representatives of capital too were increasingly critical of monetary policy. The FBI were now describing the return to gold as having been a deliberate attempt to force down British production costs and prices, and were claiming that it had been a 'major cause' of Britain's economic difficulties. Similar views were also now shared by many smaller industrial and commercial groups, such as the MAIE, while the vast majority of capitalist opinion, including that of the ABCC and even the City, was now of the view that economic re-organisation would no longer be sufficient to resolve Britain's difficulties, and that drastic cuts in tax, public spending, and wages, as well as the introduction of protective tariffs and the fostering of closer economic links with the Empire were now necessary in order to reduce production costs and improve competitiveness.[10]

Once again the governing authorities sought to distance themselves from these criticisms. Calls for greater state intervention were rejected on the basis that this would merely alleviate the pressure for economic adjustment and would render the state increasingly responsible for economic conditions, and instead government officials continued to insist on the need for reducing prices and public spending, and remained keen for the Bank to continue assisting with industrial re-organisation. Consideration of how to deal with the rising level of state expenditure (especially on unemployment) was now hived off to the newly established May committee and the Gregory commission in order that the government could avoid having to deal with these issues directly, and officials were also increasingly anxious to reduce and contain public debate of monetary policy.

Snowden for example publicly reasserted the government's commitment to maintaining the independence of the Bank of England, and responded to pressure in the House of Commons by stating that it would now be 'improper' to comment on monetary policy issues before the Macmillan enquiry had delivered its report, while the Prime Minister, Ramsay MacDonald, insisted that Britain's economic problems were not due to monetary factors but to a failure to adapt to changing global conditions.[11]

Bank of England officials too remained anxious to avoid responsibility for economic conditions, and remained emphatic that their involvement with industry would be both temporary and limited. Norman for instance was resolutely of the view that firms would have to get 'their own house in order' before being supplied with capital from the Bank, and maintained that 'just as we must now go into

Industry so we must be sure that we get out of it!'. In addition, the Governor also told the Macmillan enquiry that although the Bank were legally independent, they were 'not at all a free agent' now that their actions were constrained by the necessities of the gold standard, and denied that high interest rates had been detrimental to the British economy, claiming that their effects were 'more psychological than real'. Instead, Norman argued that Britain's troubles were not due to monetary policy but to 'misfortunes' such as the undervaluations of France and Belgium, and to the failure of industry to modernise and adapt. As he put it:

> I have never been able to see myself why for the last few years it should have been impossible for industry starting from within to have readjusted its own position ... I believe that had it been done the whole face and prospect of industry would look different to-day.[12]

For all these difficulties however, the gold standard nonetheless continued to provide officials with a credible and a largely depoliticised framework for economic policy management. Although the high political freedom of Britain's governing authorities continued to be constrained by the lack of domestic economic adjustment, officials were still now under less pressure than they had been prior to the return to gold. While monetary policy was now an increasingly political issue, while discontent over the effects of the gold standard was now rising, and while the persistence of high unemployment had led to the defeat of the Conservatives at the general election, the regime was still proving to be considerably effective at enabling officials to displace responsibility for economic conditions and policy-making. The vast majority of the City remained staunchly supportive of the gold standard and did not regard it or the behaviour of the authorities to be a central cause of Britain's economic difficulties, and although the FBI and the TUC were now becoming increasingly restive, both continued to place most of the responsibility for Britain's predicament on other factors such as the economic policy behaviour of foreign nations (primarily the United States and France), and the malevolent influence of City financiers, who were believed to have manipulated monetary policy in their own interests. For the TUC, the solution to Britain's economic problems was still considered to be a process of industrial re-organisation and adjustment, with Milne-Bailey of the TUCGC explaining that the vast majority of labour opinion did not hold monetary policy to be a key factor in 'all or even the chief difficulties of British industry', and FBI representatives were also of the view that the authorities were not primarily to blame. As Robert Glenday (the head of the FBI's General Economics Department) and Roland Nugent explained, the main cause of Britain's difficulties was thought to be 'the operation of the gold standard internationally', and the Bank of England was believed to have 'done its best' to help British industry. Indeed with the gold standard having placed the Bank 'in a position in which its freedom of movement was definitely restricted', the FBI now considered that they had 'put up a very fine fight against impossible circumstances.'

In addition to this, criticism of monetary policy was now overwhelmingly directed at the need to make the international system work properly, and there were as yet no real calls for the abandonment of the regime. The general view of the labour movement was that the gold standard should be reformed rather than replaced, and indeed a properly functioning international system was considered to be 'indispensable to the restoration of national and world economic prosperity'. Moreover, the TUC were now unsure how or even if a managed money policy could be made to work, and as Milne-Bailey again put it, for most the notion of leaving the gold standard was thought to be 'a thoroughly unsound idea'. Yet again, similar views were also held by the FBI. The Federation remained opposed to any attempt at resolving Britain's economic problems with expansionary measures on the grounds that this would merely lead to renewed inflation and a further erosion of competitiveness, and the general view was that 'a very determined effort' should now be made 'to get the old system going' before considering the introduction of any alternative measures. Indeed, such was the weight of opinion now leaning in this direction that many of those who had been sharply critical of the return to gold in 1925, including Keynes, Henderson, and Stamp, were now opposed to any notion of leaving the regime. As they explained in a report for the EAC, while the return had added to the difficulties of the British economy, other factors such as the inflexibility of capital and labour were also largely to blame, and departing from the system would now create more problems than it would possibly solve.[13]

Going...going...gone!

Although by 1931 it was now impossible to disentangle the economic effects of the gold standard strategy from those of the world recession, the experience of this policy in Britain had nonetheless been decidedly mixed. While wholesale prices had fallen by more than a third since 1924, and while retail prices were now 15% lower, the average level of wages had fallen by less than 4%, exports and invisible earnings had both fallen by a quarter (although imports had fallen by more than a third), and GDP had fallen slightly. Moreover, unemployment had soared from less than 1.5 million to the unprecedented height of 3.25 million, industrial production had recently dropped back to the levels of 1925, and while productivity in terms of output per worker had increased by about a sixth, there had been little in the way of economic restructuring. Britain's pattern of economic activity remained overwhelmingly dominated by the old export trades, and while these continued to stagnate, the expansion of newer and more advanced industries remained insufficient to make up the shortfall. In addition to this, sterling was now coming under renewed pressure as the emergence of a large budget deficit began to raise question marks over Britain's future gold standard status in the eyes of the financial markets. As the Prime Minister, Ramsay MacDonald put it, the present industrial and financial situation was now 'giving us all deep concern'.[14]

The political effects of the return to gold however had been somewhat more beneficial. Though it was now under increasing strain, the regime had nonetheless provided officials with a depoliticised means of managing the domestic circuit of capital, had successfully displaced pressure over economic conditions and policy-making away from the state, and had enhanced the high political freedom of the governing authorities. Furthermore, the discipline of the gold standard had also helped to undermine the position of the labour movement, and had proved effective in containing class unrest. Trade union membership had fallen by around 10% since 1924; the annual average number of working days lost since the return had been lower than that for the period from 1919 to 1924 (three quarters lower if the effects of the general strike are excluded) and had fallen to almost half the levels seen during the Great Unrest from 1910 to 1914; while the annual average number of industrial disputes had fallen to less than half the number seen in both of these periods. In addition to this, the spectre of a postwar advance by the working class had been successfully neutralised, and the distribution of wealth in Britain remained essentially the same as it had been twenty years previously. For all the fears and concerns about the growth of labour radicalism, the top 10% of the population still owned more than 90% of the wealth.[15]

The intensification of economic difficulties during 1931 however now also led to a breakdown in the industrial truce, and to a sharpening of class antagonisms. Although both capital and labour were in agreement about the need to resolve Britain's economic problems from within the confines of the gold standard, their proposed means for doing so were diametrically opposed. For the FBI, the NCEO, the ABCC, and the City (as well as the majority of the British press), industrial re-organisation and monetary reform were no longer considered to be sufficient to overcome the growing economic crisis, and protective tariffs, closer Empire links, and dramatic cuts in taxation, wages, and public spending were now thought to be essential in order to reduce production costs, raise profits, and improve competitiveness. The labour movement however were vehemently opposed to such measures. Reductions in wages and public spending, it was argued, would merely reduce economic demand and intensify the slump, and a programme of greater state spending, public works, and higher progressive taxation was now thought to be necessary in order to overcome Britain's ills. Moreover, while monetary policy was now seen to be of 'overwhelming importance' amidst growing displeasure with the way the gold standard was operating, and while the notion of easing Britain's problems through a devaluation was gaining popularity, the general feeling within labour circles remained in favour of economic re-organisation and modernisation, and the general view was that monetary changes were 'one of the conditions of better trade rather than a direct cause of it'.[16]

The majority of Britain's officials however remained directly opposed to the pursuit of expansionary or interventionist policies, and as such continued to side primarily with the views of capital. Although Hawtrey now thought the gold standard to be 'quite intolerable', the majority of Bank and Treasury opinion remained resolutely in favour of maintaining the regime and of addressing Britain's growing budgetary difficulties through cuts in tax and public spending, with the Bank of England and Snowden both insisting that they would take whatever measures were necessary in order to defend the pound.[17] Despite a further easing of global credit conditions however, and despite a fall in domestic interest rates to 2.5% (their lowest levels since 1909), the crisis in the international circuit of capital continued to worsen during the summer. This reached a new level of intensity with the collapse of Credit Anstalt (the largest bank in Austria), which severely damaged international confidence and sparked a fierce scramble for liquidity throughout Europe. With Britain having now accumulated a volume of short-term liabilities that was far in excess of its short-term assets due to the borrowing and lending strategy pursued by the City since the return to gold, and with many of these assets now also being frozen as a result of the liquidity crisis, Britain too was severely affected by the financial crash, leading foreign investors to grow increasingly nervous about the future security of sterling.[18]

At the same time, the report of the Macmillan inquiry into the effects of monetary policy also failed to ease the pressure on the authorities. Despite emphasising the need for lower production costs, industrial re-organisation, and for maintaining the gold standard at $4.86, a large fall in the pound shortly after the publication of the report prompted a sharp rise in interest rates to 4.5% and compelled the Bank to seek supportive credits from the United States and France. By now though, the majority of Bank and Treasury officials were of the view that any solution to the crisis would require firm action by the government in order to rectify the budgetary imbalance, particularly by reducing the level of spending on unemployment benefits.[19] Towards the end of July, with the pressure mounting, Norman fell ill and was replaced for the duration of the crisis by the Deputy-Governor, Sir Ernest Harvey. Almost immediately, Harvey's nerve was also put to the test by the publication of the May report, which further undermined foreign confidence by predicting a huge budget deficit of £120 million for the next financial year, and by arousing public hostility and outbreaks of civil disorder with its recommendations for dealing with the crisis through increased taxation and severe cuts in public spending, two-thirds of which was to come from unemployment benefits.[20]

In September the crisis entered its final phase. At a meeting with trade union leaders, Snowden and MacDonald emphasised the necessity of both defending the parity and balancing the budget, with the Chancellor warning that failure to do so would lead to a collapse of the pound and to widespread 'chaos and ruin'. The TUCGC however refused to accept any means of balancing the budget through cuts in unemployment benefits, with Citrine arguing that this would merely encourage an employers' attack on wages. Unable to reach an agreement with the unions, the government sought to buy more time with further credits from the United States, though were now informed that any further loans would require large cuts in public spending. On proposals for cutting unemployment benefit however the Cabinet were also sharply divided by eleven votes to nine. Fatally wounded by this schism, the minority Labour government subsequently collapsed, though MacDonald and Snowden duly re-emerged, amidst cries of a 'bankers' ramp', at the head of a Conservative dominated 'national' coalition government, ostensibly constructed as a temporary means of defending the gold standard and of guiding Britain through the financial crisis. This was quickly followed by the introduction of an emergency budget, which introduced £80 million of new taxes and cut unemployment benefits by 10%, and by the ready provision of some £80 million worth of French and American credits for the defence of sterling.[21]

Although the re-politicisation of monetary policy as a result of the economic crisis and the direct intervention of the government had now severely undermined the effectiveness of the gold standard as a means of protecting officials from political pressure, the crisis had yet to destroy the credibility of the regime. Representatives of capital for example welcomed the establishment of the national government and continued to call for cuts in wages and public spending rather than a change in monetary policy as the key means of resolving the crisis, and although the labour movement were vehemently opposed to the new government and were continuing to call for higher tax and public spending, the government's commitment to the gold standard was nonetheless considered to be resolute. As the TUCGC put it, a devaluation was now 'politically impossible.' Moreover, the Labour Party, the TUC, and even the ILP all continued to accept the need for a balanced budget, and even Keynes was now vacillating between calls for the abandonment of gold, for a devaluation, and for giving the international gold standard one 'last opportunity'.[22]

Foreign confidence in the government's commitment to maintain the gold standard at $4.86 however was now gravely weakened. As ministers became increasingly preoccupied with a forthcoming general election rather than with taking the necessary measures required to bolster the pound, and as social unrest began to rise in response to the imposition of public spending cuts, a renewed efflux of gold from the Bank of England was soon underway. This loss of confidence was further exacerbated by an apparent outbreak of mutiny at a British naval base in Invergordon over proposed salary cuts, which sent shockwaves through official circles and around the world. By mid-September, with the Bank's credits for the defence of sterling becoming dangerously low, and with a further rise in interest rates ruled out for fear that this might be seen as a panic measure, and may itself unleash a full-scale panic, Bank officials finally conceded defeat and formally requested that the government relieve it of its legal obligation to sell gold. To this the Cabinet agreed without dissent, and on the 21st Britain suspended its adherence to the gold standard.[23]

The aftermath

The decision to abandon the gold standard received a favourable reception. The FBI, the TUC, and the majority of the press welcomed the departure, there was no financial panic in the City, and the ABCC described the decision as having been a sound one given the circumstances involved. For state officials however, the loss of the gold standard was accompanied by an acute fear that sterling would now collapse, and that this would lead to an uncontrollable resurgence of inflation. To counter this threat, interest rates were immediately raised to 6% in spite of the dangers, and a series of economic controls were imposed, including a prohibition on foreign lending and a temporary six month tariff. Despite these measures however, the exit from the gold standard was also followed by an increase in global financial instability as many countries opted to follow Britain's example and abandon the regime, and while sterling did not collapse it nonetheless fell heavily, despite an overwhelming victory for the national government in the October general election, reaching a low point of $3.24 in December.[24]

Jettisoning the gold standard however failed to ease the pressure on the governing authorities. Indeed, since economic conditions and policy-making were now major political issues, and since the authorities were now deemed to bear a large part of the responsibility for such matters, the pressure on state officials continued to grow. The labour movement remained vehemently hostile to the national government, mounting nationwide demonstrations in response to the cuts in public spending and calling for a programme of increased state intervention in order to deal with the economic crisis; both the Labour Party and the TUC argued that the only means of resolving Britain's difficulties was through greater international co-ordination in economic policy and through more extensive links with the Empire; while the labour left pressed for more substantial measures including widespread nationalisation, public works, and higher taxation. In addition to this, the labour movement were now also placing the primary responsibility for Britain's poor economic performance on the return to gold at the prewar par, and were explicitly stating their strong opposition to any future restoration of the system. As the TUC put it, going back to the gold standard at $4.86 would be a 'dangerous mistake' that would merely produce price instability and lead to 'widespread industrial conflict', while the prospect of a return at a lower exchange rate was also rejected on the basis that this would merely provide temporary benefits and would be detrimental to Britain's long-term competitiveness.[25]

Representatives of capital too were continuing to put pressure on the government. The dominant view in industrial, commercial, and financial circles was that the exit from gold was not a panacea for Britain's difficulties, and that any resolution of these problems still required the introduction of protective tariffs and greater Empire links, as well as an improvement in competitiveness through cuts in taxation, public spending, and wages (although in practice few employers were now willing to pursue this for fear of re-inciting labour unrest). The FBI also called for 'the closest possible co-operation between Government and Industry' in order to ensure that the policy mistakes of the past were not repeated, and to ensure that the views of industry were fully taken into account. In addition to this, while many within capitalist circles still favoured an eventual return to gold (especially within the City), the majority of domestic capitalist opinion concurred with the labour movement, arguing that the return to gold in 1925 had been detrimental to Britain's economic performance, and stating that there should be no repeat of this policy unless it could be demonstrated clearly and unequivocally that this would be in Britain's economic interests.[26]

The new economic policy regime that was constructed against this backdrop was based on the same underpinning objectives as the strategy of a return to gold at $4.86. The main aims of the governing authorities were still to contain class struggle, to maintain pressure for greater economic competitiveness and adjustment, and to minimise the direct involvement of the state in order to diminish political pressure over economic conditions and policy-making. The notion of establishing a managed money policy for example, an idea that was now attracting renewed support from the labour movement and was once again being vigorously promoted by Keynes, was rejected by officials on the basis that direct state control would have an adverse effect on foreign confidence in the pound, and that it would therefore make sterling more difficult to manage and would leave the way open for even greater criticism. The governing authorities also claimed that a policy of regulating sterling in accordance with movements in commodity prices would be destabilising, and that this would not only lead to a run on the pound whenever prices fell, since the market would now assume an inflationary response, but would also generate political dangers whenever sterling rose, since this would renew the deflationary pressure on prices and wages. Given the impossibility of a managed money policy then, and given that the gold standard strategy was now thought to have shown the impossibility of reducing wages without provoking labour unrest, the dominant view within official circles was that the immediate course of action should therefore be to allow sterling to fall in order to produce a mild inflation, thus raising profits and thereby easing the pressure for cuts in money wages while simultaneously eroding their real value.[27]

The main components of the new regime for economic policy management were installed during the first half of 1932. With a recovery in sterling convincing officials that the threat of a collapse had now passed, interest rates were reduced to 2% by June (where they remained until 1939), a more permanent 10% tariff was introduced, and a trade policy of Imperial preference was adopted. These measures were buttressed by the maintenance of a tight fiscal discipline, with officials insisting on the need to maintain a balanced budget; by the introduction of a loosely managed exchange rate regime, with the establishment of an Exchange Equalisation Account (EEA) to provide the Bank of England with funds in order to keep sterling steady at around $3.50; and by the construction of an informal currency bloc known as the 'Sterling Area' based around the Empire and countries with close economic links to Britain.

With economic conditions and policy-making now overtly political issues, state officials also remained anxious to minimise their direct involvement in such matters. Control over tariffs was farmed out to an independent and ostensibly non-political Import Duties Advisory Committee; 'inappropriate' countries (namely those still on the gold standard) were deterred from joining the Sterling Area since this would risk undermining the advantages of a depreciated pound by encouraging other countries to devalue, and would also impose a moral responsibility on state officials to help with any difficulties that should arise; while the accounts of the EEA were kept strictly secret in order to conceal the depleted condition of Britain's reserves and to avoid encouraging speculation against the pound. Moreover, despite the more direct role for the Treasury under this new regime, operational policy decisions remained very much a matter for the Bank of England. As Norman put it, the Bank had retained 'an extraordinarily free hand' and were not called upon 'to justify the complete discretion which the Treasury allow us in matters of day to day practice.' In addition, both Bank and Treasury officials also remained keen to ensure that there was no unwarranted ease in the pressure for economic adjustment and improvements in efficiency. As Robert Kindersley and Henry Clay, economic advisors to the Bank, warned for example, it was now essential to make sure that lower interest rates did not 'defer the re-adjustment of industry by making it easier for redundant, inefficient and water-logged concerns to avoid elimination', and as they maintained, what was needed was a 'contraction of over-expanded industries', technological re-organisation and 'the development of new lines of production'.[28]

While this new economic policy regime was considered by the governing authorities to be a useful means of dealing with the problems accompanying the collapse of the gold standard, the long-term objective of economic policy was nonetheless to secure another return to gold at the old parity of $4.86.[29] While to many people the problems associated with the return to gold in 1925 were now thought to be obvious, to many key state officials these difficulties were considered to have been anything but inevitable. Neville Chamberlain (the latest Chancellor of the Exchequer) for example blamed Britain's economic difficulties on international factors, and maintained that 'there was no reason why the return to gold should not have been a great success', and while Norman later confessed to thinking that the return 'was probably a mistake', he nevertheless asserted that he would still 'do the same thing again', since 'a great deal of what has happened ... was not necessary' but 'might have been different'. Indeed, such views were also later echoed by Niemeyer, who remained a stalwart defender of the gold standard strategy. As he argued:

> It is perhaps easy to attribute to it all sorts of later misfortunes which might well have arisen anyhow from political and economic conditions which it was hoped in 1925 to avert in part by this very attempt at stability.[30]

Throughout the 1930s however, Britain's governing authorities were also aware that another return to gold at $4.86 was not now possible due to the high level of domestic antipathy towards the regime, and to the continued deterioration and instability in global conditions. As the depression continued to worsen, international co-operation also continued to break down (especially following the high profile collapse of a world economic conference in 1933), reparations and debt repayments fell by the wayside, and protectionist measures became almost universal as nations sought to shield themselves from the crisis through the pursuit of 'beggar-thy-neighbour' economic policies, which included a large devaluation by the United States in 1934.[31] With the re-imposition of deflationary pressure now considered to be too economically and politically dangerous, especially given the persistence of high unemployment, the general view of British officials was that there could be no return to gold unless the various difficulties afflicting the regime had been resolved, and that until such time low interest rates therefore needed to be maintained in order to avoid any further rise in unemployment and any resurgence of labour unrest. Graham-Harrison, the Financial Secretary to the Treasury, explained for instance that the choice was now 'between a low exchange and an attempt to cut wages severely', with the latter course of action thought to contain the risk that 'the position might develop in the same way as 1925 and 1926', while H. A. Siepmann, another economic advisor at the Bank of England, pointed out that 'the memory of our previous return to par with all the evil consequences commonly attributed to it would surely prevent our being allowed to climb back again'. In sum, as Chamberlain maintained 'even the most tentative approach to stabilisation' was now, in the circumstances, 'quite unthinkable'.[32]

Concluding remarks

This chapter has shown how the continually languid nature of the British economy combined with the emergence of a crisis in the international circuit of capital to progressively undermine the gold standard strategy. Poor economic growth and persistently high levels of unemployment generated rising dissatisfaction with monetary and economic policy, and while the credibility and depoliticising aspects of the regime survived intact, albeit in a weakened state, the deterioration in economic conditions eventually culminated in renewed class unrest, a growing budgetary crisis, and an enforced abandonment of the gold standard itself. Despite the departure from gold in September 1931 however, Britain's governing authorities sought to construct a new regime for economic policy management based on the same underlying principles. The key priorities were to contain class unrest within politically safe limits, to provide favourable conditions for capital accumulation while sustaining pressure for improved competitiveness and economic adjustment, and to minimise the state's directly visible involvement with the economy. Although another return to the gold standard at the prewar parity remained the ultimate aim of state officials until the latter years of the 1930s, this proved to be impossible to achieve given the persistently high level of international instability and the strength of domestic antipathy both towards the regime itself and to any prospect of further deflation. The gold standard strategy was now finally consigned to history.

7
Britain's Membership of the Exchange Rate Mechanism

Introduction

As well as establishing grounds for a reinterpretation of Britain's return to the gold standard in 1925, an open Marxist approach also provides a useful means of analysing other episodes of exchange rate policy-making. In this chapter, Britain's membership of the Exchange Rate Mechanism (ERM) from 1990 to 1992 is examined from this alternative theoretical perspective. While this is commonly understood to have been primarily motivated by economic concerns, and, in similar terms to the return to gold, to have been a major policy disaster, it is also possible to interpret this episode in a rather different manner. In contrast to conventional analyses, Britain's membership of the ERM is instead considered here to have been the central component of a wider governing strategy designed to address growing economic and political difficulties within the British state through the imposition of financial discipline and through the depoliticisation of monetary and economic policy-making. Moreover, it is also considered to have been a relatively successful strategy for Britain's governing authorities. Although membership of the ERM did not lead to any significant improvement in Britain's competitiveness compared to its main economic rivals, it nonetheless facilitated a substantial reduction in inflation, provided an effective means of containing class struggle, and for the most part enabled officials to effectively displace responsibility for economic conditions and policy-making away from the state, thereby enhancing their governing autonomy.

The Exchange Rate Mechanism

The ERM was the central component of the European Monetary System, which was established in 1979 as a means of restoring monetary stability within the European Community (EC) following the collapse of the Bretton Woods system. Nations participating in the ERM were required to establish a centrally defined parity for their exchange rate with the European Currency Unit (a notional currency made from a weighted average of all EC currencies), through which a series of bilateral parities were thereby established with all other ERM currencies. This central rate was to be maintained within a narrow 2.25% fluctuation band on either side of the parity for 'full' ERM members, or within a broader and transitional range of 6% for countries that were not yet ready for such a rigorous constraint. Intervention in defence of the parity was obligatory once a currency reached the limits of its fluctuation margin, and various support mechanisms, including the provision of extensive short-term credits, were available for this purpose if required.

In a similar fashion to the gold standard, the ERM thus served to constrain the exchange rates of participating nations within tightly defined limits, thereby linking together their national price levels, and compelling them to pursue economic policies that were broadly in line with those pertaining throughout the system. Any country experiencing excessive inflation or deflation relative to the ERM average would experience a corresponding fall or rise in the external demand for its goods and services, and hence a fall or rise in its exchange rate within the ERM. Eventually, once the exchange rate reached the limits of its fluctuation band, this would force the imposition of countervailing measures, such as changes in monetary or fiscal policy, in order to maintain the currency within its limits.

In practice however, since the risk of speculation against the exchange rate was far greater for member states experiencing above-average rates of inflation, and since countries joining the ERM did so primarily for anti-inflationary reasons, membership of the ERM effectively entailed a commitment to follow the monetary policies of the least inflationary country. In reality, this tied its participants to the monetary policies of the German Bundesbank, whose political independence and constitutionally enshrined commitment to the maintenance of price stability had long endowed it with a strong anti-inflationary credibility, and had effectively installed the German Deutschmark (DM) as the ERM's dominant, or 'anchor' currency. Membership of the ERM thus offered participating countries an effective means of importing the anti-inflationary credibility of the Bundesbank for themselves, enabling them to impose financial discipline upon the expectations and behaviour of capital and labour, and to thereby contain and reduce inflation with fewer economic costs and political difficulties than might otherwise be necessary. To strengthen these disciplines and to further enhance these benefits, ERM participants also committed themselves to the promotion of economic convergence with a view to achieving the ultimate goal of economic and monetary union (EMU), and were obliged to gain the consent of all other ERM members should they wish to realign their currency beyond the limits of its fluctuation margin, thereby making it extremely difficult for countries pursuing lax economic policies to simply devalue their way out of trouble.[1]

Britain however was not an original participant in the ERM, and instead joined the regime relatively late in October 1990. The timing of this entry coincided with an intensification of serious economic and political difficulties both domestically and within the ERM itself, and in September 1992 Britain was ignominiously forced to abandon the regime after less than two years as a member following a huge speculative attack on the pound. This has led to a conventional interpretation of this policy episode as having been a complete policy disaster. Although the decision to join the regime is principally believed to have been taken for entirely admirable economic reasons, notably to reduce inflation, the Conservative government of the day are believed to have joined at the wrong time given the conjuncture of growing internal and external difficulties, and at the wrong exchange rate, with sterling being effectively overvalued by around 10% at its ERM parity of DM2.95. As such, while the ERM eventually proved to be successful in reducing inflation, as with the return to the gold standard, it is also thought to have undermined the competitiveness of Britain's exports, to have entailed the maintenance of high interest rates in defence of the pound, and to either have led to, or to have exacerbated a precipitous recession. In turn, these problems are also believed to have led to a sharp increase in the political difficulties facing the government, which are thought to have far outweighed any political advantages that officials might have hoped to gain through a heightening of Britain's influence within the European Community. In particular, sterling's withdrawal from the ERM on 'Black Wednesday' is believed to have wrecked the government's economic policy credibility and to have been a key factor in their political destruction at the 1997 general election. Given this, it is therefore usually argued that these difficulties could have been reduced or even avoided had Britain joined the ERM either sooner, not at all, and/or at a lower and more appropriate exchange rate.[2]

In contrast to this conventional wisdom however, an open Marxist analysis of this policy episode offers a rather different view of events. Indeed, from this perspective Britain's membership of the ERM is not considered to have been a policy disaster, but is in fact seen as having been a relative success for the governing authorities. In general terms, ERM membership is understood to have been the key component of a governing strategy designed to contain class struggle, to provide favourable conditions for capital accumulation, and to increase the high political freedom of the core executive. More specifically, and again in common with the return to the gold standard, it is thought to have been designed to address growing economic and political difficulties within the British state through the imposition of financial discipline and through the depoliticisation of monetary and economic policy-making. In terms of results, while the economic effects of the strategy were ultimately mixed, in political terms the ERM was largely successful in providing officials with a credible and a depoliticised framework for regulating the circuit of capital, and with an effective means of displacing pressure over economic conditions and policy-making.[3]

The economic and political crisis

The decision to join the Exchange Rate Mechanism in 1990 was set against a backdrop of growing economic and political difficulties within the British state. Principally, these stemmed from the continuing failure of the governing authorities to adequately address the long-running problem of Britain's relative economic decline, and from a persistent rise in the demands and the expectations of capital and labour throughout the postwar period. As with its predecessor, Britain's engagement in the Second World War once again undermined its international position and forced the state to assume an unprecedented level of control over the economy, thereby eroding the discipline of the market and transforming economic conditions and policy-making into overtly political issues. In sharp contrast to the First World War however, the conflict was not followed by any concerted efforts at state retrenchment, but by the construction of an economic policy framework based on the accommodation of working class demands and an acceptance of state intervention. This led to the establishment of a postwar settlement based around the creation of a welfare state, a mixed economy, and an ostensible commitment to both 'corporatism' and to the use of 'Keynesian' demand management in order to maintain full employment and rising prosperity.

However, while this class accommodation helped to maintain social stability it also ensured that the state remained the primary locus of responsibility for economic conditions and policy-making during the postwar era. This was aggravated by the inherently unsustainable nature of the postwar settlement itself, as the continually expanding role of the state undermined the ability of Britain's governing authorities to deal with the rising pressure from capital and labour that this generated. With Britain's economy now remaining effectively insulated from the need for productive improvements and re-organisation by the heightened levels of dirigisme, and with state officials unwilling to try and impose such changes directly due to the now-politicised character of policy-making, Britain's relative economic decline was allowed to continue unabated, and the pressure on the governing authorities grew progressively stronger. At the same time then, as the demands on the British state were growing ever-larger, its ability to satisfy them was therefore becoming ever-more diminished.

This inherent contradiction in the postwar settlement though was not immediately problematic. The emergence of the largest and most extensive boom in the history of world capitalism during the 1950s enabled officials to gloss over the deterioration in Britain's relative economic performance, and helped to maintain economic growth and low unemployment with relatively few difficulties. By the 1960s however the underlying weakness of the British economy was becoming increasingly evident, and by the end of the decade the global boom itself was starting to unwind, leading to the worst economic and political crisis in Britain since the early 1920s. Britain's growth of GDP, industrial production, investment, and productivity were now all lower than those of its main competitors, unemployment grew from around a quarter of a million in 1956 to 1.3 million by 1979, while retail prices experienced an almost five-fold increase over the same period. Industrial unrest too was on the rise, with the annual average number of new stoppages between 1968 and 1979 now almost three times higher than the annual average from 1945 to 1967, and with the annual average number of working days lost having multiplied by almost four times.[4]

By the end of the 1970s official concerns about rising inflation and social disquiet were becoming acute. Presenting the crisis as the inevitable result of an over-expanded state and an excessively powerful trade union movement (a particularly resonant claim following the Winter of Discontent), the incoming Conservative government of 1979 argued that the key to resolving Britain's difficulties lay with reducing the role of the state in economic affairs, with curtailing the power of the unions, and with extending the discipline and incentives of the free market. This, it was thought, would not only help to raise economic productivity and competitiveness, but would also enhance the governing autonomy of the authorities by reducing the expectations of capital and labour, and by therefore reducing the demands being made on the state. As Nigel Lawson, then the Financial Secretary to the Treasury later explained, it was now increasingly necessary 'to adjust expectations to reality' and to disengage the state from its directly visible involvement with the economy in order to avoid 'politicising the wage bargaining process'.[5]

The failure of monetarism

Despite proclaiming its support for membership of the ERM 'when the time was right', the initial strategy adopted by the Conservative government was instead founded upon the tenets of 'monetarism'. This was embodied in the Medium Term Financial Strategy (MTFS), which aimed to contain the growth of the money supply within a pre-specified target range through the imposition of high interest rates and public spending cuts. By establishing a clearly visible rule for economic policy management, the government hoped that this would provide them with a credible framework for tackling inflation, raising productivity, curtailing wage demands, and reducing the direct economic involvement of the state. As Lawson again explained, the MTFS was designed to impose an anti-inflationary 'shock treatment' on capital and labour, and to provide the government with 'a self-imposed constraint on economic policy-making, just as the Gold Standard ... had been in the past, and the ERM came to be.'[6]

The introduction of the MTFS however also coincided with the emergence of another downturn in the global economy, leading to a steep recession during the early 1980s. While interest rates reached record heights, industrial production fell sharply, the balance of trade deteriorated to its worst ever position, and unemployment began an inexorable rise to 3.2 million by 1985. Nevertheless, the recession was not without its advantages for the authorities. Between 1981 and 1983 the rate of earnings growth fell by more than a third and the rate of inflation more than halved, while the annual average growth rate of output tripled from 1980 to 1985. The discipline of rising unemployment combined with stiff trade union 'reforms' also helped to undermine the strength of organised labour. From 1980 to 1983 trade union membership fell by 13%, while the annual average number of new stoppages and working days lost now fell to less than half the levels endured during the 1970s.[7]

Despite these benefits however, by the mid-1980s the MTFS was widely considered to have failed. The rising cost of unemployment benefit had seriously disrupted the government's efforts to reduce public expenditure, earnings growth had continued to outstrip the growth of productivity, and despite the attempt to reassert the control of market forces, economic conditions and policy-making remained politicised. Representatives of both capital and labour still considered the governing authorities to be largely responsible for the poor state of the British economy, while the attempt to disengage the state from its direct economic involvement was also compromised as officials were forced to adopt a series of interventionist measures in order to prevent the collapse of firms in key industrial sectors. Moreover, while inflation had fallen during the early 1980s, the money supply itself had some-what paradoxically increased, causing the government to frequently overshoot its monetary targets, and undermining the theoretical assumptions on which the MTFS was based.

Faced with these difficulties, several key state officials, most notably Lawson (now the Chancellor) and Geoffrey Howe (the ex-Chancellor and now the Foreign and Commonwealth Secretary), were led to con-clude that the fall in inflation had been due chiefly to a rise in the value of the pound. By 1981 a combination of high interest rates and a rise in the price of oil (now an important factor in the exchange rate given Britain's North Sea oil reserves) had driven sterling up by around 30% since the 1979 general election. This was thought to have deliv-ered a large deflationary shock to the economy by reducing import costs and by eroding the competitiveness of British exporters, thereby offsetting the effects of the expanding money supply by putting down-ward pressure on prices. In addition to this, the apparent link between the exchange rate and inflation had also been demonstrated by a sub-sequent slide in the pound, which fell from $2.40 in 1981 to $1.05 by January 1985 due to a rise in the dollar and a fall in oil prices, and by an accompanying rise in the retail price index from 4.5% in 1983 to 6% by 1985.[8]

In this light, both Lawson and Howe now came to see membership of the ERM as a useful means of addressing Britain's economic and political problems. Joining the regime, they argued, would not only help to provide exchange rate stability, but would also enable the gov-ernment to establish a new and credible anti-inflationary framework for economic policy to replace the now discredited MTFS. Placing a tight constraint on the value of the pound would send out a clear signal to both capital and labour that they could no longer 'look to exchange rate depreciation to solve their difficulties' as they had persistently done throughout the postwar period, but would instead have to 'lower their inflationary expectations' and 'conduct their affairs in a more prudent way'. Furthermore, a strategy of ERM membership was also seen to offer distinct political benefits. In particular, this would raise Britain's status and influence within the European Community, and would also enable the government to impose their anti-inflationary discipline from the 'outside', since this would now appear to emanate from the impersonal structures of the EC itself rather than from the politically motivated behaviour of the government. The key advantages of this were that it would thereby enhance the credibility of the government's anti-inflationary commitment, since the international arrangements of the ERM would be more difficult to abandon than those of the domestically based MTFS, and that it would effectively insulate officials from disquiet over key economic policy-making decisions by ostensibly removing them from the sphere of national democratic control. In sum, as Lawson put it, the regime would offer the 'most desirable form of financial discipline', would give the government's economic policy a sorely needed 'shot in the arm', and would provide the Conservative party with the new impetus needed to carry them 'up to the election and beyond'.[9]

Support for the ERM however was not confined to a few government ministers. By 1985 the City, the Confederation of British Industries (CBI),[10] and the TUC were all pressing for membership on the grounds that this would ensure lower inflation and economic policy certainty, while the majority of senior officials at the Bank of England and the Treasury, along with most of the Cabinet, were also in favour of entry. Despite this groundswell of support however, opposition from Margaret Thatcher effectively torpedoed the proposal. The Prime Minister was implacably hostile to any notion of subordinating British monetary policy to that of the Bundesbank, and insisted that joining the ERM would in fact impose an unacceptable constraint on the government's freedom of manoeuvre. Under the influence of Brian Griffiths (the head of the No. 10 Policy Unit), and her independent economic advisor Sir Alan Walters, Thatcher claimed that membership would be economically and politically dangerous, since tying British monetary policy to an external anchor would run the risk of being forced to maintain an adversely high level of interest rates in defence of the pound, and since entering the regime for its anti-inflationary benefits would constitute a damaging admission of failure in the government's own ability to raise competitiveness. As such, the Prime Minister therefore concluded that given these difficulties, 'the attempt to use ERM membership to influence the expectations of management and work-forces would be an equal failure'.[11]

'A safe and secure discipline'

Despite recovering from the recession, the performance of the British economy during the latter half of the 1980s was mixed. From 1985 to 1988 output per man hour rose by an annual average of almost 5%, business investment rose by an annual average of almost 9%, and unemployment fell from 3.2 to 2.4 million. On the other hand, the balance of trade continued to deteriorate, productivity growth continued to lag behind the growth in earnings, and labour unrest increased, due most notably to a lengthy and bitter conflict between the government and the National Union of Mineworkers. At the same time, with entry into the ERM having been ruled out by Thatcher, and with monetarism having now been quietly jettisoned, the government also spent the second half of the decade constructing a new economic policy framework. This was based around a programme of privatisation and supply-side measures designed to improve economic flexibility and to further reduce the economic involvement of the state.[12]

While this was being installed however, the tensions between Thatcher and Lawson over Britain's future relationship to the ERM were becoming increasingly public, leading to growing uncertainty about the government's economic policy direction. In 1987, on Lawson's instruction, the Bank of England and the Treasury began to pursue a policy (allegedly unknown to Thatcher) of 'shadowing' the deutschmark by intervening in the market in order to keep sterling within a range of DM2.80 to DM3.00. This *de facto* membership of the ERM though, also coincided with a series of large cuts in tax and interest rates (which by May 1988 had reached their lowest level for a decade) as the government sought to engineer an electorally popular economic boom. While this enabled the Conservatives to secure a third consecutive term in office, the 'Lawson boom' as it became known, also led to a re-emergence of inflationary pressures. In turn, these were further stoked up by the Chancellor's exchange rate policy, which precluded a rise in interest rates and forced the Bank of England to sell sterling in order to prevent the pound, whose value was now being driven up by speculation fuelled by the unexpectedly strong growth in the British economy, from rising above its ceiling of DM3.00. In spring 1988, with the economy rapidly overheating and with inflation starting to take off, Thatcher, who had now apparently discovered that sterling was being manipulated in line with the deutschmark, forced the Chancellor to abandon his efforts, and to allow the pound to float freely once more.[13]

As economic conditions and policy-making became the subject of increasingly heated political debate, and as Thatcher continued to refuse entry into the ERM, Lawson now began to direct his energies towards persuading the Prime Minister of the virtues of central bank independence. In a similar fashion to the ERM, the Chancellor argued that this would enable the government to regain its anti-inflationary credibility, and would displace political pressure over monetary policy by passing the control and the responsibility for interest rate decisions over to the Bank of England. Such a move, Lawson explained, would therefore not only 'provide a beneficial jolt to inflationary expecta-tions', but would also serve to 'depoliticise interest rate changes'. Despite these advantages however, Thatcher's intransigence remained unyielding. In a repeat of her objection to the ERM, the Prime Minister claimed that granting independence to the Bank of England would also send out a signal that the government's own attempts at constraining inflation had failed, and that it would therefore constitute a politically damaging 'admission of failure of resolve on our part'.[14]

Against this backdrop the pressure on Thatcher to allow Britain to join the ERM sharpened during the summer of 1989. Increasingly annoyed at the Prime Minister's continued obstinacy, especially since the government's official policy on the ERM was still one of joining 'when the time was right', Lawson and Howe now made the unex-pected move of threatening to resign during a European Community summit in Madrid if Thatcher did not make it clear exactly when this would be. Under duress, the Prime Minister responded with an announcement that Britain would enter the ERM when certain key conditions had been met, namely when the process of creating the Single European Market had been completed, when all exchange con-trols within the EC had been abolished, and when the level of inflation in Britain had fallen to the average level within the ERM itself. While this was clearly a step forward from an outright rejection of ERM mem-bership, since these conditions were unlikely to be met at any time soon, Thatcher was nonetheless convinced that the issue had now been effectively neutralised.[15]

Yet nothing could have been further from the truth. In October the simmering conflict between Lawson and Thatcher came to a head when the Chancellor sensationally resigned following the Prime Minister's refusal to sack Sir Alan Walters (who ironically also resigned shortly afterwards) for the latest in a long line of attacks on the ERM in which he described the regime in the press as being 'half baked'.[16] At the same time, faith in the government's economic competency was also crumbling as the credit-fuelled indulgence of the Lawson boom began to turn into recession. By 1990 unit labour costs, wage demands, producer prices, bankruptcies, and unemployment were all rising, profits, output, and productivity growth were all in decline, inflation had more than doubled since 1985 (at 9.5% compared to 3.4%), interest rates were at a five year high of 15%, and real GDP growth had virtually ground to a halt. Further still, the stratospheric levels of business confidence that had been reached during the heady days of the Lawson boom had now collapsed, sterling was under renewed pressure, and after more than a decade of Conservative rule Britain's international position was continuing to decline. To round this all off, while labour unrest was now at a relatively low level compared to the mid-1980s, political and economic disquiet was also growing. Unease within the Conservative party over the twin issues of Europe (especially the drive towards monetary union) and Thatcher's increasingly autocratic style of leadership had led to a small but symbolic leadership challenge, popular discontent was mounting in the country at large over the issue of the poll tax, and the government's electoral popularity was shrinking. Dissatisfaction ratings recorded by Market and Opinion Research International (MORI) had risen to 71% from a low of 49% in 1987, and the Conservatives had recently slumped to their worst ever local election results.[17]

Particularly disconcerting for the governing authorities amidst all of this, was the fear that rising inflation would not only continue to undermine Britain's global competitiveness but that it would also lead to a return of the severe political and social unrest of the 1970s. As the new Chancellor, John Major, later described the scene, the government's economic policy was now 'falling apart', and there was an increasing 'atmosphere of crisis' throughout the country. Moreover, officials also recognised that addressing these difficulties would entail difficult and unpopular measures. As Norman Lamont (the Chancellor from November 1990) later explained, the process of reducing inflation would entail 'higher interest rates, frustrated hopes, bankruptcies, and lost jobs', while as Major warned, 'defeating inflation would be a long and painful haul'. Nonetheless, the Chancellor was firmly of the opinion that the dangers of continued inflation were such that efforts to counter it were now 'unavoidable' and had to be imposed 'even if the cost was high'. Or as Lamont infamously professed, rising unemployment and a recession would be a price 'well worth paying'.[18]

Faced with such difficulties, membership of the ERM started to look like an increasingly attractive proposition for state officials. In an echo of Lawson's earlier arguments, Major too concluded that joining the regime would enable the government to impose a credible anti-inflationary discipline by sending out a strong signal that competitive deficiencies would no longer 'be bailed out by a devaluation of the currency'. This, he claimed, would put pressure on both capital and labour to raise productivity, and would facilitate 'the destruction of inflation' by forcing prices, and especially wages, to conform to internationally prevailing levels. In this assessment Lamont also concurred, stating that the discipline imposed by the ERM would force the growth of earnings in Britain to 'fall to levels comparable with the rest of Europe'. In addition, it was also recognised that the need to defend the exchange rate parity within the ERM would constrain all aspects of economic policy-making, effectively placing an external straitjacket on the government's discretionary capacities. As Lamont was to again explain, ERM membership would require that fiscal policy be used 'to buttress monetary policy', while as Major put it, the ERM would not represent an 'additional optional discipline', but would provide the government with 'the total framework for policy'. Indeed, with the government's economic policy credibility now firmly on the ropes, the Chancellor not only considered the ERM to be 'the only coherent policy on offer', but thought that entry into the regime was rapidly becoming 'inevitable'.[19]

On top of these economic benefits, officials were also aware of the attractive political advantages offered by the ERM. Extending Britain's influence within the EC was now believed to be increasingly necessary in order to slow down the drive towards monetary union, while on a domestic level, the provision of a clear and credible framework for economic policy would help to unite the ever-more fratricidal Conservative party, and to reduce the inflationary expectations of capital and labour, thus making it more likely that electorally sensitive interest rates could be reduced without jeopardising the value of the pound. Further still, by confining the future direction of economic policy-making and by effectively placing it under the control of an externally defined system, membership of the ERM would also enable the government to remove key economic policy decisions from the realm of democratic control and accountability, and to thereby displace pressure over these issues away from the state. By depoliticising economic conditions and policy-making in this way, the ERM would, as Major acknowledged, provide the government with 'a convenient scapegoat' for Britain's problems, thus enabling them to impose a tough economic discipline while simultaneously shifting responsibility for its effects onto an exogenous regime. As the Chancellor prosaically observed, 'we needed to get re-elected, the economy needed tough decisions'.[20]

Into the ERM

While the pressure for Britain to join the ERM continued to build within official circles, representatives of both capital and labour were also continuing to press for membership. To the City the ERM was seen to offer a means of restoring its position as a pre-eminent financial centre, while to the CBI the key benefits were considered to be the provision of economic policy stability and the imposition of wage pressure upon labour. Favouring an entry rate of around DM3.00, the Confederation argued that a major advantage of ERM membership would be that it would help to check the growth of wages above levels warranted by improvements in productivity, and that it would thereby force pay settlements to 'reflect economic performance'. In this way, joining the ERM would help to avoid the threat of 'a wage-price spiral leading to a more prolonged resurgence of inflation or a more severe squeeze on profit margins'. To representatives of labour on the other hand, the anti-inflationary discipline of the ERM was also believed to be a key reason in favour of joining. The Labour Party considered its support for the regime to be a useful means of enhancing its own economic policy credibility, while the TUC argued that the ERM would not only help to secure economic policy stability and prevent an excessive rise in the cost of living, but by removing the ability of industry to 'devalue its way out of difficulties', would also ensure that the British economy became and remained internationally competitive. In order to ensure that this pressure was not wholly prohibitive however, the TUC also called for a 'competitive' entry rate into the regime of below DM3.00, on the grounds that this would deliver a boost to exports, and that it would thereby help to reinvigorate economic growth and reduce unemployment.[21]

By the summer of 1990 the pressure on Thatcher to sanction entry into the ERM was mounting on all sides. The majority of the Cabinet, most senior officials at the Treasury and the Bank of England, and representatives of both capital and labour were all in favour of joining, while speculation on Britain's entry into the regime was now pushing up the value of the pound and adding further momentum to the proceedings. Indeed, as Richard Ryder, the Economic Secretary to the Treasury, had recently told the House of Commons, it was no longer a question of if Britain would join the ERM, but was rather 'simply a question of when'.[22] As Thatcher's position within the Cabinet became increasingly isolated and ever-more diminished, the Prime Minister was now finally and reluctantly forced to relent, and though none of the previously specified conditions had yet been fulfilled, the green light was given for sterling to enter the ERM within the 6% fluctuation band.

Following this decision, the focus for official discussions now centred around the timing and the rate at which Britain should join the regime. On the first of these issues Treasury officials, though concerned about the prospect of joining while on the verge of recession, now favoured an entry during September or October, contending that this would give time for Britain to fulfil the Madrid conditions, which the government had by now softened to a mere proviso that British inflation should be moving towards the ERM average, and arguing that this would thereby ease the economic and political strains of the move. On the question of the entry rate however, officials were somewhat less concerned to secure a smooth transition, and were more anxious to ensure that sterling was fixed at a level that would provide strong anti-inflationary pressure. On this basis, the eventual rate chosen for entry was DM2.95, giving the pound a fluctuation range of between DM2.77 and DM3.13. Although this central parity broadly coincided with the approximate market value for sterling at the time of entry, a rate of DM2.95 was nevertheless a relatively high level given the speculative rise in the pound (from DM2.75 in April), and given that the level of British inflation at 9.5% was still significantly higher than that pertaining in other ERM countries.[23] Indeed, as Thatcher and Major both later acknowledged, sterling's ERM parity was deliberately set at a relatively high level in order to put downward pressure on prices and to ensure credibility in the government's anti-inflationary commitment. The possibility of entering at a lower rate was rejected on the grounds that this would have antagonised Britain's ERM partners, and that it would have required lower interest rates in order to prevent sterling from rising above its upper ERM limit, thereby leading to a renewal of inflationary pressures.[24]

On 5th October Britain finally joined the Exchange Rate Mechanism. The decision was warmly received by the majority of labour, business, press, public, and political opinion, and at Thatcher's behest was also accompanied by a cut in interest rates from 15% to 14% in order to bolster support for the move. The timing of the reduction however raised immediate question marks about the seriousness of the government's anti-inflationary intentions, and this, in conjunction with a rise in the deutschmark and the Spanish peseta, soon forced sterling down towards the bottom of its ERM band. Moreover, the easing of credit conditions also failed to ease the pressure on the economy, which continued to sink into recession. By the summer of 1991 manufacturing output had fallen by 7.5% since joining the ERM, unemployment had increased by more than a third (its largest rise for almost a decade), and business optimism had slumped following a sharp rise in bankruptcies. In addition, the balance of trade was still in deficit, GDP and investment remained in decline, and the growth of earnings continued to outstrip that of productivity, with output per man hour now rising at its lowest rate for ten years.[25]

Political difficulties too continued to plague the government. In particular, growing social unrest over the poll tax and growing discontent within the Conservative party over Thatcher's style of leadership combined in an explosive manner, with Geoffrey Howe's resignation from the government at the end of October 1990 precipitating a chain of events which culminated in the replacement of the Iron Lady with the mere amalgam of the still relatively unknown Chancellor, John Major. These domestic tensions were also compounded by rising international instability, with the outbreak of military conflict against Iraq, ongoing difficulties throughout the former Soviet Union following the collapse of Communism, and the onset of a recession in the world economy all adding to the prevailing mood of uncertainty. With public support for the government also remaining weak, the situation, as Major was forced to admit, was now looking increasingly tempestuous. As he put it, the governing authorities were facing 'a sea of troubles'.[26]

Nevertheless, the first year of Britain's ERM membership was still deemed to be a success by the government, and the regime effectively established a credible and a largely depoliticised framework for economic management. Though generally weak within the ERM, the pound attracted no heavy speculative attention, inflation fell to less than 6%, and by the early months of 1991 a weakening of the deutschmark and the peseta allowed the government to implement a series of further cuts in interest rates, which by September had fallen to

10.5%. Moreover, despite the recession the government were now under less pressure over economic conditions and policy-making than they were prior to entering the ERM, and than is likely to have been the case had they continued to remain outside the regime. While the Labour Party continued to attack the government for its handling of the downturn, and while the TUC began to call for a realignment of ERM currencies in order to ease the pressure on the economy, both remained firmly in favour of ERM membership and firmly accepted the need for its economic discipline. As the TUC maintained, it was now becoming increasingly essential 'to improve Britain's relatively poor levels of productivity if adverse consequences are to be avoided'. Capitalist opinion too remained relatively propitious for the governing authorities. The City were still firmly supportive of the government's economic policy framework, with share prices reaching record levels in September 1991, and while the CBI repeatedly called for a lowering of interest rates, they also continued to support Britain's membership of the ERM and believed that the economy was now poised for a recovery. Such views were also mirrored by public opinion generally, and while economic conditions remained an issue of some considerable concern, opinion polls nonetheless indicated that people were becoming increasingly optimistic about Britain's economic future.[27]

In addition to this, the government's electoral prospects were now also starting to improve. Although they remained unpopular in the polls, the government's dissatisfaction ratings were now almost 10% lower than they were before joining the ERM, and dissatisfaction ratings for the Major government during 1991 never rose above 66%, a level that the Thatcher government never managed to fall below during 1990. Moreover, after twelve months in the ERM the Conservatives were now edging ahead of Labour in the polls, while the Prime Minister himself registered a not too disheartening average of 52% in his own personal satisfaction ratings. In relative terms then, things had clearly improved for the government.[28]

State officials also remained steadfastly committed to the pursuit of the ERM strategy, and were adamant that there would be no unwarranted relaxation in economic policy in order to ease the strains of the recession. By September 1991 John Major was feeling sufficiently confident in the success of the government's approach to declare that they had now 'got inflation licked', while trade union calls for a devaluation were rejected both by the Prime Minister and by Norman Lamont, the new Chancellor of the Exchequer, who described the suggestion as 'fools gold', and who counselled that such a move would shatter the government's economic policy credibility and lead to even higher levels of interest rates. Instead, Lamont insisted that while the process of reducing inflation had invariably been 'painful', it was nonetheless 'producing results' and British industry was now 'immeasurably better placed ... than it was ten years ago'. The Chancellor also re-emphasised the government's commitment to drive out inflation, portending that a failure to do so would lead to a continued decline in Britain's global competitiveness and to an accompanying rise in 'uncertainty and strife', and warned that as such, the rising tide of unemployment would now therefore have to keep growing until pay settlements fell 'to the levels prevailing in other ERM countries'.[29] Moreover, such sentiments were not confined to the Prime Minister and the Chancellor, but were also evident elsewhere within official circles. The Governor of the Bank of England, Robin Leigh-Pemberton, maintained for example that both the ERM and the value of the pound had now been successfully established as 'facts of life to be taken into account when taking decisions about prices and wages', and remarked with some satisfaction that capital and labour would now simply have 'to recognise conditions for what they are, and adjust behaviour'. In a similar vein, a government White Paper on industrial relations published during the summer also argued that if British wage costs continued to rise faster than those of competitor nations then 'the inevitable consequence' would be 'lost jobs and a lower standard of living'. Britain, it warned, could simply not 'afford to risk slipping back into the inflationary pay settlements, low productivity and strike prone industrial relations of the 1970s'.[30]

Down and out

In February 1992 the government sought to strengthen its commitment to the ERM by signing up to the Maastricht Treaty on European Union. This tightened the anti-inflationary discipline and credibility of the regime by establishing a series of institutions and binding procedures for the purpose of facilitating greater policy co-ordination between EC states, and by creating a set of tough convergence criteria to which countries wishing to participate in the process of EMU would have to adhere. Despite obtaining opt-outs from what were considered to be the more unpalatable aspects of the Treaty, namely the social chapter and the third and final stage of the move towards full EMU, the Conservative government nevertheless pledged itself to implementing the second stage of the process, which required the establishment of central bank independence, thereby signalling its intention to further entrench the principles underlying its economic policy framework.

Despite this bolstering of the government's commitment to the ERM, its economic and political difficulties nevertheless increased throughout 1992. At the heart of this was the emergence of a conflict between the requirements of maintaining the value of sterling within the ERM, and the need to address growing domestic pressure for a relaxation of economic policy in order to ameliorate the effects of the recession, which was now proving to be deeper and longer than anyone had expected. The main cause of this conflict was the development of an economic boom in Germany following the process of reunification, which had compelled the Bundesbank to increase its interest rates by 2.75% since the beginning of 1991 in order to counter the threat of rising inflation. In conjunction with this, a series of interest rate cuts in the United States designed to counter the threat of a domestic recession now led to a flight of capital out of the dollar and into the deutschmark, causing it to appreciate and putting strong pressure on all currencies within the ERM.

For Britain, this meant that relatively high levels of interest rates would have to be maintained in order to hold sterling within its fluctuation margins, even though the economy was still in the icy depths of recession. Despite a large cut in income tax, GDP continued to fall, industrial output remained stagnant, and although unemployment now reached the height of 2.8 million by the summer (almost two-thirds higher than at the time of Britain's ERM entry), wages continued to rise above the rate of inflation. In addition to this, the budget deficit now grew to an enormous £46 billion as government borrowing was forced to rise in order to cover the loss of tax revenue and to meet the escalating costs of unemployment and related benefits, while discontent over economic conditions and policy-making was also starting to mount. The notion of devaluing the pound within the ERM was now growing steadily in popularity within both industrial and trade union circles, and strong rumblings of unease were also starting to emanate from the government's own backbenches. With the vocal support of Thatcher, this Parliamentary pressure for a devaluation (with some Conservative MP's even calling for the abandonment of the ERM itself), now forced the government to delay its efforts to ratify the Maastricht Treaty, thereby undermining its attempt to strengthen its anti-inflationary discipline.[31]

For all these problems however, membership of the ERM was still continuing to provide a beneficial political and economic strategy for the authorities. Inflation remained in decline and the credibility of the government's commitment to maintain the exchange rate was still largely unchallenged, despite the growing pressure on sterling, and despite the introduction of further reductions in interest rates to 10% by May in an attempt to revive the economy. Moreover, productivity growth had now increased since entering the ERM, labour unrest had fallen to a record low (with the smallest number of disputes and working days lost since records began), business confidence was continuing to improve, and political conditions were also starting to look more salubrious. Though remaining harshly critical of the government's handling of the recession, both the Labour Party and the TUC also continued to support membership of the ERM, and despite their complaints the CBI were also favourably predisposed to the government's approach. Though continuing to call for lower interest rates, the outgoing chairman of the CBI's Economic Situation Committee, David Wigglesworth, recognised for example that there was only a 'limited scope available to the government' given the constraints of the ERM, while Howard Davies, the CBI's newly-appointed Director General, also lent support to the government, claiming that they were being 'rightly tough on inflation', that devaluation had 'little to commend it', and that abandoning the ERM was 'even more unattractive'.[32]

Furthermore, while public levels of dissatisfaction with the government remained virtually unchanged, officials were nonetheless successfully managing to avoid most of the blame for Britain's economic difficulties. According to one opinion poll, only 4% of respondents now laid the blame for the recession squarely at the door of the Major government, while in contrast nearly half blamed it on the global economic downturn or on the policies of the previous Thatcher government. Moreover, while the number of people who were now expecting the economy to improve had fallen slightly compared to the previous year, public optimism over economic conditions remained significantly higher than in the period preceding Britain's entry into the ERM. More significantly still, in the spring general election the government successfully managed to buck all expectations to win a fourth term in office in spite of the recession, with the issue of monetary policy barely registering on the agenda during the course of the campaign, and with the increasingly deep splits within the Conservative party over the question of Europe also remaining well submerged. For

John Major, it was a further extension of what was already proving to be the longest electoral honeymoon for a post-war British Prime Minister.[33]

Such heady feelings of optimism though were soon to be dashed, and by the summer the government were facing a crisis that would ultimately force it to abandon the ERM. A key point in the unravelling of this crisis was the rejection of the Maastricht Treaty by Denmark in a referendum at the beginning of June. Since a condition of the Treaty was that it needed to be ratified by all its signatories in order to be adopted, the Danish rejection now cast a long shadow over its future. Shortly afterwards the political skies were darkened still further as the French government declared that they too would hold a referendum on the Treaty during September, giving rise to the prospect that the entire project of European monetary integration could soon collapse. Since this would remove the incentive for participating governments to continue pursuing the tight economic policies needed in order to satisfy the specified convergence criteria, and since they would now instead have every incentive to enhance their electoral popularity by adopting a more relaxed economic policy stance, the credibility of the various exchange rates within the ERM itself, as the precursor to EMU, was now undermined. At the same time, problems within the structure of the ERM were also starting to emerge. The absence of any significant realignments within the regime during the last three years had given rise to the impression, which many participating governments were keen to foster, that the ERM was now operating as a completely fixed exchange rate system, despite the fact that the necessary economic convergence for this purpose had not yet been achieved. As the clouds of uncertainty over Europe's monetary future continued to gather, and as the world's financial markets now started to question the appropriateness of the various exchange rates within the ERM, dangerous speculatory pressures began to muster.

These developments had a direct and a severe impact upon Britain. As high interest rates continued to dampen economic activity and to push up unemployment, and as the possibility of further rises in defence of the pound became increasingly apparent, the pressure on sterling started to intensify. Despite intervention by the Bank of England, towards the end of August the pound fell to the bottom of its fluctuation band. Britain's governing authorities however remained resolutely committed to maintaining sterling within the ERM, and were adamant that leaving the regime was not a viable option. As Lamont pointed out, not only would it be 'extremely difficult' to abandon the ERM given the widespread support for the system, but such a move would also be 'profoundly disruptive' on the internal politics of other participants due to the impending referenda on Maastricht, and would therefore attract an inevitably hostile response. Moreover, the Prime Minister, the Chancellor, and the majority of senior Bank and Treasury officials were also certain that jettisoning the ERM would greatly complicate the management of monetary and economic policy, and that it would lead to a dramatic loss of confidence in the government's anti-inflationary credibility. In turn, officials feared that this would prompt a sharp fall in the pound, a resurgence of inflation, and would therefore require even higher levels of interest rates than were being endured at the present time in order to avoid a financial catastrophe. A second option however, that of easing the pressure on the economy through a devaluation, was also rejected by the authorities on the grounds that any competitive advantage gained would soon be wiped out by a rise in inflation, and with Lamont warning that this too would lead to a loss of confidence and would precipitate a slump in sterling that would be 'unprecedented in the last forty years'. To put a further and more pernicious spin on the government's predicament, officials were also aware that seeking to defend the pound within the ERM through the use of higher interest rates now contained its own set of dangers, since this would not only add to Britain's economic and political difficulties, but would increase the pressure for higher rates throughout the system, thereby adding to the prevailing instability and endangering the ratification of the Maastricht Treaty in the French referendum.[34]

The only solution to this Gordian dilemma was considered by the government to be a cut in interest rates by the Bundesbank. Repeated attempts to secure such a reduction however were consistently rejected by Bundesbank officials, and when the concession of a cut in rates was finally offered in return for a wider realignment of ERM currencies, this avenue was rejected by the French government, who feared that it would undermine their prospects of ensuring a positive result in the impending referendum. With no cut in sight, by the beginning of September the situation was giving Britain's governing authorities increasing cause for alarm. The Bank of England had now expended a large portion of its reserves in support of the pound, and were borrowing a further ten billion ECU's for this purpose, while the British government sought to demonstrate their resolve for the support of sterling by publicly announcing a £7.25 billion foreign exchange loan for its defence. In an attempt to calm the growing anxieties surrounding the

ERM, a meeting of EC finance ministers was also called in order to present a united front to the markets and to display their determination to avoid any revaluation. By now though, the growth of speculation was gaining an inexorable momentum. A range of Nordic currencies linked to, but not in the ERM, were experiencing increasing difficulties, and on September 14th the Italian lira was forcibly devalued by 7%, sending out an untimely reminder that the ERM was not a fixed exchange rate system, and that change was in fact entirely possible.

The response of the Bundesbank to this devaluation, a belated and a disappointing 0.25% cut in interest rates, indicated that Germany was not prepared to shoulder the burden of sustaining the present distribution of parities within the ERM. To compound this impression, the president of the Bundesbank, Helmut Schlesinger, was also cited in the press as stating that Britain was suffering from a lack of competitiveness, and that sterling too would benefit from a devaluation. With the Bundesbank clearly refusing to come to the defence of the pound, the speculation against sterling now rose dramatically. Despite a series of increasingly desperate measures by the governing authorities, including massive intervention by the Bank of England (amounting to some £15 billion during the crisis as a whole), and a sharp rise in interest rates from 10% to 12%, and then finally to 15%, the attempt to salvage the ERM strategy ultimately proved to be futile. On September 16th, or 'Black Wednesday' as it came to be known, the government were finally compelled to admit defeat, and sterling's membership of the ERM was suspended.[35]

The lodestar

Britain's participation in the ERM had been clearly tumultuous. During its time as a member of the regime, GDP had fallen by 3%, manufacturing output had fallen by more than 4%, investment had dropped by 11%, the growth of business profits had slumped to half the annual average for the 1980s, and unemployment had grown by two thirds from 1.8 million to 2.9 million. In addition, both capital and labour had continued to resist the pressure for economic adjustment. Average earnings had increased by more than 12% despite the recession, and while output per man hour had improved by an annual average of just over 3%, this was almost a third lower than the annual average rise of around 4.5% achieved during the 1980s, and had enabled Britain to make only a slight gain on its main international rivals. By 1992,

British productivity remained about a sixth lower than the G7 average, almost a fifth lower than German levels (even accounting for the inefficiency of the former East German economy), and more than a third lower than levels in the United States and France.[36]

If the economic costs of being in the ERM had been harsh, then the political costs of abandoning it were even more so. Despite insisting that Britain's departure from the regime was a temporary affair, officials recognised that a return to the ERM was now politically impossible and that the key task was to instead construct a new framework for economic policy management. In this however, Britain's governing authorities also remained anxious to reassert their anti-inflationary commitment and to maintain the depoliticisation of economic policy decisions. As Lamont warned, the loss of the ERM posed a 'great danger' that 'decision-making would now be seen as entirely political', and as he defiantly remarked, 'we have not gone through the last couple of years – the sacrifices, efforts and difficult policies that have been pursued – to throw it all away.'[37] The preferred choice of the Chancellor though, the establishment of an independent Bank of England (a policy also unsurprisingly favoured by the Bank themselves), was rejected by the Prime Minister, who argued that this would fail to depoliticise interest rate decisions, and that it would merely leave the government with the responsibility for something over which it no longer had any control. Instead, the central component of the government's new economic policy strategy was based on the adoption of an explicit inflation target of between 1% and 4%, with the stated intention being to hit a 2.5% target by the end of the Parliamentary term in 1997. This was buttressed by the publication of a quarterly report on inflationary developments and prospects by the Bank of England, and from 1994 by the publication every six weeks of minutes of the meetings between the Governor of the Bank and the Chancellor. While these measures were designed to avoid the perceived pitfalls of central bank independence, they were also designed, as Lamont explained, to 'act as a discipline on the Government and [to] make it more difficult for interest rate decisions to be political.'[38]

Within this overarching framework, the government also sought to revive the flagging British economy. While various additional measures to constrain inflation were introduced, such as restrictions on public spending and a large rise in taxation, a series of policy relaxations were also implemented to help stimulate economic growth. Interest rates were now reduced to 6% (their lowest level for twenty years), public sector borrowing reached more than £45 billion by 1995, and sterling was allowed to depreciate to more than 15% below its ERM parity by 1996. Nevertheless, while the loosening of the ERM straitjacket now helped to facilitate an economic expansion, unemployment remained above its pre-ERM level, the growth of industrial production continued to lag behind Britain's main international rivals, and the balance of trade remained poor. More significantly still for the government, the experience of the ERM had fundamentally split the Conservative Party over the issue of Europe, and had completely destroyed their image of economic policy competency. Although the government managed to stagger through the remainder of their term in office, their fortunes in the opinion polls slumped and the Conservative Party's ultimate defeat in the general election of 1997 proved to be its worst for more than a hundred years. As John Major was to later lament, 'Black Wednesday' had truly been 'a political and economic calamity'.[39]

However, while the humiliation of being forced to abandon the ERM was undeniably disastrous for the government, this should not be taken to mean that the strategy had been a complete failure. Indeed, for all its difficulties membership of the regime had delivered real benefits for the governing authorities during its period of operation. Though sterling spent most of its time in the ERM below its parity, the pound had still been relatively stable and protected from speculatory pressure, interest rates had been reduced by 5% before their last minute rise, inflation had fallen by almost 6% to reach its lowest level since 1986, and though earnings growth had continued to rise faster than productivity, it had nonetheless fallen from around 10% to 6%. Moreover, in the period following Britain's exit from the ERM, earnings growth now fell to its lowest levels for the entire period of Conservative rule, and inflation remained firmly in check, reaching its lowest level for thirty years in 1993, and fluctuating thereafter between 1.5% and 3.5% until the electoral pounding of 1997.[40]

In political terms the ERM had also proved to be beneficial. Labour unrest was dramatically curtailed and organised collective resistance to capitalist exploitation was successfully redirected into less dangerous channels of individual struggle. While the number of cases referred to the Advisory, Conciliation, and Arbitration Service (ACAS) rose by more than 40% during Britain's membership of the ERM, and while the number of cases taken to an Employment Tribunal almost doubled, there were now more than 50% fewer new stoppages, and more than 75% fewer working days lost during 1990 to 1992 than there were during the previous five year period.[41] Moreover, while economic conditions and policy-making remained politically contentious issues given the severity of the recession, the regime also proved to be largely successful in furnishing officials with a means of shielding themselves from social discontent. Representatives of both capital and labour accepted the need for Britain to remain in the ERM, the blame for Britain's economic difficulties was primarily directed at targets other than the present government, the credibility of the Conservatives' economic policy stance was temporarily restored, and their electoral popularity improved during the period of ERM participation, enabling the government to triumph against all the odds in the 1992 general election. Indeed, while bemoaning its long-term consequences, John Major was clearly convinced of its more immediate merits. As he put it: 'The ERM offered us the lodestar we needed and, for all the finger pointing after 'Black Wednesday' in 1992, it worked.'[42]

Given these factors then, it is therefore entirely reasonable to assume that Britain's governing authorities experienced fewer difficulties within the ERM than would have been experienced by remaining outside the regime. While such a claim is obviously counterfactual, it seems equally obvious that had the government pursued the latter course of action then its economic policy credibility would have continued to flounder (especially given the lack of any coherent alternative to the ERM); the level of criticism being directed at state officials for the poor condition of the economy would have increased given the politicised nature of policy-making and the wide degree of support for membership of the ERM; and even higher levels of interest rates would have been needed in order to avoid an inflationary loss of confidence in the pound. In turn, this would also have added to the difficulties facing the British economy, which was already sliding into recession prior to (and hence for reasons other than) its entry into the ERM, and would have thereby heaped further political misfortune upon the government, who in all likelihood would have been forced to bear a greater share of the responsibility for the downturn. It is also highly probable (indeed it is almost certain) that Britain's relative economic decline would have continued without relent given the entrenched resistance of capital and labour to improved efficiency and economic adjustment, and while any attempt to ameliorate the effects of the recession through the pursuit of a more relaxed economic policy stance would have merely stoked up greater economic and political difficulties for the future, any attempt to force an improvement in Britain's economic performance through direct state intervention would have been virtually unthinkable for the governing authorities themselves, since this would have heightened their responsibility for economic conditions and would have therefore added still further to the opprobrium being aimed in their direction. In sum then, to blame the ERM for the political calamities which befell the Conservative government during the 1990s is somewhat akin to blaming the lifeboat for the sinking of the Titanic.

Concluding remarks

As with Britain's return to the gold standard in 1925, Britain's membership of the ERM from 1990 to 1992 is conventionally understood to have been motivated by narrowly defined economic reasons, and is commonly interpreted as having been a major policy disaster. Britain's governing authorities are believed to have joined the regime at the wrong time and at the wrong exchange rate, with the overvaluation of the pound being seen as a key factor in the subsequent difficulties faced by the British economy, and in the ensuing political traumas experienced by the Conservative Party. In contrast to this conventional view however, from an open Marxist perspective this policy episode can be interpreted as having been driven by wider economic and political factors, and to have been a relatively successful governing strategy for Britain's state officials. While Britain's economic performance under the regime was mixed, in political terms the policy helped to contain class struggle and to provide a greater degree of governing autonomy than would otherwise have been available. In the following chapter, New Labour's approach towards the question of joining the single European currency is also examined in a similar manner.

8
Britain and the Single European Currency

Introduction

Britain's return to the gold standard in 1925 and the decision to join the ERM in 1990 were both central components of a governing strategy designed to contain class struggle, to secure favourable conditions for capital accumulation, and to increase the governing autonomy of state officials. These objectives were to be achieved through the imposition of competitive pressure on capital and labour, and through the depoliticisation of economic conditions and policy-making. In this chapter, the possibility of British entry into the single European currency is also examined from this perspective. This shows that joining the euro would provide New Labour with a means of extending their existing governing strategy, enabling them to impose a tighter anti-inflationary discipline upon the British economy while simultaneously enabling them to disclaim responsibility for the unpopular effects of this process through the depoliticisation of key economic policy decisions. However, despite the clear benefits of such a move, the likelihood of the New Labour government being able to successfully realise these advantages remains slim. In particular, the persistently high level of domestic antipathy to the prospect of 'scrapping the pound' seems certain to preclude British entry into the regime.

The road to nowhere

The route to the single European currency, known as the euro, was as long as it was winding. The origins of the process can be traced back to the creation of the common market in 1957, with the subsequent expansion of trade within the European Community giving rise to a

145

need for greater monetary co-operation between member states in order to ensure a smooth flow of international payments. During the 1960s this imperative was further enhanced as the onset of a global economic crisis led to a rise in exchange rate instability which disrupted the operation of the common market and put EC relations under growing strain. To resolve these problems, by the end of the decade EC members had decided to initiate a drive towards EMU, and in 1970 set up the Werner group in order to determine the specific means by which this was to be achieved.

In 1971 the Werner report was published, outlining an ambitious three phase programme for the completion of EMU within ten years. As part of phase one, EC members were required to establish a precursor to monetary union known as the 'snake-in-the-tunnel', a mechanism in which participating states would maintain their exchange rates within a pre-specified range of each other. Progress in this direction however was rapidly scuppered by a further deterioration in global economic conditions, which led to divergent economic performances within the EC, to the collapse of the Bretton Woods system, and to a further rise in exchange rate volatility. This made the snake increasingly difficult to maintain, and led to the eventual abandonment of the Werner plan by the end of 1973. While the failure of the snake appeared to signal the early death of the attempt to achieve EMU however, by the end of the 1970s new life had been breathed into the project with the creation of the European Monetary System. This was designed to provide the EC with a 'zone of monetary stability', and was to form a new and improved basis for co-operation between member states as part of the new and renewed drive towards economic and monetary union.

Real progress towards the creation of a single currency though was not made until the mid-1980s. In 1986 the Single European Act committed its signatories to extend the principles of the common market by overseeing the creation of a single liberalised market in goods, services, and labour by 1992, and as a corollary of this, in 1988 the EC established the Delors committee in order to devise a new plan for reaching the goal of EMU. The following year the committee presented its findings, and as with the Werner report also envisioned that this could be achieved via a three stage process. Among the various steps that would need to be completed *en route* were the creation of a European Central Bank (ECB) in order to provide a single European monetary policy; the achievement of a greater degree of economic convergence and policy co-operation between participating nations; and the maintenance of European exchange rate stability, with all those taking part in the process of EMU being required to hold their currencies steady within the narrow band of the ERM prior to the final move to monetary union.

No sooner was the single market programme completed and the implementation of the Delors plan underway however, than the crisis which engulfed the ERM threatened to bring the entire edifice of EMU crashing down. From the summer of 1992 the growing difficulties surrounding the ratification of the Maastricht Treaty on European Union were accompanied by a series of enforced devaluations throughout the European Monetary System, eventually forcing ERM members to widen their fluctuation margins to an effectively meaningless 15% on either side of the remaining parities. By the autumn of 1993, all hopes of ever seeing EMU once more appeared to have been extinguished.

In the event though, such anxieties proved to be ephemeral. The crisis in the ERM was found to be far from terminal and within a year the long march towards monetary union had resumed its onward course. By 1994 the final ratification of the Maastricht Treaty had given the project renewed impetus, and by the end of 1996 all of the remaining ERM currencies (with the exception of the Irish punt) had returned to the narrow 2.25% fluctuation band. In 1997 their commitment to meeting the convergence criteria outlined by the Treaty was further buttressed by the provisions of the Stability and Growth Pact, which constrained government borrowing to a maximum 3% of GDP except in 'exceptional and temporary' circumstances, and on the 1st of January 1999 the single currency itself was finally launched (albeit nominally), with eleven of the fifteen European Union (EU) member states irrevocably fixing their exchange rates against each other. Three years later the euro finally became a fully-fledged reality with an virtually flawless introduction of notes and coins, and a process that had been almost fifty years in the making was now complete.

While a flotilla of EU members had now reached the shores of the single currency, the British ship of state remained firmly moored outside the newly established Eurozone. Indeed, for all its rhetoric about placing Britain 'at the heart of Europe', New Labour's thumping victory in the 1997 general election had been achieved without any clear policy on the question of the single European currency. Although the prospect of joining the euro drew wide (but by no means universal) support from representatives of both capital and labour, a combination of factional differences within the Labour Party and fears of antagonising the largely euro-sceptical views of the press and the general public had dictated that the New Labour leadership proceed with caution. By the late summer though, the lack of a clear policy on the euro coupled with a public bout of in-fighting between key members of the government's inner circle (at the core of which stood the euro-enthusiastic Prime Minister, Tony Blair, and his more guarded Chancellor, Gordon Brown) was leading to growing press speculation that New Labour would seek to join the single currency during the first wave of membership beginning in 1999. As uncertainty and instability in the financial markets now began to grow, and as sterling fell to its lowest level for fifteen years, the new government's alarm bells began to clang about the potential threat to its tortuously gained and still-fragile image of economic competency. The result was an intense flurry of internal negotiations, leading to the rapid assembly and deployment of a compromise policy which stated that Britain would not be seeking to join the euro during the lifetime of the present Parliament barring a fundamental and unforeseen change in economic circumstances.[1]

This hastily developed view on Britain's relationship to the world's largest single market was placed on a more substantive footing in October with an announcement by the Chancellor that the government were in favour of joining the single currency 'in principle', but only when five now infamous economic tests had been met. These were namely: (1) whether there was sufficient convergence between Britain and the Eurozone economies; (2) whether the British economy was sufficiently flexible to make the necessary adjustments to life within the Eurozone; (3) whether membership could be expected to have a beneficial effect on investment; (4) whether it would be advantageous for the financial sector; and (5) whether it would prove to be good for employment. While the deliberately vague content of these tests was intended to preserve the government's freedom of manoeuvre over any eventual decision (or indecision as the case may be), the effect in practice was also to hand an effective veto to Gordon Brown, the self-appointed 'guardian of the policy', since any interpretation and assessment of the tests would ultimately need to be carried out by the Treasury. To make things even more difficult for Britain's euro-enthusiasts, the government had by now also committed itself to a policy known as the 'triple-lock', in which any decision to join the single currency would have to be taken firstly by the government, secondly by a vote in Parliament, and thirdly, by the British people themselves in the form of a national referendum. The signs for British entry into the euro at any time soon then, were not encouraging.

Nevertheless, while this policy framework continued to provide the bedrock for New Labour's official stance on membership of the single currency, and while the decision not to decide proved to be a successful means of preventing the issue from becoming permanently lodged in the higher echelons of the domestic political agenda, various members of the Prime Minister's coterie continued to cast envious glances in the direction of the Eurozone. In February 1999 Blair himself exuberantly announced the introduction of a National Changeover Plan designed to prepare British business for life with the euro, declaring this to be a 'change of gear' in the government's principled gravitation towards the single currency, while during the summer of 2000 the divisions within New Labour's inner circle over the issue were again publicly aired, with pro-euro noises being brutally silenced by the Chancellor, who vigorously reasserted the government's official policy of non-commitment. In 2001 however, the Prime Minister's sentiments in favour of the single currency again resurfaced during the general election campaign, as Blair warned that it would be 'isolationist' to rule out entry into the single currency, and as he optimistically claimed that the British people were 'open to persuasion' on the issue.

Despite such incursions, the upper hand in the shaping of the euro-debate has nonetheless remained distinctly with the Chancellor. This was clearly revealed in June 2003 when the Treasury published its assessment of the five economic tests. This announced that only one had so far been passed (namely the benefits to the City), and that while progress had been made, the government would not therefore be recommending that Britain join the euro at the present time. While this was also accompanied by an announcement that the government were now introducing a 'reform agenda' in order to improve economic flexibility and to clear the way for a possible re-assessment on membership in the future, the signs that Britain would soon be deemed fit for entry into the euro remained unpropitious. As far as the process of monetary union was concerned, while the rest of Europe had finally completed its long and arduous journey, New Labour's Britain, it seemed, remained firmly stuck on the road to nowhere.[2]

New Labour's governing strategy

In common with all British governments, New Labour's primary aims have been to contain class struggle, to ensure favourable conditions for capital accumulation, and to achieve and maintain a sufficient degree of governing autonomy for the pursuit of high political goals. In order to achieve these objectives, the New Labour authorities have sought to address the perennial problem posed by Britain's continued relative economic decline with a rejection of 'old-style' Keynesian social democracy and with the devout acceptance of a neo-liberal free market agenda (albeit one tempered by the vacuous rhetoric of the 'third way') in an attempt to minimise the direct involvement of the state in economic affairs. A key part of this has been the adoption of a governing strategy based on a series of monetary and fiscal rules designed to establish a credible anti-inflationary discipline and to provide officials with a securely depoliticised framework for regulating the circuit of capital. The need for such a framework, and the difficulties involved in the pursuit of a discretionary governing strategy, are believed by New Labour officials to have been amply demonstrated not only by the protracted economic and political crises of the 'Keynesian' era, but also by the vacillations of the Conservative governments from 1979. As Ed Balls, the Chief Economic Advisor to the Treasury explains, the continual replacement of one set of 'rules' by another, namely the shift from monetarism to shadowing the deutschmark, to membership of the ERM, and to inflationary targeting, all helped to create the impression that economic policy under the Conservatives 'was being manipulated for short-term motives'. Moreover, this too undermined their ability to pursue high political aims, since

> setting interest rates, and all the short-term activity which came with that task, took at least half the time and energy of past Chancellors, as well as being a monthly source of disagreement between No. 10 and No. 11 Downing Street.[3]

The first of New Labour's policy rules consists of an operationally independent Bank of England. Rapidly introduced after the May 1997 general election victory, this involved handing formal control of interest rates over to a newly created Monetary Policy Committee (MPC) headed by the Governor of the Bank and made up of a majority of Bank officials (the remainder being periodically appointed by the Chancellor) subject to a governmentally determined remit of maintaining a symmetrical 2.5% inflation target. To support this, the government also introduced the so-called 'Open Letter' system, designed to inject flexibility and transparency into this process by publishing the monthly minutes of MPC decisions, and by compelling the Governor to publicly explain the actions of the Bank in the event that inflation should diverge substantially from the designated target. The key aims underpinning Bank of England independence therefore, have been to furnish the authorities with a credible anti-inflationary mechanism by effectively removing interest rate decisions from the political sphere of democratic accountability, and to thereby enable both the government and the Bank to displace responsibility for such issues. As Gordon Brown maintains, these arrangements were designed firstly to provide 'a long term policy' in order to address the problem of Britain's relative economic decline insofar as this was the result of 'short termism and the pursuit of stop-go economics', and secondly, to remove the suspicion that interest rate decisions were being influenced by 'short-term party political considerations'. Or as Eddie George, then the Governor of the Bank explained, operational independence was intended to provide 'a strategic division of responsibilities' between the government (which sets the objectives for monetary policy) and the Bank (which executes the technical decisions), thereby helping to ensure that both 'are separately accountable for their respective roles in the monetary policy process'.[4]

To complement this framework for monetary policy, the government's fiscal policy is based upon two primary rules. The first of these is the 'golden rule', which commits the government to restrict public borrowing for the purpose of investment over the economic cycle only (a move designed to ensure a fiscal balance or surplus); the second is the 'sustainable investment rule' through which the government is pledged to keep net public debt below 40% of GDP over the same period. In addition, these measures have also been supported by a continuing commitment to the provisions of the Stability and Growth Pact, and by an initial two year adherence to the public spending limits of the outgoing Conservative administration, described as 'eye wateringly tight' by the departing Tory Chancellor, Kenneth Clarke. More recently, the government's fiscal stance has been further strengthened by the provisions of its reform agenda. The Bank of England's inflation target has been tightened from the 2.5% limit defined by the retail price index (RPIX) to a 2% limit as defined by the internationally used harmonised index of consumer prices (HICP) in order to ensure that 'inflation expectations in the UK remain in line with those of the Euro area'; a regular report on fiscal stability is to be presented to Parliament, with the stated aim being to enhance transparency and accountability; and a fiscal version of the 'Open Letter' system is to be introduced in order to allow the government to temporarily diverge from their fiscal rules in the event that Britain's output gap reaches a pre-specified target without damaging the long-term credibility of their economic policy framework.[5]

To underpin this regime, New Labour have also sought to bolster the supply-side performance of the British economy. This has involved retaining many of the trade union 'reforms' introduced by the Conservatives, which have turned Britain's labour market into the most lightly regulated in the Western world, and by subjecting the collective ears of the nation to an almost unrelenting barrage of rhetoric exhorting the need for 'prudent' financial management, for public sector and welfare state reform (including 'affordable' pay settlements, perpetual 'modernisation', and a greater role for the private sector), and for ever-greater improvements in economic flexibility and productivity. Layered on top of this, the government have also fervently espoused a discourse of globalisation in which the world market is presented as an inexorable and increasingly competitive external constraint to which the British economy must either adjust or perish. While Blair frequently stresses the need to adapt to a world that is becoming 'more and more integrated', Brown speaks of the increasing need for Britain to improve its flexibility and dynamism in order to meet the 'next wave of globalisation' and its concomitant challenge of 'a long-term global restructuring of industry'. This is namely a process of:

> low value-added production shifting from the highly industrialised to the industrialising countries; competitive advantage in manufacturing and services increasingly coming from high value-added technology-driven products.[6]

To date however, the efficacy of this governing strategy has been somewhat mixed. In terms of securing a sufficient degree of governing autonomy it has thus far proved to be relatively successful. Serious political difficulties (particularly those deriving from economic matters) have, until recently, largely been avoided; inflationary expectations since 1997 have for the most part been low and stable (indeed the question of inflation has not figured in voters' top ten concerns since 1995); the government have enjoyed a sustained and apparently unassailable electoral dominance over the Conservatives (enabling the Labour Party to secure a second full term in office for the first time in its history); and questions concerning the management of the economy, including the subject of the single currency, have been largely absent from the domestic political agenda. As Ed Balls succinctly observes, New Labour's policy rules have provided them with 'time, space and long-term credibility.'[7]

In economic terms however the picture is somewhat less clear-cut. In many respects, the period from 1997 to 2002 was one of relative stability and prosperity in which Britain successfully managed to resist the pull of a global economic downturn. While many countries around the world succumbed to the effects of the slowdown, Britain enjoyed a third less unemployment than in the period from 1990 to 1996, experienced a fall in interest rates to historically low levels, a halving in the average growth rate of inflation and unit costs, and a rise in consumer confidence. At the same time, both labour unrest and trade union membership have remained at historically low levels. However, despite this, many trouble spots remain uneased by New Labour's economic policy stance. Since 1998 Britain has endured its longest manufacturing slump for two decades, its lowest rate of GDP growth since the early 1990s, and in 2002 suffered its largest drop in exports for thirty years and the largest fall in business investment since records began. Inflationary expectations too have recently exhibited signs of rising, and in the summer of 2003 reached their highest levels since November 1999. In addition to this, Britain has also continued to lose ground to its main international competitors. From 1997 to 2002, Britain had the highest average rate of inflation of all the G7 nations, the second lowest rate of investment growth as a share of GDP, the highest rise in manufacturing unit labour costs, and the slowest growth in productivity.[8]

The benefits of the euro

In basing the qualifying criteria for joining the single currency upon its five economic tests, the government have effectively sought to present the question of membership as being fundamentally one of 'economics' rather than 'politics'. Although it is also acknowledged that full participation in the Eurozone would enhance Britain's political influence within the EU, the benefits of membership have been primarily couched in economic terms, with the main advantages for example being seen to include an increase in trade and exchange rate stability with EU nations, greater cost transparency, and higher levels of inward investment. On these grounds, the frequently repeated mantra of the New Labour hierarchy has therefore been that it is the government's intention to join the single currency 'provided the economic conditions are met', and providing that such a step can be shown to be in 'the national economic interest'.[9]

By discursively framing the debate in this way however, the government have sought to confine discussion about the political impact of euro-membership to questions regarding the constitutional intricacies of the decision. In this, the key matter has been presented as being whether or not the move would represent an unacceptable breach of Parliamentary sovereignty. This too however has been put forward as a matter to be primarily resolved by reference to economic criteria. Though recognising that the project of economic and monetary union is 'an intensely political act', Blair for example maintains that the political and constitutional issues do not offer 'an insuperable barrier' to membership as long as 'the economic issue' is overcome, and as Brown puts it, membership of the euro would not mean an abnegation of sovereignty, but would rather signify a pooling of sovereignty that would give Britain a greater say 'on issues of great economic importance to our country'. Thus:

> The constitutional issue is a factor in the decision, but it is not an overriding one. Rather, it signifies that in order for monetary union to be right for Britain the economic benefit should be clear and unambiguous.[10]

Despite presenting the issue as a question of economics however, the decision of whether or not to join the single currency is inherently and profoundly political. This is not simply due to the fact that any decision on the euro will have a significant impact on Britain's relationship with its EU partners, but also derives from the broad and imprecise manner in which the economic criteria themselves have been designed, since these not only leave room for, but in fact require a subjective interpretation. As Gus O'Donnell, the Treasury's Head of Macroeconomic Policy and International Finance has pointed out, the decision on whether or not to join the euro will ultimately be a political issue since 'economics can never be clear and unambiguous'.[11] Even more fundamentally though, any decision to participate fully in the project of EMU would have far-reaching implications for the very nature of democratic accountability within Britain itself, since this would involve an irrevocable loss of control over key economic policy issues to the ECB. Despite the significance of this however, such a step would not represent a qualitatively different governing approach for New Labour, but would in fact signify a strengthening and an extension of their existing governing strategy with potentially significant benefits on several fronts.

In an identical fashion to Britain's return to the gold standard and to its membership of the ERM for example, one major advantage of joining the single currency for the government would be that this would enhance its anti-inflationary credibility and enable it to impose greater pressure on capital and labour to improve productivity, raise competitiveness, and to modernise its pattern of economic activity. In the first instance, the constraints on inflationary expectations and hence on price-wage setting behaviour would be tightened, since the level of interest rates affecting the British economy would now be determined by the Governing Council of the ECB, an institution charged with keeping Eurozone inflation within a narrow 2% limit, and one subject to even less political influence than the Bank of England. Secondly, since joining the euro would entail the loss of domestic exchange rate and monetary policy instruments, any decline in national competitiveness relative to other Eurozone economies would now be expressed through higher unemployment and lower output rather than a fall in the value of the pound. The effects of this, as the Treasury itself notes, would be to transform price and wage movements into 'the primary adjustment mechanisms' of the British economy, and to anchor British prices to levels within the Eurozone 'with little scope for slippage'. Thirdly, the adoption of the single currency would also enhance the economic discipline on capital and labour by further exposing domestic producers to the 'competitive opportunities' of the single European market. As the Treasury again maintains, the combination of greater price transparency, reduced transaction costs, and adherence to a single EU-wide economic policy framework would increasingly sensitise firms to differentials in labour costs and business regulations, thereby making it 'even more essential' to maintain economic flexibility.[12]

To a large degree however, the economic impact of joining the euro would depend upon the particular exchange rate chosen for entry into the regime. While there has to date been little discussion of this point, the government's official position is that it is in favour of 'a stable and competitive exchange rate' that is conducive to the maintenance of internal and external equilibrium (i.e. macroeconomic balance) over the medium term. As Ruth Kelly, the Economic Secretary to the Treasury, has put it for example:

the exchange rate at which sterling would enter the single currency must be consistent with economic fundamentals in the United

Kingdom and compatible with sustainable convergence between the UK and other euro area economies.[13]

A key difficulty with this approach however is that ascertaining precisely which exchange rate will be most compatible with Britain's 'economic fundamentals' remains, like the government's five economic tests, largely a matter for conjecture. Recent estimates of sterling's 'equilibrium rate' for instance have ranged widely from €1.15 to €1.60, and the Treasury itself has even played down the practical use of the concept, stating that there are 'many uncertainties' involved. Moreover, as the Treasury have also pointed out, any attempt to predict what an equilibrium exchange rate would be for an unknown future state of the British economy remains fraught with problems since while 'explaining past exchange rate movements is inherently difficult – forecasting the future path is harder still'.[14] Indeed, the very notion that there is a single value for the national currency which at any given moment can produce a single possible macroeconomic balance is itself highly spurious, since it is possible for a wide range of exchange rates to produce an equally wide range of macroeconomic equilibria, though with varying levels of unemployment, output, prices, and trade. Given this, any decision about the level of the exchange rate at which to enter the euro would not therefore be determined by a process of economic modelling designed to discover the 'correct' value of the pound, but would instead be a fundamentally political decision made according to the priorities and objectives of the government at the time. As such, there are in fact several reasons why Britain's state officials might favour a relatively high, rather than a 'competitive' or an 'equilibrium' rate of entry.

The key to this assertion rests with New Labour's unyielding insistence on the need for greater levels of productivity, flexibility, and competitiveness from capital and labour. Calls for the government to ease the pressure imposed on British industry by a comparatively high exchange rate between 1996 and 2002 for example (as sterling recovered from its post-ERM depreciation to an average of around €1.62 during this time) were persistently rejected by ministers on the basis that any moves to artificially lower the value of the pound would be destabilising, would lead to rising inflation, and would merely allow Britain's competitive deficiencies to continue. Instead, the government's response was to assert that sterling's rate of exchange was a matter for the market, and that both capital and labour therefore needed to adjust their own performance accordingly. As Brown, while purporting to understand the 'concerns of exporters' put it, 'unless we face up to the fact that we have a productivity gap with our competitors, then we will as a nation be failing to meet the challenges of the future'.[15] Furthermore, despite a fall in the pound to around €1.40 during the first half of 2003, the notion of gaining a competitive advantage by entering the single currency at a depreciated exchange rate (a move which in any case would almost certainly be vetoed by other Eurozone countries) has also been rejected on the grounds that this would undermine the government's hard won macroeconomic policy credibility. As Ruth Kelly again insists, there will be no attempt to 'massage down' the value of the pound prior to any entry into the euro, and as Balls warns, 'any short-term attempt to manipulate the exchange rate ... would put both the inflation target and ... wider stability at risk'.[16]

While joining the euro at a depreciated or an 'equilibrium' exchange rate would therefore do little to address the problem of Britain's relative economic decline, since the former would merely ease the pressure to compete, and since the latter would merely seek to maintain the existing macroeconomic position, entering at a relatively high rate would, in contrast, enable the government to increase the competitive discipline on capital and labour. Indeed, while the relatively high value of sterling since 1996 is thought to have had an adverse effect on the balance of trade by encouraging the growth of imports at the expense of exports, it is also considered by the government to have been broadly beneficial to Britain's overall economic performance by imposing competitive pressure via higher export prices, and by therefore 'attracting labour and other resources into the industries where they were most needed'.[17] As such, it is possible that a strategy of joining the single currency at a relatively high level (for example between €1.60–€1.65) could therefore re-impose the discipline of an appreciated exchange rate, though now with the extra credibility of their being no prospect whatsoever of a devaluation. This could augment the pressure on capital and labour to cut costs, moderate wage rises, move away from declining economic sectors, and adopt more efficient, flexible, and productive working methods and practices.

Moreover, while a high rate strategy would not be without its political risks, Britain's authorities would also be well equipped with a range of arguments to deploy in its defence. Should the government opt for entry within a short-to-medium time scale for example, then it could rightly be pointed out that a rate of between €1.60 and €1.65 was not only broadly consistent with sterling's medium term market value, but that it was also broadly consistent with the range of best estimates for the equilibrium entry rate itself, while the ability of the government to pursue such a policy would be further enhanced by the general level of domestic acceptance for a relatively high exchange rate. Indeed, as one recent report has noted, the 'disinflationary squeeze from the high pound' has now been present for so many years 'that many people seem to take it for granted.'[18]

In addition to this, the economic discipline of entering the euro at a relatively high level would be further heightened by the constraints that this would impose upon the government's fiscal room for manoeuvre. While it would remain technically possible for the government to respond to deflationary pressures with an expansionary fiscal policy, and while the Treasury itself has stated that joining the euro would place a 'greater premium' on fiscal policy as an adjustment tool, the discretionary use of such measures would in fact now be restricted in several ways. The provisions of the Stability and Growth Pact as well as those of the government's own rules on fiscal conduct for example, would both continue to limit its discretionary freedom of manoeuvre, and since the loss of exchange rate and monetary controls would now transform fiscal policy into the government's last remaining major macroeconomic weapon, and since the temptation to use it for political purposes would therefore now be increased, the need for credibility and hence for the minimum use of discretion would be intensified. Indeed, the Treasury itself has also admitted that discretionary fiscal measures would not only be relatively inefficient as an adjustment mechanism due to the time-lags between policy decisions, implementation, and effects, but that the heightened need for credibility would also ensure that their use would have to be confined to purely 'temporary' instances, and to be tightly circumscribed by specific regulations and procedures outlining precisely how and in what circumstances they could be permitted. Furthermore, the maintenance of a tight fiscal stance would also be easier for the government to justify under a relatively high exchange rate (especially when faced with economic difficulties), since it could be legitimately argued that any policy relaxation would merely provide a temporary ease in the need for competitive improvements and that such measures would thus store up even greater difficulties for the future.[19]

In addition to these economic advantages, membership of the single currency would also provide the government with substantial political benefits. Primarily, the move would serve to strengthen and entrench the depoliticising effects of its existing rules-based governing strategy and further enhance its high political freedom. By adopting the euro in place of the pound, and by handing control of interest rates over to the ECB, the move would not only eliminate national democratic control over exchange rate and monetary policy issues, but would also blur the lines of accountability, thereby enabling the government to legitimately claim that it was no longer responsible for key economic policy decisions, and enabling the ECB to legitimately claim that it was simply performing a technical and non-political function as determined by the member states of the EU. Furthermore, since joining the euro would not simply place the issues of exchange rate and monetary policy outside the realm of democratic control, but since it would also place further constraints on the government's use of fiscal policy, the move would thereby enable New Labour to disclaim direct responsibility for economic policy-making in general, and would thus help to displace such issues from the domestic political agenda. This would prove to be a particularly useful facet of membership given the economic discipline involved in joining the Eurozone, especially if the government should choose to adopt a high rate of entry, since it would enable unpalatable economic pressures to be imposed while simultaneously protecting officials from the adverse social and political consequences of this process. Moreover, such effects would also be strengthened if, as the government has repeatedly stated, membership of the euro were to be conditional upon obtaining a positive result in a national referendum, since this would then enable them to point out that the decision to join had effectively been made by the British people themselves, and to legitimately claim that the burden of responsibility should be borne accordingly.

The future prospects

Despite the potential economic and political advantages for Britain's state authorities of joining the single currency, there nonetheless remain a number of formidable obstacles to the adoption of a governing strategy based upon membership of the euro. The first of these concerns the economic performance of the Eurozone itself. With many of its members presently experiencing extensive difficulties against the backdrop of a global economic downturn, and with the euro having until recently been relatively weak on the world's financial markets, the argument that membership of the single currency is essential for Britain's national economic interest and that continuing to remain outside the Eurozone will therefore be inherently detrimental has been seriously weakened. This has been further compounded by the contrasting performance of the British economy, which despite continuing to fall behind internationally and despite suffering from recessions in the manufacturing and agricultural sectors has not experienced any wholesale problems for over a decade. Unless Eurozone economies markedly improve, and/or domestic economic conditions significantly deteriorate, then it seems unlikely that the potential economic advantages of the euro will possess sufficient weight to carry the argument.[20]

In addition to this, the prospects for achieving a significant improvement in competitiveness by utilising membership of the single currency to impose economic discipline, especially through the use of a high entry rate, remain uncertain. As has been shown, similar attempts at imposing discipline through the gold standard and the ERM floundered in the face of strong resistance to economic adjustment from capital and labour, while the more recent pressures of a high pound from 1996 have also failed to reverse the relative decline in Britain's international position. The implications of this for any hopes that New Labour might entertain about joining the single currency at a relatively high exchange rate are therefore significant, since while it remains too early to say whether the government's reform agenda will be able to improve economic flexibility (in fact a failure to do so may itself improve the attractiveness of attempting to enforce discipline through external means), there is little to suggest that capital and labour would now be any more predisposed to respond to an appreciation of the currency with improved efficiency than they were in the past. Given this, a key danger of such a strategy would therefore be that the attempt to impose such pressure would itself generate serious economic difficulties, and that in a similar fashion to the gold standard and the ERM strategies, this could undermine the stability and perhaps ultimately the very legitimacy of New Labour's euro-project.

Perhaps the most fundamental obstacle to British membership of the single currency however, remains the persistently high level of domestic antipathy towards it. While divisions within the government and the Cabinet have recently been publicly negated once more by the adoption of an avowedly pro-European offensive, the fault-line between Blair as the main euro-enthusiast, and Brown as the cautious holder of the 'Treasury veto' over the decision, remains a major and unresolved source of friction which may continue to preclude British entry. An important factor too is the continued success of New Labour's present strategy of depoliticisation through domestic means, since in the absence of any serious difficulties, the need for an external strategy of depoliticisation will remain diminished. More significant than governmental caution though is the opposition of the British public itself, which at best continues to regard the prospect of joining the euro with disdain. Despite support from many sections of British society, including the City, the CBI (albeit when the conditions are right), and the TUC (with the caveat that Britain enters at a 'sustainable exchange rate'), it is the opposition of the largely euro-sceptic press to 'scrapping the pound' which continues to resonate most with the general public. Indeed, opinion polls throughout New Labour's reign have consistently indicated that while a third of the British electorate would vote in favour of joining the euro, more than half would definitely vote against it.[21] To make matters even worse for Britain's euro-philes, recent polls indicating that the public are becoming increasingly disillusioned with, and distrustful of New Labour itself (particularly given the vacillating and spurious justifications given for going to war with Iraq and the subsequent events of the Hutton inquiry), have put a large dent in any hopes that a positive reassessment of the five economic tests could be delivered in the near future. Despite the planned introduction of a Draft Bill to prepare the way for a referendum on membership of the euro, it therefore seems likely that unless some means can be found of stemming this erosion of trust and support, the so-called 'sixth test' for joining the single currency, namely whether the government believes it actually can win a referendum, will continue to dictate that Britain remains outside the Eurozone.

Concluding remarks

For New Labour, signing Britain up to the single currency would signify a strengthening and an extension of its rules-based depoliticised governing strategy. This would offer the advantages of imposing further competitive discipline upon capital and labour, especially if combined with a relatively high exchange rate, and of enhancing the government's freedom of high political manoeuvre through further removing key economic policy issues from the sphere of democratic accountability. Despite this however, it remains unlikely that the pursuit of a governing strategy based on membership of the euro would be able to deliver substantial economic or political benefits. The resistance of capital and labour to greater competitive pressure is likely to remain strong, while persistently high levels of domestic hostility to any notion of abandoning the national currency seem certain to preclude the government from calling, let alone winning, a referendum on the subject. Any hopes that Britain might join its European compatriots in the project of economic and monetary union at any time soon then, are likely to remain firmly disappointed.

9
Conclusion: Exchange Rate Policy-Making Reconsidered

Towards a more open approach

While the question of exchange rate policy-making has to date been largely marginalised as a topic for political-economic examination, its centrality to a wide range of national and international factors, including levels of economic output, employment, prices, and trade, as well as political relations both within and between states themselves, makes this process one of core analytical concern. A central theme of this book has been that this process can be best explained by using an 'open Marxist' theoretical perspective. While conventional approaches to exchange rate policy-making (defined here as the 'rational choice', the 'country characteristics', and the 'interest group' approaches) can offer coherent, and to a degree useful analyses, they remain methodologically problematic given their failure to adequately consider the fundamental question of social form. By taking the starting point for analysis to be the various 'components' of society, namely its division into apparently separate and autonomous 'public' and 'private' spheres, 'political' and 'economic' structures, and sectorally motivated interest groups, and by offering no theoretical means of explaining why society should be organised and arranged in such a manner, these approaches are unable to conceptualise the wider constraints that are imposed on the policy-making process by the composition and development of capitalist society itself.

In contrast to conventional theories, an open Marxist approach begins with the question of social form, by conceptualising society as a unified whole, and by seeking to understand how its various component parts are derived from, and related to its organisational composition. As such, this is able to offer a view of exchange rate

163

policy-making that is rooted in the context of a wider social theory. From this perspective, the various elements of which society appears to be constructed are not seen as independently existing things that interact in an external manner, but are instead seen as integral parts of a process of social development. More specifically, they are considered to be the theoretical expressions of relations between people that are determined during the process of social production. In turn, this process is organised along the lines of class exploitation, and is therefore conditioned by the development of an indeterminate class struggle. While the reproduction and maintenance of this class divide is facilitated in capitalist society by the mechanism of the 'value form' (the particular means of integration for a society based on commodity exchange), its internal dynamic, which is described by Marx as the 'circuit of capital', is nonetheless inherently unstable and vulnerable to crises which result from its class composition.

A particular weakness of the circuit of capital is its inherent dependency on labour power and money. The provision of these elements involves continual action by the capitalist state, which, as a territorial fragment of global capitalist society, is itself conditioned by, and subject to the competitive pressures of the world economy. These force states to ensure that national conditions for capitalist exploitation conform to those pertaining on a global level (lest capital will gravitate towards more profitable climes and produce progressively serious economic and political crises), and are transmitted through the operation of the exchange rate regime, as the primary means through which a national economy is integrated into the international circuit of capital. Exchange rate policy-making then, forms a key component of the wider governing strategy that is designed by state managers with a view to containing class struggle, to providing favourable conditions for capital accumulation, as well as to ensuring a sufficient degree of governing autonomy for the pursuit of more subjective high political aims. The particular exchange rate regime that will be adopted or maintained at any one time, is therefore dependent upon the specific context and objectives of the governing strategy that is being pursued by the core executive.

At certain times state officials may find it to be necessary and/or desirable to engage in a 'politicised' governing strategy based on the directly visible involvement of the state in economic affairs. This can be achieved through either a floating, managed, or fixed-but-adjustable exchange rate regime, and offers the useful advantage of enabling the authorities to directly claim the plaudits for any economic policy success they may engender. All the same, such an approach nonetheless remains inherently dangerous, especially given the crisis-ridden nature of capitalist society, since the emergence of economic difficulties may necessitate overt and unpopular state action in order to secure continued capital accumulation. This can directly expose the class character of the state itself, and risks transforming an economic crisis into a crisis of political authority. As such, a generally more useful approach for state officials is to pursue a governing strategy of 'depoliticisation'. By taking core aspects of economic policy-making away from the discretionary control of the state, and by placing them instead under the control of 'independent' and ostensibly 'non-political' bodies and/or policy rules, a successful strategy of depoliticisation can facilitate the imposition of competitive discipline on both capital and labour, and can simultaneously allow officials to disclaim responsibility and hence accountability for such measures. Moreover, such an approach can also be achieved through the use of a floating, managed, or fixed exchange rate regime. The use of the former are associated with the imposition of a domestically oriented policy rule such as monetary targeting or central bank independence, and can thereby enable officials to depart from, or even abandon their strategy should they encounter any serious difficulties. Such flexibility however, can also prove to be a source of weakness, since a policy rule that is relatively easy to break may in the event be found to lack credibility. In contrast, the use of a fixed exchange rate regime can offer a more rigorous basis for a strategy of depoliticisation. International commitments can be more costly to break, and may therefore prove to be more credible than their domestic counterparts, while an externally constituted source of economic discipline can offer a more legitimate constraint on policy-making discretion, and can thereby provide a more effective scapegoat for the imposition of any unpalatable and unpopular measures. In this way, a governing strategy of depoliticisation based on a fixed exchange rate regime can prove to be a more effective means of containing class struggle, providing favourable conditions for capital accumulation, and strengthening the governing autonomy of state officials, than either a politicised framework of economic management, or a depoliticised regime based on a floating or managed exchange rate.

From the gold standard to the euro

The claims made by this alternative theoretical framework have been substantiated through an examination of three key policy-making episodes in Britain: the return to the gold standard in 1925; membership of the ERM from 1990 to 1992; and the current situation regarding New Labour's attitude towards joining the single European currency. These empirical analyses have demonstrated the utility of a governing strategy of depoliticisation based on a fixed exchange rate regime, and have in turn provided a new and alternative means of interpreting and assessing these policy developments.

The first and most comprehensive of these analyses, given the direct availability of primary documentation, was that of Britain's return to the gold standard in 1925 at the prewar exchange rate of $4.86. This is conventionally understood to have been motivated by an eclectic mix of factors, including notions of national pride and prestige, a desire to return to prewar conditions, the self-interest of key officials, and the undue policy influence of the City. In terms of its impact, this policy is traditionally interpreted as having been a complete disaster, with a mistaken overvaluation of the pound and/or inhospitable global circumstances leading to economic stagnation, chronically high unemployment, and a rise in industrial unrest. In contrast, this book has argued that the return to gold at the prewar parity was the key element in a governing strategy designed to address long-term economic and political difficulties within the British state, and that in these aims it was, in fact, relatively successful.

The backdrop to the gold standard policy is to be found in developments from the last third of the nineteenth century, with the emergence of relative economic decline, a progressively outdated pattern of economic activity, and an increasingly militant challenge from the labour movement. These pressures were further exacerbated by the impact of the First World War, which forced Britain to adopt a floating exchange rate regime for the first time, which led to the politicisation of economic conditions and policy-making, and which raised the expectations of capital and labour as to what could be expected from the state in the postwar period. In this context, a return to the gold standard at $4.86 was seen by the governing authorities to offer several distinct advantages. In economic terms, credibly re-entering the pound into a fixed exchange rate regime at a deliberately overvalued level would impose financial pressure upon capital and labour in an attempt to reduce and contain inflation (believed to be a key cause of declining competitiveness and the main source of labour unrest), and to encourage an economic modernisation through the adoption of more efficient methods and practices, and through an adjustment away from old and declining industries and into newer and more advanced lines of production. In political terms, this move would also help to insulate the core executive from the adverse consequences of these economic effects through the depoliticisation of monetary and economic policy-making. By returning control of interest rates to the politically independent Bank of England, by placing the Bank themselves within the confines of an external regime backed by the vast majority of domestic opinion, and by subordinating the general direction of economic policy to the maintenance of the exchange rate, the gold standard would enable the governing authorities to effectively discipline the expectations, and hence the behaviour of capital and labour, and to displace responsibility and hence accountability for the unpopular consequences of their economic policy stance away from the state.

While failing to achieve all of its aims, this strategy proved to be a relative success for Britain's state officials. Although it proved unable to overcome the entrenched resistance of capital and labour to economic modernisation, and although the lack of any significant adjustment or breakthrough in competitiveness allowed Britain's economic difficulties to continue, and ultimately led to the collapse of the strategy itself, the gold standard nonetheless provided officials with a credible and largely depoliticised framework for regulating the domestic circuit of capital. This proved adept at containing class unrest, and at successfully displacing social disquiet over economic conditions and policy-making. The credibility of Britain's commitment to maintain the convertibility of sterling at $4.86 was not seriously challenged until the summer of 1931, representatives of both capital and labour primarily attributed Britain's economic difficulties to factors other than the behaviour of the state authorities, and officials were now under less pressure than they had been with the politicised economic policy regime from 1919 to 1925.

The collapse of this strategy in September 1931 was followed by the construction of a new framework for economic policy management. This was characterised by an enforced shift to a loosely managed exchange rate regime, by a series of measures designed to stimulate economic growth, and by a growing politicisation of economic affairs. At the same time however, the underlying objectives of this new regime remained the same as those which had informed the gold standard strategy. The key priorities were to contain class struggle within politically safe limits, to improve Britain's economic competitiveness, to sustain pressure for a shift in its pattern of economic activity, and to enhance the governing autonomy of state officials by keeping their directly visible involvement with the economy to a minimum. Given this, the ultimate aim of the authorities was to secure another return to the gold standard at the old exchange rate of $4.86, though in the event such a move turned out to be impossible given the high level of international instability and the extent of domestic antipathy to the regime.

This analysis of exchange rate policy-making in relation to the gold standard strategy is also mirrored by an examination of Britain's membership of the ERM from 1990 to 1992. While this policy episode is conventionally understood as having been driven by narrowly defined economic concerns, and while it is typically considered to have been an abject policy failure, an open Marxist perspective again offers a rather different interpretation of events. From this viewpoint, as with the return to gold, Britain's participation in the ERM is seen as the key component of a wider governing strategy that was designed to address growing economic and political difficulties within the British state through the imposition of financial discipline and through the depoliticisation of monetary and economic policy-making.

The background to the ERM strategy was to be found in the protracted difficulties associated with Britain's continuing relative economic decline, and in the failure to resolve the contradictions of its postwar settlement. This was based on the acceptance of an expanded state, the adoption of a fixed-but-adjustable exchange rate regime, and an overtly politicised mode of economic management. While this proved to be a generally successful means of containing postwar class unrest, at the same time the settlement also fostered a perpetual increase in the demands being placed on the British state, though provided no means of enforcing the requisite economic adjustments needed to ensure that these could be met. The result was that Britain's relative economic decline was allowed to continue unabated, and although this proved to be initially unproblematic given the development of an enormous global boom, the onset of a world recession from the late 1960s led to rising levels of labour unrest and growing social disillusion as the gap between expectations and reality began to widen. This further exacerbated Britain's economic difficulties, eventually led to the abandonment of the Bretton Woods system, and plunged the country into a seemingly endless round of political turmoil. Attempts to address this malaise during the 1980s through a retrenchment of the state and the depoliticisation of economic policy decisions via the imposition of a domestically based anti-inflationary rule also proved to be less than successful. Britain continued to lose ground to its international rivals, political pressures forced the government to return to a discretionary mode of policy-making, and by the end of the decade the country was once again faced with a looming economic crisis and a resurgence of social discontent.

The decision to join the ERM was an attempt to address these problems. By credibly joining a fixed exchange rate regime at a deliberately overvalued level, Britain's governing authorities sought to impose economic pressure on capital and labour by sending out a signal that uncompetitive practices would no longer be accommodated by a decline in the value of the pound, and hence that domestic economic performance would now have to conform to the levels pertaining within the ERM. In addition to this, by placing monetary and economic policy as a whole under the control of an 'externally' constituted regime, the Exchange Rate Mechanism would also enable the government to remove key economic policy decisions from the realm of democratic control and accountability, thereby displacing pressure over such matters away from the state. In this way, membership of the ERM would allow the government to impose economic pressure on capital and labour, while legitimately disclaiming responsibility for its effects.

As with the return to the gold standard, the ERM strategy was also relatively successful. While the pressure of the regime did not overcome the resistance of capital and labour, and while it also therefore failed to produce any significant improvement in Britain's relative competitiveness or any substantial shift in its pattern of economic activity, it nonetheless provided officials with a credible and a largely depoliticised framework for managing the circuit of capital. Class unrest was effectively contained and fragmented, and although the severity of the recession put the governing authorities under pressure, on the whole the responsibility for economic conditions and policy-making was successfully displaced away from the state, thereby securing a greater degree of governing autonomy for the core executive than would otherwise have been possible.

Britain's enforced ejection from the ERM in September 1992 also contained direct parallels to the collapse of the gold standard strategy. As the absence of any significant economic improvement heightened the strains of maintaining the exchange rate, sterling was once again subjected to an intense and fatal speculative attack. Moreover, with a re-entry into the ERM now deemed to be politically impossible, this was also followed by the construction of a new framework for economic management which retained the underlying principles of the previous strategy. While this was based on a return to a floating exchange rate regime and on the introduction of measures designed to encourage a recovery from the recession, officials also turned to the adoption of a domestically oriented policy rule in an effort to maintain the anti-inflationary pressure and to minimise their directly visible involvement with the economy. Unfortunately for the government however, while this new strategy now proved to be relatively successful in economic terms, the political damage wrought by 'Black Wednesday' proved to be irreparable. In 1997 the old Conservative regime was swept away by an electoral monsoon.

Many of the similarities between the governing strategies of the gold standard and the ERM are also reflected in the present situation concerning New Labour's attitude towards membership of the single European currency. Principally, this would enable the government to strengthen its existing strategy based on a floating exchange rate and on the depoliticisation of core economic policy decisions through Bank of England independence and a series of fiscal rules. In economic terms, the advantages for New Labour of joining the euro are that this would enhance its anti-inflationary credibility and would enable it to impose greater pressure on capital and labour for improved productivity, competitiveness, and economic modernisation. By irrevocably fixing the level of the exchange rate to the euro, by handing control of interest rates over to the ECB, by constraining the direction of economic policy as a whole, and by further exposing domestic producers to the competitive disciplines of the single European market, such a move would tighten the economic policy constraints on the British economy and would send out a powerful signal that competitive deficiencies would not be accommodated by the adoption of more relaxed policy measures. These pressures could be further enhanced by utilising a relatively high entry rate into the single currency, since this would raise relative export prices, would strengthen the constraints on the government's discretionary capacities, and would further legitimise the maintenance of a tight fiscal policy stance.

In political terms, joining the single currency would also have a fundamental impact. Placing core economic policy decisions in the hands of an external regime would further remove such issues from the realm of national democratic control, and would thereby enable the government to legitimately claim that it was no longer responsible or accountable for such matters. These depoliticising effects would themselves be further enhanced should entry into the single currency be preceded by a positive result in a national referendum, since in the event that any difficulties should arise this would allow the government to point out that the decision to join had effectively been made by the British people themselves. In this way then, membership of the euro could replicate the effects of the gold standard and the ERM strategies, by allowing unpalatable economic pressures to be imposed while simultaneously protecting officials from the adverse social and political consequences of this process.

Despite the clear benefits that participation in the single currency could provide for the government, the likelihood is that they will not be successfully realised. Continuing resistance from capital and labour to pressure for economic adjustment is likely to prove stubbornly resilient, while a persistently high level of domestic hostility to the idea of scrapping the pound is likely to preclude the winning, or even the calling of a national referendum. In this sense, the situation concerning the New Labour government and the single European currency is more akin to that which faced Britain's governing authorities following the enforced abandonment of the gold standard in the 1930s, in that the pursuit of a depoliticised governing strategy based on a fixed exchange rate regime is likely to remain frustrated by popular opinion. For New Labour then, the odds are that the euro will remain an impossible dream.

Concluding remarks

While exchange rate policy-making has to date remained a marginal and a specialised topic of study, the central importance of this process for a wide range of political and economic factors indicates the need for greater attention. This book has argued that an open Marxist approach can provide a more useful means of analysing this process than existing theories. By starting with the question of social form, this alternative framework allows the various components of a society to be analysed as integral parts of a unified whole, and thereby provides a view of the policy-making process that is rooted in the organisational composition and development of capitalist society itself. On this basis, exchange rate policy-making is seen as part of a wider governing strategy designed by the core executive to contain class struggle, to provide favourable conditions for capital accumulation, and to improve their high political freedom of manoeuvre. In turn, this alternative theoretical perspective has been substantiated through an empirical analysis of three key policy-making episodes in Britain. While validating the general claims of an open Marxist approach, these analyses have also provided a new means of interpreting and assessing these policies. This has laid the firm foundation for a re-examination of other key policy episodes, and has provided firm evidence for the central importance of exchange rate policy-making to any understanding of high-level economic and political developments. This too demonstrates the need for exchange rate policy-making to be given a greater degree of analytical prominence. If this is successfully achieved, then a hitherto marginal area of study can be made open in more ways than one.

Notes

Chapter 2   The Political Economy of Exchange Rate Policy-Making

1. For contrasting perspectives on the theoretical division of the literature see the alternative typologies offered by Eichengreen (1995) and Hefeker (1997); For examples of the more technical and normative literature (as opposed to analyses of exchange rate policy-making *per se*) see Tower and Willett (1976); Miller *et al* (1989); Argy and de Grauwe (1990); Claassen (1991); Åkerholm and Giovannini (1994); Williamson (2000).
2. Examples of the 'rational choice' approach include Helpman (1981); Cukierman and Meltzer (1986); Hamada (1987); Giavazzi and Pagano (1988); Aghevli and Montiel (1991); Miller and Sutherland (1992); Bordo and Kydland (1995); Bayoumi and Bordo (1998).
3. Examples of the 'country characteristics' approach include Argy (1990); Savvides (1990); Giovannini (1993); Delbecque (1994); Honkapohja and Pikkarainen (1994); Milesi-Ferretti (1995); Edwards (1996); Oatley (1997); Caramazza and Aziz (1998); Frankel (1999); IMF (1999); United Nations (2000).
4. Examples of the 'interest group' approach include Vaubel (1990); Havrilevsky (1994); Walsh (1994, 2000); Hefeker (1997); Frieden (1998, 2000).
5. On these points also see Oatley (1997), pp. 16–18.
6. On 'open Marxism' see for example Burnham (1994); Bonefeld *et al* (1995).
7. See Marx (1913, 1973).
8. de Ste Croix (1983), pp. 43–4; also see Marx (1847), p. 162; Bonefeld *et al* (1995); For interpretations of class in terms of political consciousness or struggle see for example Elster (1985); Roemer (1986); Evans (1999).
9. Marx (1991), p. 927; also see Bonefeld *et al* (1995), p. 20.
10. See de Ste Croix (1983), pp. 51–2; Bonefeld *et al* (1995).
11. On the concept of 'value' see Marx (1990, 1992); and also Rubin (1975).
12. On the circuit of capital see Marx (1992), Chs. 1–4.
13. Marx (1992), p. 180.
14. See Rubin (1975); de Brunhoff (1978), pp. 9–36.
15. For a more in-depth analysis of these issues see Glyn and Sutcliffe (1972); Mandel (1975); Gamble and Walton (1976); Rowthorn (1977); Goldthorpe (1978); Fine (1979).
16. See Clarke, (1988), p. 17; Holloway (1995). pp. 138–41; Burnham (1996), p. 99–100.
17. For 'fractionalist' analyses of the state see Crouch (1979); Longstreth (1979); Jessop (1983); Ingham (1984); Van der Pijl (1984); for a 'structuralist' view see Poulantzas (1973); Block (1977, 1980); for an 'instrumentalist' perspective see Miliband (1969).
18. For an 'open Marxist' view of the state see Clarke (1988); Bonefeld (1993).
19. Clarke (1988), p. 138.

20. Barker (1978).
21. Marx (1973), p. 408; (1991), p. 205.
22. Picciotto (1991), p. 217.
23. Bonefeld *et al* (1995), p. 8.
24. Burnham (1996), p. 105; Holloway (1996), pp. 116ff.
25. See Barker (1978); Clarke (1988); Bonefeld *et al* (1995).
26. de Brunhoff (1978), *passim*, especially Appendices II and III; Bonefeld *et al* (1995), p. 13.
27. Buller (1999), p. 697; also see Bulpitt (1983, 1996); Holm (2000).
28. See Bulpitt (1983), Chs. 2–4; (1996), pp. 124–7; Bulpitt and Burnham (1999), pp. 17–18.
29. See Fine (1979), p. 178; Bonefeld and Burnham (1996).
30. See Burnham (2001), pp. 127–33.
31. On the subject of depoliticisation see Bonefeld and Burnham (1996); Burnham (1999, 2001).
32. Such factors for example formed the basis of the aborted 'operation ROBOT' scheme for re-establishing the convertibility of sterling during the 1950s. On this see Bulpitt and Burnham (1999).
33. On the advantages of a floating exchange rate regime see Sohnen (1969); Williamson (1983), pp. 37ff; Kenen (1988).
34. On the operation of fixed exchange rate regimes see Williamson (1983), pp. 46–56; Giavazzi and Pagano (1988); Giovannini (1993), pp. 111ff.

Chapter 3   Contextualising the Return to Gold

1. On the mechanism and history of the gold standard see for example Brown Jr (1940); Scammell (1965); Eichengreen (1993).
2. See Gregory (1926), p. 56; Brown Jr (1940), pp. 173–8; Youngson (1960), pp. 26–7; Moggridge (1972), pp. 86–97; Sayers (1976), p. 135; Tomlinson (1990), pp. 43–60.
3. See Brown Jr (1940); Sayers (1960); Youngson (1960), pp. 231ff; Winch (1969); Moggridge (1972), pp. 98–100; Howson (1975); Williamson (1984).
4. See Keynes (1925), p. 10; Williams (1959); Youngson (1960), ps. 27, 234; Moggridge (1972), ps. 86, 97; Pollard (1976); Longstreth (1979); Ingham (1984).
5. See Skidelsky (1969); Lowe (1978); Williamson (1984), pp. 110–11; Middleton (1985); Peden (1991).
6. See Keynes (1925); Moggridge (1969, 1972); Pollard (1969, 1976); Winch (1969), pp. 68ff; Pressnell (1978); Dimsdale (1981); Redmond (1984); Peden (1988); Eichengreen (1992).
7. See Gregory (1926), pp. 45ff; Einzig (1932), pp. 44–58; Brown Jr (1940); Williams (1959), pp. 47–51; Sayers (1960), pp. 93–7; Youngson (1960), pp. 234–7; Aldcroft (1967, 1983); Howson (1975), p. 31.
8. See Cole (1948); Ashworth (1960); Alford (1996), Chs. 1–3.
9. On Britain's relative economic decline see for example Elbaum and Lazonick (1987); Newton and Porter (1988); Dintenfass (1992); Alford (1996), Chs. 1–4.
10. Calculated from Butler and Butler (1994), p. 373.

11. On these events see Cole (1948), pp. 284ff; Hall and Schwarz (1985); Aris (1998).
12. See Morgan (1952), pp. 306ff; Rose (1995); Alford (1996), pp. 111–16.
13. Morgan (1952), Ch. 1, pp. 306ff; Johnson (1971).
14. Modern Records Centre (hereafter MRC) MSS.200/F/4/24/1–2. FBI Bulletins (1917–1919 issues); The National Archives (hereafter TNA) T185/1–2. FBI memo to the Cunliffe Committee 10/7/18; 'Labour and the New Social Order' (Labour Party), 1918; Labour Party Annual Reports 1917–1918; also see Cole (1948), pp. 366–86; Johnson (1968), pp. 219–46.
15. First Interim Report of the Committee on Currency and Foreign Exchanges After the War (hereafter referred to as the Cunliffe committee), (1918). Cd. 9182; Final Report of the Cunliffe committee, (1919). Cmd. 464.; TNA:T172/1499B. 'Post-War Reports and Conferences', (undated Treasury document); Bank of England Archives (hereafter BE) G1/420. Cokayne to Strong. 23/9/18, 19/11/18.
16. Report of the Balfour Committee on Commercial and Industrial Policy (1918). Cd.9035; Evidence by Sir Otto Niemeyer to the Committee on Finance and Industry, 4/6/30. Minutes of Evidence Vol. 2.
17. MRC:MSS.200/F/3/S1/31/1. 'Report upon Post-War Priority and Rationing of Materials' (Ministry of Reconstruction), 1918; TNA:T172/895. Cokayne to Bonar Law 16/10/18; TNA:CAB23/9. Cabinet Meeting 28/1/19; TNA:CAB23/ 15. 'Draft Minutes of a Meeting …', 5/8/19.
18. First Interim and Final Reports of the Cunliffe committee; Hawtrey (1933), pp. 83–90; BE:EID4/102. 'The Fiduciary Issue' (Hawtrey), 6/5/27.
19. TNA:T185/1–2 and TNA:T1/12434. Cunliffe committee minutes 25/2/18, 19/3/18, 7/5/18, 8/7/18, 9/7/18.
20. BE/OV9/480. 'Substance of a Lecture …' (Niemeyer), 22/2/29; On the benefits of an independent central bank also see notes by Montagu Norman in BE:G1/464; and BE:ADM16/2. 'Central Banks' (unsigned), 15/2/21.
21. TNA:T172/1499B. 'How Does a Gold Standard Work in Regulating Credit?' (Hawtrey), undated. Insert mine.
22. TNA:T185/1–2 and TNA:T1/12434. Cunliffe committee minutes and minutes of evidence 4/3/18, 18/3/18, 7/5/18, 10/6/18, 8/7/18, 9/7/18, 11/7/18, 16/10/19.
23. Calculated from Butler and Butler (1994), p. 373.
24. TNA:CAB24/74. 'The Labour Situation', Ministry of Labour reports. January and February 1919; TNA:CAB24/75. Notes of a Conference of Ministers' 25/2/19, 26/2/19; TNA:CAB24/90, TNA:CAB27/59, and TNA:CAB27/60. various Cabinet meetings; also see Johnson (1968), pp. 301–2; Wrigley (1990).
25. First Interim and Final Reports of the Cunliffe committee; BE:ADM34/8. Norman Diaries 30/1/19.
26. TNA:CAB24/74. 'Proposed Industrial Enquiry', 11/2/19; TNA:CAB24/75. various including, 'Rehabilitation of Trade and Provision of Employment' 17/2/19, 21/2/19; 'Notes of a Conference of Ministers', 25/2/19; 26/2/19; also see Cole (1948), pp. 389ff; Johnson (1968), pp. 391ff.
27. Figures calculated from Feinstein (1972), Table 65; also see Morgan (1952), ps. 61–6, 267ff; Johnson (1968), pp. 402–9.
28. TNA:CAB27/72. Cokayne to Chamberlain 25/9/19; 'Note by the Chancellor', 26/7/19; TNA:CAB23/15. 'Draft Minutes of a Meeting …'

5/8/19; TNA:T172/1384. various including, 'Memo. as to Money Rates' (Cokayne), 25/2/20; Niemeyer to Blackett 3/2/20; 'Cheap or Dear Money' (Hawtrey), 4/2/20; 'Dear Money' (Blackett), 19/2/20; BE:ADM34/8–9. Norman Diaries 7/7/19–18/7/19, 9/3/20.

29. Final Report of the Cunliffe committee; BE:G1/420. Cokayne to Strong 19/11/19; TNA:T1/12437. Bradbury to Chamberlain 6/12/19; House of Commons Debates. 15/12/19. Vol. 123, Cls. 43–6; also see Morgan (1952), pp. 150ff; Johnson (1968), pp. 461–89; Tomlinson (1990), pp. 58–65; Wrigley (1990), pp. 174ff.

30. Figures calculated from Feinstein (1972), Tables 1, 51, 52, 57; Butler and Butler (1994), ps. 373–4, 383; On the events of 'Black Friday' see Cole (1948), pp. 386ff; Wrigley (1990), pp. 211ff.

31. BE:G3/177. Norman to Strong 23/5/21; Labour Party Annual Report 1920, p. 9; Wrigley (1990), pp. 211ff; Figures calculated from Butler and Butler (1994), ps. 373–4, 383.

32. BE:G3/177. Norman to Strong 17/2/21–23/5/21; BE:OV37/20. Norman to W. H. Clegg 28/2/21; TNA:T176/5 Pt. 2. Untitled document (Niemeyer), 5/10/21; also see Brown Jr (1940); Eichengreen (1992).

33. 'International Economic Policy' (Labour Party), 1919; Labour Party and TUC Annual Reports 1920–1922; MRC:MSS.292/135.01/1. 'Draft Manifesto on Unemployment' (Labour Party), 12/1/21; MRC:MSS.292/110.1/1. 'The Attack on Wages and Hours Standards' (TUC/Labour Party), 1922; MRC:MSS.292/452/3. 'On the Evils of Industrial Interruption and Trade Dislocation Caused by the Fluctuations of the Exchanges and Other Problems Arising out of the Banking System', TUC General Council (hereafter TUCGC), 1922.

34. MRC:MSS.200/F/4/24/2–8; FBI Bulletins (1920–1922 issues); MRC:MSS.200/ B/3/2/C204 Pt. 1. 'The Trade Depression' (FBI), 7/10/21; MRC:MSS.200/F/3/ S1/8/13. 'Lower Production Costs and Trade Revival' (FBI), 14/2/22; BE/G30/6. various; also see Layton (1925); Turner (1984), p. 10; Cronin (1991), pp. 78–9; Kynaston (1999).

35. BE:ADM16/2. various including Norman to P. Jay. 6/9/20; BE:G3/176. Norman to P. Jay 8/9/20, 22/9/20; TNA:T176/37. Untitled memo (Niemeyer), 22/7/20.

36. BE:OV37/20. Norman to W. H. Clegg 28/2/21.

37. TNA:CAB27/115. various including Blackett to Chamberlain 10/8/20; 'Draft Interim Report of the Unemployment Committee', September 1920; TNA:CAB27/119. 'Trade in Relation to Unemployment', 26/9/21; TNA: T172/1208. various including: Notes of an interview with Norman by Hilton Young, 27/9/21; Niemeyer to Horne 3/10/21, 7/10/21; Unsigned and untitled Treasury document. September 1921; TNA:T176/5 Pt. 2. Untitled document (Niemeyer), 5/10/21; TNA:T176/13 Pt. 1. 'Relations Between the Treasury and the Bank of England'; BE:ADM34/9. Norman Diaries 23/12/20, 28/12/20; BE:G3/177. Norman to Strong 13/10/21; MRC:MSS.200/F/4/24/4. FBI Bulletins (1921 issues).

38. BE:G3/178. Norman to Strong 24/2/22; TNA:T176/5. Pts. 1–2. Horne to Niemeyer, July 1921; 'Bank Rate' (Hawtrey), 5/7/21; 'The Genoa Currency Resolutions' (Hawtrey), 4/2/22; Blackett to Chamberlain 8/6/21; Untitled memo (Niemeyer), July 1921; Unsigned and untitled Treasury document.

September 1921; untitled document (Niemeyer), 5/10/21; TNA:T172/1208. Niemeyer to Horne 3/10/21, 7/10/21.
39. BE:G3/178. Norman to Strong 21/3/22; TNA:T176/5 Pt. 1. 'Monetary Policy' (Hawtrey), October 1923; Niemeyer to Norman 21/11/23; Untitled memo. (Norman), 21/11/23.
40. BE:G3/177. Norman to Strong 23/7/21; 13/10/21; BE:G3/178. Norman to Moll 22/2/22; Norman to the Governor of the National Bank of Roumania 22/2/22; BE:G3/179. Norman to A. R. Wagg 5/7/23; BE:ADM16/2. 'Central Banks', 15/2/21; also see Clay (1957), Ch. 5; Boyle (1967), pp. 202–6; Sayers (1976), pp. 121–23; Cottrell (1997).
41. MRC:MSS.292/110.1/1. 'The Attack on Wages and Hours Standards' (TUC/Labour Party), 1922; MRC:MSS.292/452/3. 'On the Evils of Industrial Interruption and Trade Dislocation Caused by the Fluctuations of the Exchanges and Other Problems Arising out of the Banking System' (TUCGC), 1922; TUC Annual Report 1920. p. 119; Labour Party Annual Report 1922, pp. 247–8.
42. BE:ADM34/9–10. Norman Diaries 23/12/20, 28/12/20, 16/2/21; MRC:MSS. 200/F/3/S1/14/2–3; 'The Trade Depression' (FBI), 7/10/22; 'Statement by the FBI', 6/12/22; MRC:MSS.200/F/3/S1/8/13. 'Lower Production Costs and Trade Revival', (FBI), 14/2/22; MRC:MSS.200/F/4/24/3–5. FBI Bulletins (1920–1922 issues); Kynaston (1999).

Chapter 4   The Return to the Gold Standard

1. Grigg (1948), pp. 98–105; Alford (1986), p. 45; Figures calculated from Feinstein (1972), Tables 51–2; Butler and Butler (1994), p. 373.
2. TNA:T176/5 Pt. 1. 'Export of Gold to America' (Hawtrey), 5/3/23; BE:C40/737. 'The Return to Gold' (Hawtrey), 19/1/23; Niemeyer to H. A. Trotter (the Deputy Governor of the Bank of England), 23/1/23; Untitled Bank of England document, 16/5/23.
3. TNA:CAB23/45. Cabinet Meeting 14/2/23.
4. See Cole (1948), pp. 376ff; Morgan (1952), pp. 298–9; Alford (1996), pp. 119–21.
5. MRC:MSS.292/135.01/1. various including, 'Proposals for Unemployment Policy' (TUC–Labour Party Joint Research and Information Dept.), January 1923; Keynes (1923); 'Monetary Policy' (Henderson), 14/7/23, in Clay (1955); Labour Research Department (LRD) Monthly Circulars, November–December 1923; Labour Party and TUC Annual Reports 1923; Wootton (1925).
6. TNA:T172/1499B. 'Post-War Reports and Conferences' (undated); MRC:MSS.200/F/4/24/7. FBI Bulletins 30/1/23, 6/2/23; various in TNA:T176/5 Pt. 1.
7. MRC:MSS.200/F/4/24/7–8. FBI Bulletins (1923 issues, especially 9/10/23); MRC:MSS.200/F/3/S1/14/5. 'Trade Depression and Unemployment' (FBI), 12/10/23; FBI Grand Council Meeting 17/10/23; also see Boyce (1988), pp. 178–9.
8. Grigg (1948), pp. 153–72; Eichengreen (1992), pp. 147–50.
9. BE:C40/737. Untitled Bank of England document, 16/5/23.

10. TNA:T176/5 Pt. 1. 'Export of Gold to America' 5/3/23, (Hawtrey); TNA:T176/13 Pt. 1. 'Relations Between the Treasury and the Bank of England ...' (undated); Parliamentary Debates. 13/6/23. Vol. 165. Cls. 607–8.
11. TNA:T176/5 Pt. 1. various including, 'Notes on a Question by Lord Vernon' (Niemeyer), 24/4/23; 'Note on FBI Memo.' (Niemeyer), November 1923; BE:C40/737. Norman to Bradbury 26/5/23; Clay (1957), pp. 145–6.
12. BE:C40/737. Bradbury to Norman 25/5/23, 28/5/23.
13. BE:ADM16/2–3. various including, 'Notes for the Treasury Committee' (Norman), undated; TNA:T176/5 Pt. 1. 'Monetary Policy' (Hawtrey), October 1923; Niemeyer to Norman 21/11/23; Norman (and Bank of England) untitled memo. 21/11/23.
14. MRC:MSS.200/F/4/24/8. FBI Bulletin 24/7/23; the Times 7/8/23.
15. TNA:CAB23/45. Cabinet Meetings 2/7/23, 25/10/23; BE:G35/4. Norman to Strong 8/10/23.
16. BE:ADM34/12. Norman Diaries 15/10/23, 2/11/23, 19/12/23; BE:G14/312. 'Notes for the Treasury Committee' (Norman), 19/12/23; also see Sayers (1976), pp. 130–6; Eichengreen (1992), pp. 147–50.
17. BE:G14/312. 'Notes for the Treasury Committee' (Norman), 19/12/23; Committee of Treasury extracts; Monthly Circulars of the LRD (1924 issues); Labour Party and TUC Annual Reports 1924–1925; Snowden (1934), pp. 633–5; also see Lovell and Roberts (1968), pp. 72–3; Sayers (1976), pp. 128–33; figures calculated from Feinstein (1972), Tables 1, 37, 57; Butler and Butler (1994), p. 373.
18. TNA:T160/197. Niemeyer to Snowden 5/4/24; BE:G14/312. 'Notes for the Treasury Committee' (Norman), 19/12/23.
19. MRC:MSS.292/135.01/1. 'A Practical Policy for Unemployment', 17/6/24; TNA:T176/5. Pt. 2. 'Memo. on Proposed Raising of the Bank Rate' (TUC/Labour Party Joint Research Dept.), June 1924; Labour Party Annual Report 1924; Strachey (1925); Wootton (1925).
20. TNA:T160/197. Evidence to the Committee on the Currency and Bank of England Note Issues (hereafter referred to as the 'Chamberlain-Bradbury committee') by the FBI (30/7/24), and by McKenna, Goodenough, and Goschen; MRC:MSS.200/F/4/24/9. FBI Bulletins (1924 issues); MRC:MSS.200/F/3/ S1/14/3. 'Taxation Policy' (FBI), 27/2/24; also see Kynaston (1999), pp. 114–15.
21. See Eichengreen (1992), ps. 147–52, 224–6.
22. TNA:CAB23/47, TNA:PREM1/76 and TNA:T208/55. various; TNA:T172/ 1499B. 'Post-War Reports and Conferences'. Undated; Monthly Circulars of the LRD, June to September 1924; Snowden (1934), pp. 596–616; Cole (1948), pp. 408ff; Feinstein (1972), Tables 51–2; Butler and Butler (1994), p. 373.
23. Labour Party and TUC Annual Reports 1924; Monthly Circular of the LRD. April 1924; Snowden (1934), pp. 596ff; Cole (1948), pp. 408ff.
24. MRC:MSS.200/F/4/24/9. FBI Bulletins 29/1/24, 5/2/24, 12/2/24, 5/7/24, 5/8/24; TNA:T160/197. Evidence to the Chamberlain-Bradbury committee by chairmen of Britain's leading banks (various dates), and by the FBI, 30/7/24; TNA:T176/5 Pt. 1; also see Kynaston (1999), pp. 114–15.
25. BE:G3/180. Norman to Blackett 21/5/24; Norman to Silberling 13/6/24, 14/6/24; BE:ADM34/13. Norman Diaries 13/6/24; BE:C40/737. Norman to Strong 27/3/25, 24/4/25; TNA:T160/197. Niemeyer to Snowden 5/4/24;

TNA:T176/5 Pt. 1. 'Sterling and the Gold Standard' (Hawtrey), 26/4/24; Williamson (1999), pp. 169ff.

26. TNA:T176/5 Pt. 1. Niemeyer to Snowden, March 1924; BE:G3/181. Norman to Strong 16/10/24.

27. BE:ADM34/13. Norman Diaries 13/6/24; BE:G3/180. Norman to Strong 16/6/24; also see Brown (1940), Ch. 12.

28. The committee was initially led by Austen Chamberlain, who was replaced by Bradbury after being made foreign secretary in the new Conservative government. On the establishment of the committee see for example BE:G35/5. Norman to Strong 26/2/25, 15/4/25; BE:G3/181. Norman to W. H. Clegg 13/10/24; BE:G3/180. Norman to Niemeyer 16/4/24; TNA:T160/197. various notes by Niemeyer.

29. TNA:T176/5 Pt. 2. 'Sterling and Gold' (Hawtrey), 4/7/24.

30. TNA:T160/197. Evidence of Norman and Addis to the Chamberlain-Bradbury committee 27/6/24; BE:G35/5. Norman to Strong. 18/2/25.

31. TNA:T160/197. Evidence by Addis to the Chamberlain-Bradbury committee 27/6/24; Comments by Niemeyer during the evidence of Goodenough 11/7/24; TNA:T172/1500A. Norman to Niemeyer 4/12/24; BE:G30/13. Norman to H. Schacht 6/12/24.

32. TNA:T176/5 Pt. 2. 'Sterling and Gold' (Hawtrey), 4/7/24; TNA:T208/54. 'Sterling and the Gold Standard' (Hawtrey), 24/7/24; TNA:T160/197. Bradbury to Farrer 24/7/24; BE:G3/181. Lubbock to Strong 25/8/24.

33. The view for example of Brown Jr (1940), pp. 609–12; Moggridge (1972), Chs. 3–4; Howson (1975), Ch. 3.

34. Hawtrey (1933), pp. 233–4; TNA:T172/1499B. 'How Does a Gold Standard Work in Regulating Credit?' (Hawtrey), undated believed 1925; Evidence by Niemeyer to the Committee on Finance and Industry, 4/6/30. Minutes of Evidence Vol. 2; BE:G14/312. Niemeyer to A. C. Turner 19/11/43.

35. TNA:T160/197. Evidence by Norman to the Chamberlain-Bradbury committee 27/6/24.

36. BE:G3/180. Norman to Strong 16/6/24; Norman to Blackett 21/5/24; Norman to Silberling 13/6/24; 14/6/24.

37. TNA:T176/5 Pt. 2. 'Sterling and Gold' (Hawtrey), 4/7/24; TNA:T208/54. 'Sterling and the Gold Standard' (Hawtrey), 24/7/24; TNA:T160/197. Comments made by Chamberlain during the evidence of F. C. Goodenough to the Chamberlain-Bradbury Committee 11/7/24; Comments by Bradbury during the evidence of Norman and Addis to the Chamberlain-Bradbury committee 27/6/24; BE:ADM16/2. Minutes of the Committee of Treasury 23/6/24.

38. TNA:T160/197. Evidence by Norman to the Chamberlain-Bradbury committee 27/6/24.

39. Copies of the draft reports and various comments by officials are in TNA:T160/197.

40. TNA:T172/1500A. Niemeyer to Norman 8/12/24; TNA:T172/1499B. Untitled Document 21/4/25; also see Evidence by Niemeyer to the Committee on Finance and Industry, 4/6/30. Minutes of Evidence. Vol. 2.

41. BE:G3/181. Norman to Strong 16/10/24.

42. BE:G3/182. Norman to Blackett 27/10/24.

43. BE:G3/181. Norman to Strong 16/10/24.

44. Sunday Express 5/5/25; Daily Mail, 5/3/25; 'Will Unemployment Increase?'
    (Henderson), 4/4/25 in Clay (1955); the New Leader 16/1/25; 13/3/25; the
    Workers' Weekly (Communist Party of Great Britain) January–March 1925;
    Monthly Circular of the LRD, March 1925; also see Boyce (1988).
45. MRC:MSS.200/F/4/24/11. FBI Bulletins 24/3/25, 30/4/25: In October 1924
    the 'FBI Bulletin' changed its name to 'British Industries', though for
    reasons of simplicity and continuity the rest of the book will continue to
    refer to it as the 'FBI Bulletin'.
46. MRC:MSS.200/F/3/E1/4/1. 'Finance' (FBI), 5/2/25; MRC:MSS.200/F/3/S1/
    14/6 and TNA:T172/1499B. various including J. S. McConechy (MAIE) to
    Nugent 24/1/25; and to Churchill, 18/4/25; G. H. Fulton to FBI 17/3/25;
    MAIE Bulletin 24/7/24.
47. Labour Party and TUC Annual Reports 1924–1925; Monthly Circular of the
    LRD (August 1924 to May 1925); Workers' Weekly (January to March 1925);
    The Socialist Standard (1925 issues); Snowden in the Observer 8/2/25.
48. MRC:MSS.200/F/4/24/11. FBI Bulletins 27/1/25, 3/2/25, 10/2/25; MRC:MSS.
    200/F/3/S1/14/6. G. H. Fulton to FBI 17/3/25; TNA:T172/1499B. Midland
    Bank Monthly Reviews (January to March 1925); A. de V. Leigh (London
    Chambers of Commerce) to Baldwin and Churchill 16/3/25; also see
    Catterall (1976), p. 44; Kynaston (1999), p. 18.
49. MRC:MSS.200/F/3/S1/14/6 and TNA:T172/1499B. FBI to Churchill 17/3/25; to
    G. H. Fulton 20/3/25, to R. A. Kerr Montgomery 18/5/28; D. L. Walker (FBI
    General Secretary) to Sir R. A. Kerr Montgomery 12/12/28; MRC:MSS.200/
    F/3/E1/4/1. 'Finance' (FBI), 5/2/25; MRC:MSS.200/F/4/24/9–11. FBI Bulletins
    (August 1924 to March 1925, especially 5/8/24); also see Layton (1925),
    pp. 184–5; Hume (1963), pp. 240–1; Boyce (1988), pp. 189–90.
50. BE:G3/181. Norman to B. Hornsby 10/11/24.
51. BE:G3/181. Norman to Strong 16/10/24; and also to W. H. Clegg 13/10/24.
52. TNA:T175/9. Norman telegrams to Lubbock 7/1/25; TNA:T160/197.
    Evidence by Norman to the Chamberlain-Bradbury committee 28/1/25;
    BE:G35/5. Norman to Strong 21/3/25.
53. TNA:T175/9. Norman telegrams to Lubbock 7/1/25.
54. Churchill to Baldwin 15/12/24, in Gilbert (1976), p. 93; Copies of
    Chamberlain-Bradbury reports in TNA:T160/197.
55. TNA:T172/1500A. Niemeyer to Norman 8/12/24; 'The Cushion' (Niemeyer),
    20/3/25; Untitled and undated document by Fisher; BE:C40/737. Lubbock
    to Norman 9–10/1/25; Niemeyer to Norman 16/3/25; TNA:T175/9. Norman
    telegrams to Lubbock 7/1/25; Niemeyer to Lubbock 9/1/25.
56. BE:G35/5; Norman to Strong 24/1/25; BE:G14/312. Norman to Strong
    24/4/25.
57. Churchill's obsession with high politics was amply revealed by Norman,
    who explained that there was no one 'more anxious to use publicity for his
    own purposes', and no-one 'more suspicious of information being disclosed
    at one moment which he intended to disclose at another.' BE:C40/737.
    Norman to Strong 24/4/25; also see Boyle (1967), pp. 179–81; Middlemas
    (1969), pp. 302–3; Ponting (1994), p. 293.
58. TNA:T175/9. Untitled Memo. (Churchill), 29/1/25.
59. TNA:T172/1499B. various including 'The Gold Standard' (Hawtrey), 2/2/25;
    'Gold Standard Bill' (Niemeyer), Undated; 'Commentary' (Niemeyer),

2/2/25; Niemeyer to Churchill 6/2/25; Untitled Memos, 7/3/25, 21/4/25; BE:G14/312. Norman to Churchill, 2/2/25; Bradbury to Niemeyer 5/2/25; TNA:T171/246. Niemeyer to Churchill 21/2/25.

60. Report of the Committee on the Currency and Bank of England Note Issues. 5/2/25. Cmd.2393.
61. BE:C40/731. Bank of England to Strong 6/2/25.
62. TNA:T171/245. Churchill to Niemeyer 6/2/25; TNA:T172/1499B. Churchill to Niemeyer 22/2/25; also see Boyle (1967), p. 188; Skidelsky (1969); Gilbert (1976), p. 96.
63. TNA:CAB23/49. Cabinet Meeting 25/3/25; TNA:T176/13 Pt. 1. Niemeyer to Churchill 4/3/25; also see Leith-Ross (1968), p. 95.
64. TNA:T176/13 Pt. 1. 'Relations Between the Treasury and the Bank of England ....' (undated).
65. The only surviving account of this meeting is in Grigg (1948), pp. 182–4.
66. Notes in TNA:T172/1500A; BE:ADM34/14. Norman Diaries 20/3/25; TNA:CAB23/49. Cabinet Meetings 25/3/25, 27/4/25.

Chapter 5   The Golden Shield

1. The restoration of the prewar par effectively constrained sterling within a fluctuation margin of around $4.85 to $4.88. On the technical details of the return see BE:G1/426 and BE:G35/5.
2. Baldwin in Middlemas and Barnes (1969), pp. 302ff; Williamson (1999), pp. 145ff.
3. BE:G3/15. 'Industry and Overseas Investments' (Hawtrey), 23/6/25.
4. BE:G35/5. Norman to Strong 8/5/25.
5. Parliamentary Debates. Vol. 183, 4/5/25.
6. Baldwin in Middlemas and Barnes (1969), pp. 302ff; Williamson (1999), pp. 145ff.
7. Churchill in the Times 18/7/25; also see Gilbert (1976), p. 128.
8. MRC:MSS.200/F/3/S1/14/6. Nugent to Sir H. Roberts 4/5/25; and F. Percival 6/5/25; MRC:MSS.200/F/4/24/11. FBI Bulletins May–September 1925; ILP Archives (University of Warwick Library), various documents including 'Twenty Points of Socialism' (J. Maxton), 1925; The New Leader 8/5/25; The Workers' Weekly 8/5/25; Labour Party Annual Report 1925, p. 93; MRC:MSS.292/135.01/1. 'Unemployment', TUC General Council (TUCGC), January 1927.
9. BE:C40/738. Norman to Sir Drummond Fraser 4/5/25; BE:G35/5. Norman to Strong 8/5/25; BE:C40/737. Norman to Strong 29/4/25; TNA:T172/1499B. Niemeyer to Churchill 7/5/25.
10. MRC:MSS.292/252.61/5–6. various; MRC:MSS.292/603/1 and 6. various including 'The Economic Position of the Coal Industry' (MFGB), May 1925; Daily Herald 27/6/25; the Times 23/7/25; Citrine (1964), pp. 132–6.
11. Cited in Farman (1972), p. 25.
12. Citrine (1964), pp. 132–9; Laybourn (1993), pp. 28–36.
13. See Addendum to the Report of the Macmillan Court of Inquiry. Cmd 2478 (1925); MRC:MSS.292/252.61/5–6. various including 'The Coal Crisis' (MFGB), 22/7/25; MRC:MSS.292/135.2/2. 'The Economic Position of the

Coal Industry' (TUCGC); MRC:MSS.200/F/3/E1/3/3. 'Some Causes of the Present Stagnation of British Trade' (FBI Grand Council), July 1925; MRC:MSS.200/F/4/24/11. 'Position of British Trade' (FBI), July 1925; FBI Bulletin 30/7/25; Labour Party and TUC Annual Reports 1925; The New Leader 7/8/25, 4/9/25; Lansbury's Labour Weekly 27/2/26, 12/6/26, 20/11/26; LRD Monthly Circular, September 1925; 'Unemployment and Monetary Policy' (Keynes), Evening Standard 22–23/7/25; Keynes (1925); Strachey (1925); Citrine (1964), pp. 132–3; Renshaw (1975), pp. 118–22.

14. BE:ADM16/3. 'Gold and Bank Rate' (Hawtrey), 11/7/25; BE:C40/738. Untitled Bank of England Document 27/7/25; Churchill in the Times 13/7/25; TNA:T176/21. Niemeyer to Baldwin 26/6/25; Sir Warren Fisher to Baldwin 25/5/25; TNA:T208/105. 'Gold Standard Results' (Niemeyer), 4/8/25.

15. TUC Annual Report 1925, pp. 158–9; The Times 18/7/25; 'The Gold Standard : A Reply to Mr Keynes' (Bradbury), Financial News 12/8/25.

16. BE:G30/14. Norman to Sir Edward Cook 14/9/25; also see BE:G35/5. Norman to Strong 21/8/25; TNA:T176/13 Pt. 2. Norman to Niemeyer 21/9/25.

17. BE:G35/5. Norman to Strong 23/11/25.

18. BE:G3/182. Norman to Blackett 27/10/25, to W. H. Clegg 8/12/25; MRC:MSS.200/F/4/24/12. FBI Bulletin 30/1/26; The New Leader (January–April 1926); TNA:T176/13. 'The Credit Situation' (Hawtrey), 5/12/25; Clay (1957), pp. 293–5.

19. Figures calculated from Butler and Butler (1994), p. 373.

20. Labour Party and TUC Annual Reports 1925 (remarks by Frank Heaviside at the Labour Party conference, pp. 262–6); MRC:MSS.292/252.61/5. 'Report of the Special TUC Conference', 24/7/25.

21. MRC:MSS.292/135.01/3. 'Notes for TUCGC Unemployment Deputation' (TUC/Labour Party), December 1925; MRC:MSS.292/135.01/6. Joint Report on the Prevention of Unemployment (1926), p. 12; MRC:MSS.292/ 252.61/6. various including 'The Economic Position of the Coal Industry' (MFGB), May 1925; 'Copies of all Official Documents and Communications Received and Issued in Connection with the Present Crisis' (MFGB), 1925; 'The Mining Dispute' (TUCGC), 1925; Daily Herald 21/5/25, 7/7/25; the Times 22/6/25; The New Leader, 26/6/25; also see Labour Party and TUC Annual Reports 1925; MRC:MSS.292/100/1. 'The Possibility of a Higher Standard of Living Under Capitalism' (TUCGC), March 1927; various in MRC:MSS.292/135.2/3; Keynes (1951), pp. 241–2.

22. TNA:CAB24/179. NCEO Deputation to the Prime Minister 20/4/26; MRC:MSS.200/F/3/S1/14/6. T. B. Johnston to the Editor of the National Review 26/1/26.

23. MRC:MSS.200/F/4/24/11–12. FBI Bulletins 30/7/25, 30/1/26; MRC:MSS.200/ F/3/S1/14/6. P. G. Swann to the FBI. 14/7/25; FBI General Economic Dept. to Rowntree & Co. Ltd. 17/8/25; Nugent to Norman 15/10/25; MRC:MSS.292/252.61/6. various including, 'The British Coalmining Industry' (MFGB), 1925; 'Position of British Trade' (FBI), July 1925.

24. MRC:MSS.200/F/3/S1/14/6. various including Nugent to P. G. Swann 21/7/25; C. Tennyson to T. B. Johnston 15/2/26, 24/2/26; MRC:MSS.200/ F/3/E1/3/3. 'Some Causes of the Present Stagnation of British Trade' (FBI), July 1925; 'Position of British Trade' (FBI), July 1925.

25. On the general strike see TNA:CAB24/179; Citrine (1964), p. 167ff; Farman (1972); Arnot (1975); Renshaw (1975); Morris (1976); Phillips (1976); Laybourn (1993).

26. See for example Renshaw (1975), ps. 108–9, 251–2; Boyce (1988), p. 193; Laybourn (1993), p. 14; Kynaston (1999), p. 126.

27. Various in MRC:MSS.292/252.61/3–6, including 'Statement on Owners Proposals' (MFGB), 27/4/26; 'The Coal Situation' (TUCGC), 6/9/26; 'Mining Crisis 1926', (TUCGC); 'Statement on the General Strike' (MFGB), 12/1/27; the Times 22/5/26; Labour Party and TUC Annual Reports 1926; MRC:MSS.126/EB/FI/46/3 and 47/5. Evidence to the Committee on Finance and Industry by the FBI (26/2/30) and by the TUCGC (12/4/30); MRC:MSS.200/F/4/24/12. FBI Bulletins (1926 issues); Cook (1926); Fyfe (1926); Snowden (1934), pp. 725–34; Citrine (1964), pp. 137–8; the Workers Weekly (1926 issues); Lansbury's Labour Weekly 22/5/26.

28. Lansbury's Labour Weekly (1926 issues); Labour Party and TUC Annual Reports 1926.

29. MRC:MSS.200/F/3/S1/14/1, 3, and 6. various including, FBI Memo. to the Prime Minister 30/11/26; 'Industry's Burden' (FBI), December 1926; MRC:MSS.200/B/3/2/C625 Pt. 7. Report on the Industrial Situation (NCEO), May 1926; TNA:T208/55. ABCC Report 22/4/26.

30. BE:OV32/2. Norman to Strong 15/4/26; BE:G8/57. Committee of Treasury Minutes 28/4/26, 5/5/26; TNA:T175/11. Churchill to Niemeyer 9/4/27; various in TNA:CAB24/179.

31. TNA:T208/55. Niemeyer to Sir Sydney Chapman 15/5/26; BE:G1/464. J. P. Morgan (New York) to E. C. Grenfell 12/5/27; Daily News 17/5/26.

32. BE:ADM34/15. Norman Diaries 20/5/26; Feinstein (1972); Clegg (1985), p. 421; Alford (1986), pp. 20–1; Gazeley and Rice (1992), pp. 326–31; Butler and Butler (1994), ps. 373–5, 383–5.

33. See Branson (1977), pp. 140–2; Best and Humphries (1987), pp. 231–2; Heim (1987), pp. 240–56; Tolliday (1987), p. 86.

34. Figures calculated from Butler and Butler (1994), p. 373; on the industrial truce discussions see various items in MRC:MSS.200/F/3/S1/14/6 and MRC:MSS.200/F/3/E1/3/11.

35. See for example TNA:BT55/49. 'The Economic Situation in the United Kingdom 1922–7' (Cunliffe-Lister), 1927; TNA:CAB24/184. 'Trade Union and Trade Disputes Bill' (Steel-Maitland), 23/3/27.

36. BE:ADM34/16. Norman Diaries 21/11/27; BE:G14/55. Committee of Treasury Extracts; BE:OV9/479. Niemeyer to Grigg 19/7/28; also see Clay (1957), pp. 320–59; Sayers (1976), Ch. 14.

37. See Kenwood and Lougheed (1971), Chs. 11–13; Marichal (1989), Ch. 7; Feinstein *et al* (1997), Table 5.2; Bulmer-Thomas (1998), p. 70.

38. See Soule (1947); Marichal (1989), Ch. 7; Beaudreau (1996), Tables A3.2, A3.6.

39. Kenwood and Lougheed (1971), pp. 186–97; Bulmer-Thomas (1998), Table 2.1.

40. BE:G1/421. Note by the Whaley-Eaton news service, spring 1927; BE:G1/464. Norman to Sir Edward Cook 4/1/27; TNA:T176/5. Pt. 2. 'Recent Price Movements' (Hawtrey), 1/3/27; TNA:T176/13. Pt. 2. 'The Monetary Outlook

According to the Times' (Hawtrey), 18/3/27; MRC:MSS.200/F/3/S1/14/6. FBI General Economic Department to Ley's Malleable Castings Co. 11/4/27; Lansbury's Labour Weekly (April 1927 issues).

41. BE:ADM34/15. Norman Diaries 8/10/26; BE:G1/464. Churchill to Norman 18/5/27; Note by Norman; TNA:T175/11. Churchill to Niemeyer 9/4/27; TNA:T208/121; 'Memo. on Draft Currency and Bank Notes Bill' (Churchill), 1927.
42. BE:G1/50. Norman to Francis Rodd 7/1/33; BE:G1/421. Strong to Norman 12/4/27; Norman to Strong 7/5/27; TNA:T175/11. Churchill to Niemeyer 9/4/27.
43. See Brown Jr (1940), pp. 452–8; Clay (1957), pp. 221–37.
44. See Sayers (1976), pp. 192ff; Eichengreen (1992), pp. 187ff.
45. MRC:MSS.292/135.01/2. 'Statement on Unemployment' (TUCGC), 1/12/28; MRC:MSS.292/262/36. 'Memo. Submitted on the Gold Reserve and its Relations with Industry' (TUCGC and Mond Group), 1928; 'Explanatory Memo. Submitted on the Memo. on "The Gold Reserve and its Relations With Industry"', 1928 (hereafter 'Explanatory Memo.'); MRC:MSS.292/265/1. 'National Finance and Banking' (TUCGC), 15/2/28; MRC:MSS.292/560.1/1. 'Development of Economic Policy' (TUCGC), November 1928; Labour Party Annual Reports 1927, pp. 264–5; 1928; TUC Annual Reports (1927), pp. 453–5; (1928), p. 230; Lansbury's Labour Weekly (1927 issues); New Leader 24/6/27.
46. MRC:MSS.292/135.01/2. 'General Memo. on Unemployment' (Mond Group), August 1928; MRC:MSS.200/F/3/S1/14/6 and 15/6. various including, V. Vickers to FBI Chairman 2/7/27, to FBI Secretary 6/7/27; FBI General Secretary to R. A. Kerr Montgomery. 12/12/28; MRC:MSS.200/F/4/24/12–13. FBI Bulletins (1927–1928 issues); Kynaston (1999), pp. 128–9.
47. TNA:T160/463. 'Mr. McKenna on the Gold Standard' (Hawtrey), 30/1/28; TNA:T172/1500B. Grigg to Churchill 14/4/28; the Times 30/10/28; also see Grigg (1948), p. 199–200; Gilbert (1976), pp. 289–95.
48. BE:ADM34/16. Norman Diaries 27/8/27; BE:G1/421. Norman to Strong 5/10/27, 28/11/27; BE:G1/422. Lubbock to Harrison 3/8/28; Norman to Strong 11/4/28; BE:G1/464. Norman to Niemeyer 6/12/27.
49. Various in TNA:T175/18 Pts. 1–2 and MRC:MSS.292/135.01/1; BE:EID4/102l. 'The Fiduciary Issue' (Hawtrey), 6/5/27; also see Gilbert (1976), pp. 289–95.
50. BE:G1/421. Norman to Strong 14/3/27; BE:G1/423. Norman to Harrison 28/11/28.
51. Labour Party and TUC Annual Reports 1927–1928; MRC:MSS.292/100/1. 'The Possibility of a Higher Standard of Living Under Capitalism' (TUCGC), March 1927; 'Improvements in Conditions in 19th and 20th Centuries' (TUCGC), June 1927; MRC:MSS.292/135.01/2; 'Unemployment: Employers' Memo. General Criticism' (TUCGC), 7/11/28. 'Statement on Unemployment' (TUCGC), 1/12/28; MRS:MSS.292/262/36. 'Explanatory Memo', (1928), p. 5.
52. MRC:MSS.200/F/3/S1/14/6 and 15/6. various including, Nugent to Sir R. A. Kerr Montgomery 16/5/28; FBI General Economic Department to Sir R. A. Kerr Montgomery 18/4/28, and to Colonel F. V. Willey 13/6/28; MRC:MSS.200/F/4/24/14. FBI Bulletins (1928 issues); MRC:MSS.292/135.01/2. 'General Memo. on Unemployment' (Mond Group) August 1928, pp. 53ff; 'Memo. Submitted on the Gold Reserve and its Relations With Industry', and 'Explanatory Memo.';

MRC:MSS.292/262/36. 'TUC Industrial Conference Report', p. 20; Yorkshire Post 28/12/28; Daily Herald 25/1/29.
53. MRC:MSS.292/110.1/1. 'The Trend of Real Wages in Britain 1850–1928' (TUCGC); MRC:MSS.292/135.01/2. Summary of Mond-Turner Meetings, 17/10/28; 'Development of Economic Policy' (TUCGC); 'Unemployment : Employers' Memorandum. General Criticism', (TUCGC Industrial Committee), 7/11/28, p. 2; Industrial Review (1928 issues); MRC:MSS.200/F/3/S1/14/1–7. 'Government Economy' (FBI), 31/3/27; Sir Max Muspratt (FBI President) to various bank chairmen 3/2/27; MRC:MSS.200/F/4/24/13–14. FBI Bulletins (1927–1928 issues).

Chapter 6   The Collapse of the Strategy

1. Butler and Butler (1994), pp. 373–4.
2. TNA:CAB24/20. Note by Churchill 25/2/29; TNA:CAB23/60. Cabinet Meeting 7/2/29; MRC:MSS.292/135.01/1. 'Interim Joint Report on Unemployment' (Mond-Turner), March 1929; MRC:MSS.200/F/4/24/15. FBI Bulletin 15/2/29; TUC Annual Report 1929, pp. 188–202; ILP Archives. 'Re-Organise Industry' (ILP). March 1929; 'National Finance' (Pethick-Lawrence), April 1929; the Times 8/2/29.
3. TNA:CAB23/60. Cabinet Meeting 7/2/29; TNA:CAB24/20. 'Unemployment' (Churchill) 25/2/29; TNA:T175/18 Pts. 1–2. various; TNA:T176/13 Pts. 1–2. various including, Blackett to Phillips 17/2/29; Bradbury to Phillips 18/2/29; Niemeyer to Phillips 18/2/29; 'Relations Between the Treasury and the Bank of England'; BE:G1/466. Untitled memo. (Hopkins), undated; 'Memo. on Certain Proposals Relating to Unemployment', May 1929. Cmd. 3331., pp. 51–3.
4. 'Final Report of the Committee on Industry and Trade', February 1929, pp. 54–8. Cmd. 3282; TNA:CAB24/20. 'Government Assistance to Rationalisation' (Cunliffe-Lister), 24/2/29; BE:ADM34/18. Norman Diaries. 5/3/29; BE:G14/55. various including Norman to Committee of Treasury 21/11/29; Blackett cited in Middlemas (1969a), p. 219.
5. BE:OV9/587. Untitled memo. by Norman (in collusion with Niemeyer), 1929; BE:G1/466. 'Some Notes on the Return to the Gold Standard' (Norman), 3/4/29; 'Resumption of the Gold Standard' (Norman), 3/4/29; 'Rationalisation', unsigned and undated Bank memo; BE:G30/19. Norman to J. W. Nightingale 1/1/29; BE:G1/455. Evidence by Norman to the Cotton Industry Committee of the Economic Advisory Council, 11/4/30.
6. BE:G1/452–3. various correspondence between Norman and George Harrison (the new Governor of the FRBNY); BE:G1/515. Harvey to Norman 26/7/29; TNA:T176/13. Pt. 2. Lubbock to Hopkins 12/8/29.
7. BE:G1/515. Sir Ernest Harvey (the Bank's Deputy Governor) to Norman 12/7/29, to J. Stamp 12/7/29; BE:ADM34/18. Norman Diaries, September 1929.
8. BE:G1/515. Harvey to Norman 12/7/29, to Stamp 12/7/29; BE:ADM34/18. Norman Diaries 30/9/29; Labour Party Annual Report 1929, pp. 237–31; the Financial Times 29/7/29; the Times 27/9/29; the Daily Herald, 28/9/29.
9. MRC:MSS.126/EB/FI/47/5. TUCGC Evidence to the Committee on Finance and Industry (hereafter referred to as the Macmillan committee), 12/4/30;

MRC:MSS/292/462/3. 'The General Price Level and Stabilisation' (TUCGC), 15/5/30; Labour Party Annual Report 1930; also see Jones and Keating (1985), pp. 51–2.

10. Evidence to the Macmillan committee by the FBI 26/2/30; and by Lakin-Smith (ABCC) 11/7/30. Minutes of Evidence Vols. 1–2; MRC:MSS.200/F/4/24/16. FBI Bulletins (1930 issues); MRC:MSS.200/F/3/E1/3/7. MAIE Bulletin. January 1930; MRC:MSS.292/135/1. 'Unemployment' (ABCC), 29/7/30; Kynaston (1999), pp. 204–5.

11. BE:G1/427. Hopkins to Harvey 24/11/30; Labour Party Annual Report 1930, p. 182; Middlemas (1969a), pp. 257ff.

12. Evidence to the Macmillan committee by Norman (an unaltered proof is in BE:G1/428), Minutes of Evidence Vols. 1–2; BE:ADM34/19. Norman Diaries 24/10/30; also see BE:G30/21. Norman to V. A. Malcolmson 12/9/30; BE:G1/455. Evidence by Norman to the EAC Iron and Steel Committee, 31/3/30; BE:G1/470. Norman to Sir Oswald Stoll 17/7/33; Evidence by Niemeyer to the Macmillan committee 4/6/30. Minutes of Evidence Vol. 2; For the views of the Bank also see TNA:PREM1/70. 'The Industrial Situation' (Henry Clay, a Bank of England advisor), 1929; BE:C43/137. 'Answers to Governor' (J. C. Osborne, the Bank's Secretary), 15/4/30.

13. MRC:MSS.292/110.1/1. 'Wages and Unemployment' (TUCGC), 7/2/29; MRC:MSS.292/135.01/1. 'Interim Joint Report on Unemployment' (Mond-Turner representatives), March 1929; MRC:MSS.292/462/3. Milne-Bailey to Mr. Firth 28/5/29; 'General Price Level and Stabilisation' (TUCGC), 15/5/30; MRC:MSS.292/560.1/1. various including 'Economic Programme' (TUCGC); MRC:MSS.200/F/3/E1/3/6–7. FBI evidence to the Macmillan committee; MRC:MSS.200/F/3/S1/15/6. Glenday to F. V. Willey 15/1/29, and to Secretary of the Society of British Aircraft Construction. 23/9/29; MRC:MSS.200/F/3/S1/19/1. FBI General Secretary to J. Pogson 9/12/29; MRC:MSS.200/F/4/24/15–16. FBI Bulletins (1929–1930 issues); BE:G1/455. EAC Committee of Economists Report 24/10/30, p. 27; Labour Party and TUC Annual Reports 1929; ILP Archives. 'Re-Organise Industry' (ILP) March 1929.

14. Figures calculated from the Report of the Committee on Finance and Industry (hereafter referred to as the Macmillan Report), 1931. Cmd.3897, p. 85; Feinstein (1972), Tables 20, 37, 51, 52, 57, 64, 65; BE/G1/455. MacDonald to E. R. Peacock 15/4/31.

15. Calculated from Branson (1977), Table 2, p. 11; Butler and Butler (1994), p. 383.

16. MRC:MSS.292/560.1/2. 'The Industrial Situation' (NCEO), 11/2/31; MRC:MSS.292/560.1/21. 'Industry and the Nation' (FBI); MRC:MSS.292/135.01/3. 'The Unemployment Situation' (TUCGC), 13/7/31; MRC:MSS.292/560.1/20. 'Economic Policy of the TUC' (TUCGC), 4/3/31; Economic Policy Statement (TUCGC), 25/3/31; the Manchester Guardian 5/8/31; the Times 10/8/31.

17. BE:G1/468. 'Industrial Depression' (Hawtrey), 5/3/31; Norman to D. Ferguson 27/1/31; BE:G14/341. various.

18. Kunz (1987), pp. 57–71; Eichengreen (1992), pp. 259ff.

19. Macmillan Report. Cmd.3897; BE:G14/316. Committee of Treasury Extracts; BE:G1/468. Harvey to Snowden 6/8/31; also see Kunz (1987), pp. 64ff.

20. BE:ADM34/20. Norman Diaries; BE:G1/109. 'Domestic Financial Policy Since 1925', Unsigned Bank of England memo; MRC:MSS.292/420/2 Pt. 2. 'The Crisis' (E. Bevin and G. D. H. Cole), 1932.
21. MRC:MSS.292/420/2 Pts. 1–2. various including 'The Trade Unions and the National Financial Situation' (1931); MacDonald to W. Citrine 21/8/31; TNA:CAB23/67. Cabinet Meeting 21/8/31; BE:G14/316. Committee of Treasury Extracts; Daily Herald 4/9/31; the Times, 26/8/31, 8/9/31; Kunz (1987), pp. 94ff.
22. MRC:MSS.200/B/3/2/C530 Pt. 2. various; MRC:MSS.292/471/1. 'Gold Standard' (TUCGC), 17/9/31; MRC:MSS.292/420/2. Pts. 1–2. 'The Financial Situation' (TUCGC), 25/8/31; 'The Trade Unions and the National Financial Situation', 7/9/31; ILP Archives. 'Oppose the Bankers "Ramp"' (ILP), 1931; Daily Herald 17/9/31.
23. BE:G1/459. MacDonald and Fisher to Norman and Harvey 19/9/31; various in TNA:CAB23/68.
24. The Times 21/9/31, 25/9/31; the Financial Times, the Daily Telegraph, the Manchester Guardian, the Daily Express, the Morning Post, the Daily Herald 22/9/31; MRC:MSS.292/135.01/3. 'Observations on Draft of Labour's way to Provide Work and Leisure' (TUCGC), 11/5/35; Keynes (1951), pp. 288–94; Clay (1957), pp. 399–400.
25. MRC:MSS.200/B/3/2/C800 Pt. 2. various including 'Imperial Conference, Ottawa 1932' (TUC), July 1932; MRC:MSS.292/420/2–3. various including 'The Crisis' (Bevin and Cole); various in MRC:MSS.292/135/1; MRC:MSS.292/462/3. 'Policy on International Gold Standard' (TUCGC), 1936; MRC:MSS.292/560.1/1–3. 'TUC and the Gold Standard' (TUCGC), 1936; Labour Party Annual Report 1932.
26. MRC:MSS.200/B/3/2/C107. T. Ashurst (CSMA) to J. B. Forbes Watson 17/6/33; MRC:MSS.200/F/3/E1/14/1. 'Future Monetary Policy' (NFISM), 24/10/31; MRC:MSS.200/F/3/E3/3/2. various including 'Industry's Monetary Policy' (FBI), 8/2/33; MRC:MSS.200/F/4/24/17–19. FBI Bulletins (1931–1932 issues); 'Industry and the Nation' (FBI); MRC:MSS.200/F/4/46/3–4. 'Industry and the Crisis' (FBI) September 1931; MRC:MSS.292/560.1/2. 'The Industrial Situation' (NCEO); BE:G1/459. J. S. McConechy (MAIE) to Chamberlain 14/11/3; Kynaston (1999), pp. 361ff.
27. BE:G1/50. 'Note by the Treasury' (unsigned), 17/8/32; BE:G1/453. Harvey to MacDonald 28/9/31; BE:G1/455. various including, 'Notes on the Currency Question' (Keynes), November 1931; Norman to N. Chamberlain 26/11/31; 'Notes on Mr Keynes' Memo' (Hopkins), 3/12/31; BE:G1/459. Untitled memo. (Niemeyer), 26/9/31; Fisher to Snowden 30/9/31; BE:G15/30. various including 'Note on the Possible Rise in Prices' (untitled and undated); 'Note of a Conversation ...' (Siepmann), 22/9/31 and 24/9/31; Views of R. G. H.' (Hawtrey), 5/10/31; BE:OV48/9. Untitled memos. by Siepmann and Niemeyer, 23/8/31, 23/9/31, 22/12/31; TNA:T175/57 Pts. 1–2. various including, 'The Future of the Pound' (Hopkins), November 1931; Untitled Memos. (Hopkins), 6/4/32, 2/4/33; TNA:T188/28. Leith-Ross to Keynes 15/10/31; TNA:T188/48. 'Note of a Conversation with Lord Bradbury' (Siepmann), 24/9/31.
28. BE:ADM34/2. Norman Diaries. 26/2/32; BE:C42/17. 'Credit Policy and Trade Recovery' (Kindersley and Clay), 13/4/32; BE:G1/50. 'Note by the Treasury'

(unsigned), 17/8/32; 'The Non-Monetary Factors Affecting Prices' (unsigned Bank memo), 1/9/32; BE:G1/459. Fisher to Snowden, 30/9/31; Untitled Document (Niemeyer), 26/9/31; BE:G15/30. Untitled memo. by Siepmann 23/9/31; BE:OV48/9. Untitled memo. by Siepmann 23/8/31; various in TNA:T160/488, TNA:T175/17 Pts. 1–2, and TNA:T175/57 Pt. 1, including, 'Note on the Programme for the World Conference' (undated and unsigned); Untitled Memos (Hopkins), 6/4/32, 30/3/33; 'Empire Currency and the Sterling Block' (Hopkins), undated; Norman cited in Clay (1957), pp. 437–8; also see Nevin (1953), pp. 76–83; Jucker-Fleetwood (1968), p. 67; Howson (1975), pp. 92–9.

29. See note 27.
30. Norman cited in Jucker-Fleetwood (1968), p. 68; BE:G14/165. various including, Norman to J. D. B. Fergusson 7/5/34; Norman to L. Fraser 9/5/34; BE:G14/312. Niemeyer to A. C. Turner 19/11/43; MRC:MSS.292/563.2/3. 'Statement by the Chancellor ... at the Monetary and Economic Conference', 14/6/33.
31. See Drummond (1981), pp. 139ff, Chs. 6, 9–10; Kindleberger (1986), pp. 202ff; Eichengreen (1992), pp. 317ff.
32. TNA:T160/770. Untitled Memo (Leith-Ross), 21/11/37; TNA:T160/840. various including, 'Treasury Report...', 15/7/35; Notes by S. D. Waley (Treasury); S. D. Waley to Hopkins 25/9/35; TNA:T160/488. various; TNA:T175/17 Pt. 2. 'Note on the Programme for the World Conference' (undated and unsigned); TNA:T/175/57 Pt. 1. Graham-Harrison (untitled) 5/3/32; TNA:T177/12 Pts. 1–3. various including 'Observations on Main Memorandum'(unsigned Treasury memo), 1932; 'Joint Meeting of Financial Sub-Committee ...' (Treasury document), 1/11/32; BE:G1/50. 'The Non-Monetary Factors Affecting Prices' (unsigned Bank memo), 1/9/32; BE:G1/455. Norman to Hopkins 11/12/32; BE:G15/30. 'Note of a Conversation with Monsieur Van Zeeland ....', 22/9/31 (Siepmann).

Chaper 7   Britain's Membership of the Exchange Rate Mechanism

1. On the operation of the ERM see Haldane (1991); Gros and Thygesen (1992); Minikin (1993); Giordano and Persaud (1998).
2. For examples of the conventional literature on Britain's membership of the ERM see Brittan (1991); Gros and Thygesen (1992), pp. 126ff; Smith (1992), pp. 164ff; Barrell *et al* (1994); Mullard (1995), pp. 99ff; Thompson (1995); Eichengreen (1996), pp. 167–92; Stephens (1996); Cobham (1997); Tsoukalis (1997); Similar views can also be found in the autobiographical accounts of several of the key actors involved. See Thatcher (1993), p. 690; Howe (1994), p. 689; Major (2000), *passim*.
3. For an open Marxist account of Britain's membership of the ERM also see Bonefeld and Burnham (1996, 1998).
4. Figures calculated from Butler and Butler (1994), pp. 374–5; Economic Trends (1994), Tables 1.20, 2.1.
5. Lawson (1992), Ch. 5.

6. Lawson (1992), p. 67, Chs. 5, 7; also see Thatcher (1993), p. 566; Howe (1994), p. 448.
7. Figures calculated from Butler and Butler (1994), ps. 373–5, 384; Economic Trends (1994), Tables 1.11, 1.16, 1.9, 1.20, 3.1, 3.2, 3.5; Daffin and Lau (2002). Chart 1; time series data from the Office for National Statistics (ONS), 2003, available at www.statistics.gov.uk; HM Treasury Pocket Databank, 22/4/03. Table 1.
8. See Stephens (1996), pp. 21–30.
9. Lawson (1992), ps. 111, 418–40, 485, 495, 504, 652, 1024–5, Chs. 39–40, Annexe II; Thatcher (1993), pp. 688–97; Howe (1994), ps. 112, 448–50; also see Stephens (1996), Ch. 2.
10. The CBI were formed in 1955 following a merger between the FBI and the NCEO.
11. See Thatcher (1993), pp. 692–700; Howe (1994), p. 450; Thompson (1995), pp. 254ff; Stephens (1996), pp. 36–52.
12. Figures calculated from Lawson (1992), Chs. 51–2; Economic Trends (1994), Tables 1.9, 1.11, 1.16, 3.1, 3.2, 3.5; Daffin and Lau (2002); and from ONS time series data, 2003.
13. See Stephens (1996), Ch. 4.
14. Lawson (1992), pp. 867–70; Thatcher (1993), pp. 706–7.
15. Lawson (1992), ps. 732, 931–4, Ch. 70; Howe (1994), pp. 577–80; Thompson (1995), pp. 264–5.
16. Lawson (1992), Chs. 76–7; Thatcher (1993), p. 718.
17. Figures calculated from Butler and Butler (1994), pp. 374–5; Economic Trends (1994), Tables 1.20, 3.1, 3.5, 5.10; opinion poll data compiled from www.mori.com; also see Bonefeld and Burnham (1996, 1998).
18. Lamont (1999), ps. 55–6, 90; Major (2000), ps. 136–160, 202, 660–2.
19. Budget speech by Lamont in the Times 20/3/91; Howe (1994), p. 639; Lamont (1999), ps. 36, 55–6, 107, 274; Major (2000), pp. 134–56.
20. Major (2000), ps. 154–60, 202, 661; also see Thatcher (1993), pp. 719–20; On the depoliticising aspects of the ERM see Bonefeld and Burnham (1996, 1998).
21. CBI Economic Situation Reports, 1989 and October 1990; TUC Annual Reports (1989), ps. 210, 424; (1990), ps. 182–3, 364, 402–28.
22. Hansard. 27/3/1990, cl. 374.
23. The Italian level of inflation for example was now at 6.5%, French inflation was at 3.6%, and German levels were at a mere 2.7%. See HM Treasury Databank, 22/4/03, Table 16.
24. See Thatcher (1993), pp. 721–2; Stephens (1996), pp. 148–53; Lamont (1999), pp. 210–11; Major (2000), p. 158–65.
25. Calculated from Economic Trends (1994), Tables 1.16, 1.5, 3.2, 3.5; HM Treasury Pocket Databank, 22/4/03, Tables 2, 3, 4, 7.
26. See Butler and Kavanagh (1992), p. 8; Major (2000), pp. 202–3; opinion poll data from www.mori.com
27. TUC Annual Report 1991, pp. 171–4 and *passim*; the Times, October 1990, January 1991, and September 1991 issues.
28. Figures calculated from Crewe (1994), p. 102; the Times (September 1991 issues); and from MORI and ICM time series data available at www.mori.com and www.icmresearch.co.uk

29. Major in the Times 14/9/91; Lamont in Hansard 19/3/1991, Cls. 165–7; (1999), ps. 104–5, 125; also see Stephens (1996), Ch. 8.
30. Major 15/10/1990. Hansard, Cls. 928–935; Leigh-Pemberton (1991); also see Lamont (1999), p. 107; 'Industrial Relations in the 1990s'. Cmd 1602 (July 1991), cited in Taylor (1994), p. 251.
31. TUC Annual Reports (1991, 1992); Financial Times, 4/1/92; Thatcher (1993), pp. 721–4; Economic Trends (1994), Tables 1.5, 3.1, 3.2; Stephens (1996), Ch. 9; Lamont (1999), ps. 8, 40–2, 150–4, Tables 1, 3, 8; Major (2000), ps. 152, 162–5, 319; HM Treasury Pocket Databank, 22/4/03, Tables 2, 3, 4, 7.
32. TUC Annual Report (1992); the Times 29/7/93; 30/792.
33. Thatcher (1993), p. 724; Lamont (1999), ps. 8, 194–7; Major (2000), pp. 152–65; Opinion poll data calculated from Crewe (1994), pp. 99–108; Kavanagh (1997), p. 76; and from MORI and ICM time series data available at www.mori.com and www.icmresearch.co.uk
34. On these events see Eichengreen (1993); Bonefeld and Burnham (1996, 1998); Stephens (1996), Ch. 9; Lamont (1999), pp. 208–225; Major (2000), Ch. 14.
35. On these events see Stephens (1996), Ch. 10; Lamont (1999), Ch. 10; Major (2000), Ch. 14.
36. Figures calculated from Economic Trends (1994), Tables 1.11, 1.16, 1.9, 3.1, 3.2, 3.5; Lamont (1999), ps. 33–5, 528, 536, Tables 3 and 8; ONS time series data, 2003.
37. House of Commons Debates, 12/11/92; Lamont (1999), pp. 274–7.
38. Lamont (1999), pp. 274–7.
39. Major (2000); Townsend (2003), Tables A.1, A.2, D.3; HM Treasury Pocket Databank, 22/4/03. Tables 20, 24; Time series data available from www.mori.com
40. Calculated from Economic Trends (1994), Table 3.1; HM Treasury Pocket Databank, 22/4/03. Tables 1, 16; also see Stephens (1996), Ch. 11.
41. Calculated from Butler and Butler (1994); Drinkwater and Ingram (2003), Appendix. Table A1.
42. Major (2000), p. 138.

Chapter 8   Britain and the Single European Currency

1. On these events see Rawnsley (2001).
2. See Rawnsley (2001), Ch. 19; Budd (2002).
3. Balls (2001).
4. Brown cited in Allen (2002); George cited in Balls (2001).
5. HM Treasury (2003a), Ch. 1.
6. Blair in the Guardian, 23/2/99; Brown (2002), Hansard Debates, Cl. 322.
7. Balls (2001); 'Sterling and the Economy', Citigroup report. May 2003.
8. Calculated from HM Treasury Pocket Databank, 22/4/03, Tables 2, 5, 7, 8, 9, 13, 16, 17, 18, 19, 21; the Guardian 23/7/03; ICM/Bank of England inflationary survey report, June 2003.
9. See for example Brown (1997, 2002); Balls (2002); Blair in House of Commons Debates, 23/2/99.

10. Brown (1997, 2002); Blair in the Guardian, 23/2/99, 23/10/01; Balls (2002).
11. O'Donnell in the Daily Telegraph 4/1/02, 5/1/02; the Times 4/1/02.
12. HM Treasury (2003a), ps. 81–8, 108; also see Dornbusch and Jacquet (2000); Trichet (2001); Hämäläinen (2003).
13. Ruth Kelly in House of Commons Hansard Debates, 15/1/02. cl. 23WH; HM Treasury (2003); also see Westaway (2003); Wren-Lewis (2003).
14. HM Treasury (2003a), pp. 67–70.
15. Brown in the Daily Telegraph, 24/7/1998.
16. HM Treasury (2003), p. 26; Ruth Kelly in House of Commons Hansard Debates, 15/1/02. cl. 24WH; House of Commons written answers to questions, 23/5/02; Balls (2001).
17. HM Treasury (2003), Ch. 5.
18. 'Sterling and the Economy', Citigroup Report. May 2003.
19. See O'Donnell (2002); HM Treasury (2003a), pp. 128–31.
20. Dornbusch and Jacquet (2000), pp. 96–8; the Guardian, 26/5/2003.
21. See Baker (2002), p. 328; opinion poll data from www.mori.com

Bibliography

Primary sources

Archives of the Independent Labour Party (University of Warwick, Coventry)
Various Pamphlets. Microfiche.

Bank of England Archives (Threadneedle St., London)
ADM16 : Sir Charles Addis' Papers
ADM34 : Norman Diaries
C40   : Chief Cashier's Policy Files
C42   : Chief Cashier's Personal Files
C43   : Gold and Foreign Exchange Files
EID4   : Home Finance
G1   : Governor's Files
G3   : Governor's Diaries, Duplicate Letters, etc.
G8   : Minutes of the Committee of Treasury
G14   : Committee of Treasury Files
G15   : Secretary's Files
G30   : Governor's Miscellaneous Correspondence Files
G35   : Strong–Norman Correspondence
OV9   : Sir Otto Niemeyer's Papers
OV32   : Federal Reserve Bank of New York
OV37   : Overseas Department–South Africa
OV48   : Overseas Department–Gold

Modern Records Centre (University of Warwick, Coventry)

MSS.126/EB/   Transport and General Workers' Union : Ernest Bevin Papers
FI/46 : Memoranda of written evidence
FI/47 : Memoranda of written evidence

MSS.200/B/   British Employers Confederation List
3/2/C107 : Economic Conferences
3/2/C204 : NCEO General Meetings
3/2/C530 : Rationalisation and Re-Organisation of Industry
3/2/C625 : Committee on Industry and Trade
3/2/C800 : Exports and Imports

MSS.200/F/   Archive of the Federation of British Industries
3/E1   : Economic Advisors' Papers (Glenday Papers)

3/E3   :   General Economic Directorate Files (Assistants' Papers)
3/S1   :   Secretary's Department (Walker Papers)
4   :   Publications of the Federation (1917–1965)

MSS.292/   *Trades Union Congress : Deposited Records*

100	:	Labour
110.1	:	Wages
135	:	Unemployment
135.01	:	Unemployment
135.2	:	Unemployment
252.61	:	General Strike
262	:	Industrial Conferences
265	:	Industrial Parliament and National Industrial Council
420	:	National Finance
452	:	Finance
462	:	Finance
471	:	Finance
560.1	:	Economics
563.2	:	Economics
603	:	Industries and Trades

The National Archives (Kew, London)

BT 55	:	Board of Trade: Records of Departmental Committees: Papers.
CAB 23	:	War Cabinet and Cabinet: Minutes.
CAB 24	:	War Cabinet and Cabinet: Memoranda.
CAB 27	:	War Cabinet and Cabinet: Miscellaneous Committees: Records.
T 1	:	Treasury Papers.
T 160	:	Treasury: Finance Department. Registered Files.
T 171	:	Chancellor of the Exchequer's Office: Budget and Finance Bill Papers
T 172	:	Chancellor of the Exchequer's Office and Miscellaneous Papers.
T 175	:	Papers of Sir Richard Hopkins.
T 176	:	Papers of Sir Otto Niemeyer.
T 177	:	Papers of Sir Frederick Phillips.
T 185	:	Committee on Currency and Foreign Exchanges: Minutes and Reports.
T 188	:	Papers of Sir Frederick Leith-Ross.
T 208	:	Treasury: Financial Enquiries Branch. Files.
PREM1	:	Prime Minister's Office: Correspondence and Papers, 1916–1940.

Official publications

CBI Economic Situation Reports.
FBI Bulletins (becoming 'British Industries' from October 1924).
Hansard.
House of Commons Debates.
Labour Party Annual Reports and Pamphlets.
Labour Research Department Monthly Circulars
MAIE Bulletin
Trades Union Congress Annual Reports.

Report of the Balfour Committee on Commercial and Industrial Policy, (1918). Cd.9035.

First Interim Report of the Committee on Currency and Foreign Exchanges After the War, (1918). Cd.9182.

Final Report of the Committee on Currency and Foreign Exchanges After the War, (1919). Cmd. 464.

Report of the Macmillan Court of Inquiry, (1925). Cmd. 2478

Report of the Committee on the Currency and Bank of England Note Issues, (1925). Cmd. 2393.

Memoranda on Certain Proposals Relating to Unemployment, (1929). Cmd. 3331.

Final Report of the Committee on Industry and Trade, (1929). Cmd. 3282.

Report of the Committee on Finance and Industry, (1931). Cmd. 3897.

Minutes of Evidence Taken Before the Committee on Finance and Industry. 2 Volumes, (1931). HM Stationery Office, London.

Economic Trends. Annual Supplement (1994). Central Statistical Office, London.

HM Treasury (1997), *UK Membership of the Single European Currency: An Assessment of the Five Economic Tests*, HM. Stationery Office, London.

HM Treasury (2003), *The Exchange Rate and Macroeconomic Adjustment*, HM Stationery Office, London.

HM Treasury (2003a), *UK Membership of the Single Currency: An Assessment of the Five Economic Tests*, HM Stationery Office, London.

Internet resources

ICM: www.icmresearch.co.uk
MORI polls: www.mori.com
Office for National Statistics: www.statistics.gov.uk

Secondary sources

Aghevli, B. B. and Montiel, P. J. (1991), 'Exchange Rate Policies in Developing Countries', in Emil-Maria Claassen (ed.), *Exchange Rate Policies in Developing and Post-Socialist Countries*, International Centre for Economic Growth, California.

Åkerholm, J. and Giovannini, A. (1994), 'Introduction', in J. Åkerholm, and A. Giovannini (eds), *Exchange Rate Policies in the Nordic Countries,* Centre for Economic Policy Research, London.

Aldcroft, D. H. (1967), 'Economic Growth in Britain in the Inter-War Years: A Reassessment', Economic History Review. Vol. 20.

Aldcroft, D. H. (1983), *The British Economy Between the Wars*, Philip Alan, Oxford.

Alford, B. W. E. (1986), *Depression and Recovery? British Economic Growth 1918–1939*, Macmillan, London.

Alford, B. W. E. (1996), *Britain in the World Economy Since 1880*, Longman, Essex.

Allen, G. (2002), 'Economic Indicators', House of Commons Library Research Papers 02/09.

Argy, V. (1990), 'Choice of Exchange Rate Regime For a Smaller Economy: A Survey of Some Key Issues', in V. Argy and P. de Grauwe (eds), *Choosing An Exchange Rate Regime: The Challenge For Smaller Industrial Countries*, International Monetary Fund, Washington D. C.

Argy, V. and de Grauwe, P. (1990) (eds), *Choosing An Exchange Rate Regime: The Challenge For Smaller Industrial Countries*, International Monetary Fund, Washington D. C.

Aris, R. (1998), *Trade Unions and the Management of Industrial Conflict*, Macmillan, London.

Arnot, R. P. (1975), *The General Strike, May 1926: Its Origin and History*, E. P. Publishing Ltd., London.

Ashworth, W. (1960), *An Economic History of England 1870–1939*, Methuen, London.

Baker, D. (2002), 'Britain and Europe: More Blood on the Euro-Carpet', Parliamentary Affairs, 55.

Balls, E. (2001), 'Delivering Economic Stability', Oxford Business Alumni Lecture, 12/6/01. http://www.hm-treasury.gov.uk

Balls, E. (2002), 'Why the Five Economic Tests?', Cairncross Lecture Speech, 4/12/02. http://www.hm-treasury.gov.uk

Barker, C. (1978), 'A Note on the Theory of Capitalist States', Capital and Class, No. 4.

Barrell, R., Britton, A. and Pain, N. (1994), 'When the Time was Right? The UK Experience of the ERM', in D. Cobham (ed.), *European Monetary Upheavals*, Manchester University Press, Manchester.

Bayoumi, T. and Bordo, M. D. (1998), *Getting Pegged: Comparing the 1879 and 1925 Gold Resumptions*, Oxford Economic Papers 50.

Beaudreau, B. C. (1996), *Mass Production, the Stock Market Crash and the Great Depression: The Macroeconomics of Electrification*, Greenwood Press, London.

Best, M. H. and Humphries, J. (1987), 'The City and Industrial Decline', in B. Elbaum and W. Lazonick (eds) *The Decline of the British Economy*, Clarendon Press, Oxford.

Block, F. (1977), 'The Ruling Class Does Not Rule: Notes on the Marxist Theory of the State', in F. Block (ed.), (1987), *Revising State Theory: Essays in Politics and Postindustrialism*, Temple University Press, Philadelphia.

Block, F. (1980), 'Beyond Relative Autonomy: State Managers as Historical Subjects', in F. Block (ed.), (1987), *Revising State Theory: Essays in Politics and Postindustrialism*, Temple University Press, Philadelphia.

Bonefeld, W. (1993), *The Recomposition of the British State During the 1980s*, Dartmouth, Aldershot.

Bonefeld, W., Brown, A. and Burnham, P. (1995), *A Major Crisis?: The Politics of Economic Policy in Britain in the 1990s*, Dartmouth Publishing Co. Ltd., Aldershot.

Bonefeld, W. and Burnham, P. (1996), 'Britain and the Politics of the European Exchange Rate Mechanism 1990–1992', Capital and Class 60.

Bonefeld, W. and Burnham, P. (1998), 'The Politics of Counter-Inflationary Credibility in Britain 1990–94', Review of Radical Political Economics, 30 (1).

Bordo, M. D. and Kydland, F. E. (1995), 'The Gold Standard as a Rule: An Essay in Exploration', Explorations in Economic History 32.

Boyce, R. (1988), 'Creating the Myth of Consensus: Public Opinion and Britain's Return to the Gold Standard in the 1925', in P. L. Cottrell and D. E. Moggridge (eds), *Money and Power*, Macmillan, London.

Boyle, A. (1967), *Montagu Norman: A Biography*, Cassell and Co. Ltd., London.

Branson, N. (1977), *Britain in the Nineteen Twenties*, Weidenfeld and Nicolson, London.

Brittan, S. (1991), 'The Thatcher Government's Economic Policy', in D. Kavanagh, and A. Seldon (eds), *The Thatcher Effect: A Decade of Change*, Oxford University Press, Oxford.

Brown, G. (1997), 'Statement on Economic and Monetary Union by the Chancellor of the Exchequer', 27/10/97. http://www.hm-treasury.gov.uk

Brown, G. (2002), Mansion House Speech, 26/6/02. http://www.hm-treasury.gov.uk

Brown, Jr. W. A. (1940), *The International Gold Standard Reinterpreted 1914–1934, Volume 1*, National Bureau of Economic Research, AMS Press Inc., New York.

Budd, A. (2002) 'Making Sense of the Euro Debate', Bristol Convocation, 4/02/02.

Buller, J. (1999), 'A Critical Appraisal of the Statecraft Interpretation', Public Administration, 77(4).

Bulmer-Thomas, V. (1998), 'The Latin American Economies, 1929–1939', in L. Bethel (ed.), *Latin America: Economy and Society Since 1930*, Cambridge University Press, Cambridge.

Bulpitt, J. (1983), *Territory and Power in the United Kingdom: An Interpretation*, Manchester University Press, Manchester.

Bulpitt, J. (1996), 'The European Question: Rules, National Modernisation and the Ambiguities of Primat Der Innenpolitik', in D. Marquand and A. Seldon (eds), *The Ideas That Shaped Post-War Britain*, Fontana, London.

Bulpitt, J. and Burnham, P. (1999), 'Operation Robot and the British Political Economy in the Early-1950s: The Politics of Market Strategies', Contemporary British History, 13(1).

Burnham, P. (1994), 'Open Marxism and Vulgar International Political Economy', Review of International Political Economy, 1(2).

Burnham, P. (1996), 'Capital, Crisis, and the International State System', in W. Bonefeld and J. Holloway (eds), *Global Capital, National State and the Politics of Money*, Macmillan, London.

Burnham, P. (1999), 'The Politics of Economic Management in the 1990s', New Political Economy, 4 (1).

Burnham, P. (2001), 'New Labour and the Politics of Depoliticisation', The British Journal of Politics and International Relations, 3(2).

Butler, D. and Kavanagh, D. (1992), *The British General Election of 1992*, Macmillan, London.

Butler, D. and Butler, G. (1994), *British Political Facts 1900–1994*, Seventh Edition. Macmillan, London.

Caramazza, F. and Aziz, J. (1998), *Fixed or Flexible? Getting the Exchange Rate Right in the 1990s*, Economic Issues No. 13, International Monetary Fund, Washington D. C.

Catterall, R. E. (1976), 'Attitudes to and the Impact of British Monetary Policy in the 1920s', Revue International D'Histoire De La Banque 12.

Citrine, W. (1964), *Men and Work: An Autobiography*, Hutchinson and Co., London.

Claassen, E. M. (1991) (ed.), *Exchange Rate Policies in Developing and Post-Socialist Countries*, International Centre for Economic Growth, California.

Clarke, S. (1988), *Keynesianism, Monetarism and the Crisis of the State*, Edward Elgar, Aldershot.

Clay, H. (1955), *The Inter-War Years and Other Papers: A Selection From the Writings of Hubert Douglas Henderson*, Clarendon Press, Oxford.

Clay, H. (1957), *Lord Norman*, Macmillan, London.

Clegg, H. A. (1985), *A History of Trade Unions Since 1889 Volume II: 1911–1933*, Clarendon Press, Oxford.

Cobham, D. (1997), 'Inevitable Disappointment? The ERM as the Framework for UK Monetary Policy 1990–92', International Review of Applied Economics, 11(2).

Cole, G. D. H. (1948), *A Short History of the British Working-Class Movement 1789–1947*, George Allen and Unwin Ltd., London.

Cook A. J. (1926), *The Nine Days*, Co-Operative Printing Society, London.

Cottrell, P. L. (1997), 'Norman, Strakosch and the Development of Central Banking: From Conception to Practice, 1919–1924', in P. L. Cottrell (ed.), *Rebuilding the Financial System in Central and Eastern Europe, 1918–1994*, Scholar Press, Aldershot.

Crewe, I. (1994), 'Electoral Behaviour', in D. Kavanagh and A. Seldon, *The Major Effect*, Macmillan, London.

Cronin, J. E. (1991), *The Politics of State Expansion: War, State and Society in Twentieth-Century Britain*, Routledge, London.

Crouch, C. (1979), 'The State, Capital and Liberal Democracy', in C. Crouch (ed.), *State and Economy in Contemporary Capitalism*, Croon Helm, London.

Cuckierman, A. and Meltzer, A. H. (1986), 'A Positive Theory of Discretionary Policy, the Cost of Democratic Government and the Benefits of a Constitution', Economic Inquiry, Vol. XXIV.

Daffin, C. and Lau, E. (2002), 'Labour Productivity Measures from the Annual Business Inquiry', Office for National Statistics.

de Brunhoff, S. (1978), *The State, Capital and Economic Policy*, Pluto Press Ltd., London.

de Ste Croix, G. E. M. (1983), *The Class Struggle in the Ancient Greek World: From the Archaic Age to the Arab Conquests*, Duckworth, London.

Delbecque, B. (1994), 'Discussion', in J. Åkerholm and A. Giovannini (eds), *Exchange Rate Policies in the Nordic Countries*, Centre for Economic Policy Research, London.

Dimsdale, N. H. (1981), *British Monetary Policy and the Exchange Rate 1920–1938*, Oxford Economic Papers, Vol. 33.

Dintenfass, M. (1992), *The Decline of Industrial Britain 1870–1980*, Routledge, London.

Dornbusch, R. and Jacquet, P. (2000), 'Making EMU a Success', International Affairs, 76(1).

Drinkwater, S. and Ingram, P. (2003), 'Have Industrial Relations in the UK Really Improved?', Department of Economics, University of Surrey.

Drummond, I. M. (1981), *The Floating Pound and the Sterling Area, 1931–1939*, Cambridge University Press, Cambridge.

Edwards, S. (1996), *The Determinants of the Choice Between Fixed and Flexible Exchange-Rate Regimes*, NBER Working Paper 5756, National Bureau of Economic Research, Cambridge, Massachusetts.

Eichengreen, B. (1992), *Golden Fetters: The Gold Standard and the Great Depression, 1919–1939*, Oxford University Press, Oxford.

Eichengreen, B. (1993), *Elusive Stability: Essays in the History of International Finance 1919–1939*, Cambridge University Press, Cambridge.

Eichengreen, B. (1995), 'The Endogeneity of Exchange-Rate Regimes', in P. B. Kenen (ed.), *Understanding Interdependence: The Macroeconomics of the Open Economy*, Princeton University Press, Princeton NJ.

Eichengreen, B. (1996), *Globalising Capital: A History of the International Monetary System*, Princeton University Press, Princeton, New Jersey.

Einzig, P. (1932), *Montagu Norman: A Study in Financial Statesmanship*, Kegan Paul, London.

Elbaum, B. and Lazonick, W. (1987), (eds), *The Decline of the British Economy*, Clarendon Press, Oxford.

Elster, J. (1985), *Making Sense of Marx*, Cambridge University Press, Cambridge.

Evans, G. (1999), *The Decline of Class Politics? Class Voting in Comparative Context*, UCP, London.

Farman, C. (1972), *The General Strike May 1926*, Granada, London.

Feinstein, C. H. (1972), *National Income, Expenditure and Output of the United Kingdom 1855–1965*, Cambridge University Press, Cambridge.

Feinstein, C., Temin, R. and Toniolo, G. (1997), *The European Economy Between the Wars*, Oxford University Press, Oxford.

Fine, B. (1979), 'World Economic Crisis and Inflation: What Bourgeois Economics Says and Why it is Wrong', in F. Green and P. Nore (eds), *Issues in Political Economy: A Critical Approach*, Macmillan, London.

Frankel, J. A. (1999), 'No Single Currency Regime is Right For All Countries: Testimony Before the Subcommittee on Domestic and International Monetary Policy of the Committee on Banking and Financial Services', US House of Representatives, 21/5/99.

Frieden, J. A. (1998), *The Political Economy of European Exchange Rates: An Empirical Assessment*, Working Paper, Harvard University, USA.

Frieden, J. A. (2000), 'Exchange Rate Politics', in J. A. Frieden and D. A. Lake (eds), *International Political Economy: Perspectives on Power and Wealth*, Fourth Edition, Bedford/St. Martins, USA.

Fyfe, H. (1926), *Behind the Scenes of the Great Strike*, The Labour Publishing Co. Ltd., London.

Gamble, A. and Walton, P. (1976), *Capitalism in Crisis: Inflation and the State*, Macmillan, London.

Gazeley, I. and Rice, P. G. (1992) 'Employment and Wages in the Interwar Period: The Case of the Staple Industries', in S. N. Broadberry and N. F. R. Crafts (eds), *Britain in the International Economy*, Cambridge University Press, Cambridge.

Giavazzi, F. and Pagano, M. (1988), 'The Advantage of Tying One's Hands: EMS Discipline and Central Bank Credibility', in T. Persson and G. Tabellini (1995), (eds), *Monetary and Fiscal Policy Volume 1: Credibility*, MIT Press, London.

Gilbert, M. (1976), *Winston, S. Churchill, Volume V, 1922–1939*, Heinemann, London.

Giordano, F. and Persaud, S. (1998), *The Political Economy of Monetary Union: Towards the Euro*, Routledge, London.

Giovannini, A. (1993), 'Bretton Woods and its Precursors: Rule Versus Discretion in the History of International Monetary Regimes', in M. D. Bordo and B. Eichengreen (eds), *A Retrospective on the Bretton Woods System: Lessons for International Monetary Reform*, University of Chicago Press, Chicago.

Glyn, A. and Sutcliffe, B. (1972), *British Capitalism, Workers and the Profits Squeeze*, Penguin, Middlesex.

Goldthorpe, J. H. (1978), 'The Current Inflation: Towards a Sociological Account', in F. Hirsch and J. H. Goldthorpe (eds), *The Political Economy of Inflation*, Martin Robertson, London.

Gregory, T. E. (1926), *The First Year of the Gold Standard*, Ernest Benn Ltd., London.

Grigg, P. J. (1948), *Prejudice and Judgement*, Jonathon Cape, London.

Gros, D. and Thygesen, N. (1992), *European Monetary Integration: From the European Monetary System to European Monetary Union*, Longman, London.

Haldane, A. G. (1991), 'The Exchange Rate Mechanism of the European Monetary System: A Review of the Literature', Bank of England Quarterly Bulletin. February 1991.

Hall, S. and Schwarz, B. (1985), 'State and Society', in M. Langan and B. Schwarz (eds), *Crises in the British State 1880–1930*, Hutchinson.

Hamada, K. (1987), *The Political Economy of Monetary Interdependence*, The MIT Press, London.

Hämäläinen, S. (2003), 'How the European Central Bank Manages the Euro and What is in Store for 2003', 14/1/03. European Central Bank. Press and Information Division. http://www.ecb.int

Havrilevsky, T. (1994), 'The Political Economy of Monetary Policy', European Journal of Political Economy, 10.

Hawtrey, R. G. (1933), *The Gold Standard in Theory and Practise*, Third Edition, Longmans, Green and Co. Ltd., London.

Hefeker, C. (1997), *Interest Groups and Monetary Integration: The Political Economy of Exchange Regime Choice*, Westview Press, Oxford.

Heim, C. E. (1987), 'Interwar Responses to Economic Decline', in B. Elbaum and W. Lazonick (eds), *The Decline of the British Economy*, Clarendon Press, Oxford.

Helpman, E. (1981), 'An Exploration in the Theory of Exchange Rate Regimes', Journal of Political Economy, 89 (5).

Holloway, J. (1995), 'Capital Moves', Capital and Class, Vol. 57, 1995.

Holloway, J. (1996), 'Global Capital and the National State', in W. Bonefeld and J. Holloway (eds), *Global Capital, National State and the Politics of Money*, Macmillan, London.

Holm, E. (2000), *High Politics and European Integration*, Discussion Paper No. 2, The Hellenic Observatory, The European Institute, LSE.

Honkapohja, J. and Pikkarainen, P. (1994), 'Country Characteristics and the Choice of Exchange Rate Regime: Are Mini-Skirts Followed By Maxis?', in J. Åkerholm and A. Giovannini (eds), *Exchange Rate Policies in the Nordic Countries*, Centre for Economic Policy Research, London.

Howe, G. (1994), *Conflict of Loyalty*, Macmillan, London.

Howson, S. (1975), *Domestic Monetary Management in Britain 1919–38*, Cambridge University Press, Cambridge.

Hume, L. J. (1963), 'The Gold Standard and Deflation: Issues and Attitudes in the Nineteen-Twenties', Economica NS, 30.

Ingham, G. (1984), *Capitalism Divided? The City and Industry in British Social Development*, Macmillan, London.

International Monetary Fund (1999), *Exchange Rate Arrangements and Currency Convertibility: Developments and Issues*, Washington D. C.

Jessop, B. (1983), 'Accumulation Strategies, State Forms and Hegemonic Projects', in Jessop, B (ed.) (1990), *State Theory: Putting the Capitalist State in its Place*, Polity Press, Cambridge.

Johnson, E. (ed.) (1971), *The Collected Writings of John Maynard Keynes. Vol. XVI: Activities 1914–1919: The Treasury and Versailles*, Macmillan, London.

Johnson, P. B. (1968), *Land Fit for Heroes: The Planning of British Reconstruction 1916–1919*, University of Chicago Press, London.

Jones, B. and Keating, M. (1985), *Labour and the British State*, Clarendon Press, Oxford.

Jucker-fleetwood, E. E. (1968), 'Montagu Norman in the Per Jacobson Diaries', NatWest Bank Quarterly Review. November 1968.

Kavanagh, D. (1997), *British Politics: Continuities and Change*, Third Edition, Oxford University Press, Oxford.

Kenen, P. B. (1988), *Managing Exchange Rates*, London, Routledge.

Kenwood, A. G. and Lougheed, A. L. (1971), *The Growth of the International Economy, 1820–1960*, George Allen and Unwin Ltd., London.

Keynes, J. M. (1923), *A Tract on Monetary Reform*, Macmillan, London.

Keynes, J. M. (1925), *The Economic Consequences of Mr. Churchill*, The Hogarth Press, London.

Keynes, J. M. (1951), *Essays in Persuasion*, Rupert Hart-Davis Ltd., London.

Kindleberger, C. P. (1986), *The World in Depression 1929–1939*, University of California Press, L. A.

Kunz, D. B. (1987), *The Battle for Britain's Gold Standard in 1931*, Croon Helm, London.

Kynaston, D. (1999), *The City of London, Volume III: Illusions of Gold 1914–1945*, Chatto and Windus, London.

Lamont, N. (1999), *In Office*, Warner, London.

Lawson, N. (1992), *The View From No. 11: Memoirs of a Tory Radical*, Bantam Press, London.

Laybourn, K. (1993), *The General Strike of 1926*, Manchester University Press, Manchester.

Layton, W. T. (1925), 'British Opinion of the Gold Standard', Quarterly Journal of Economics, 34 (2).

Leigh-Pemberton, R. (1991), 'The Economy and ERM Membership', Bank of England Quarterly Bulletin, 31.

Leith-Ross, F. (1968), *Money Talks: Fifty Years of International Finance*, Hutchinson, London.

Longstreth, F. (1979), 'The City, Industry and the State', in C. Crouch (ed.), *State and Economy in Contemporary Capitalism*, Croon Helm, London.

Lovell, J. and Roberts, C. (1968), *A Short History of the T. U. C.*, Macmillan, London.

Lowe, R. (1978), 'The Erosion of State Intervention in Britain, 1917–24', Economic History Review, Second Series, Vol. 31, 1978.

Major, J. (2000), *John Major: The Autobiography*, HarperCollins, London.

Mandel, E. (1975), *Late Capitalism*, NLB, London.

Marichal, C. (1989), *A Century of Debt Crises in Latin America: From Independence to the Great Depression, 1820–1930*, Princeton University Press, Princeton, New Jersey.

Marx, K. (1847), 'Moralising Criticism and Critical Morality: A Contribution to German Cultural History Contra Karl Heinzen', in K. Marx and F. Engels (1976), Collected Works, Vol. 6, Lawrence and Wishart, London.

Marx, K. (1913), *A Contribution to the Critique of Political Economy*, Charles H. Kerr and Co., Chicago.

Marx, K. (1973), *Grundrisse: Foundations of the Critique of Political Economy*, Penguin Books Ltd., Middlesex.

Marx, K. (1990), *Capital: A Critique of Political Economy Volume I*, Penguin, London.

Marx, K. (1991), *Capital: A Critique of Political Economy Volume III*, Penguin, London.

Marx, K. (1992), *Capital: A Critique of Political Economy Volume II*, Penguin, London.

Middlemas, K. (1969), *Thomas Jones: Whitehall Diary, Volume I, 1916–1925*, Oxford University Press, London.

Middlemas, K. (1969a), *Thomas Jones: Whitehall Diary, Volume II, 1926–1930*, Oxford University Press, London.

Middlemas, K. and Barnes, J. (1969), *Baldwin: A Biography*, Weidenfeld and Nicolson, London.

Middleton, R. (1985), *Towards the Managed Economy: Keynes, the Treasury and the Fiscal Policy Debate of the 1930s*, Methuen, London.

Milesi-Ferretti, G. M. (1995), 'The Disadvantage of Tying Their Hands: On the Political Economy of Policy Commitments', The Economic Journal, 105, November.

Miliband, R. (1969), *The State in Capitalist Society*, Weidenfeld and Nicolson, London.

Miller, M. Eichengreen, B. and Portes, R. (1989) (eds), *Blueprints for Exchange Rate Management*, Academic Press Ltd., London.

Miller, M. and Sutherland, A. (1992), 'Britain's Return to Gold and Entry into the EMS: Joining Conditions and Credibility', in P. Krugman and M. Miller (eds), *Exchange Rate Targets and Currency Bands*, Cambridge University Press, Cambridge.

Minikin, R. (1993), *The ERM Explained: A Straightforward Guide to the Exchange Rate Mechanism and the European Currency Debate*, Kogan Page Ltd., London.

Moggridge, D. E. (1969), *The Return to Gold 1925: The Formulation of Economic Policy and its Critics*, Cambridge, Cambridge University Press.

Moggridge, D. E. (1972), *British Monetary Policy, 1924–1931: The Norman Conquest of $4.86*, Cambridge University Press, London.

Morgan, E. V. (1952), *Studies in British Financial Policy, 1914–25*, Macmillan, London.

Morris, M. (1976), *The General Strike*, Penguin, Middlesex.

Mullard, M. (1995), 'Public Expenditure Decisions', in M. Mullard (ed.), *Policy-Making in Britain: An Introduction*, Routledge, London.

Nevin, E. (1953), 'The Origins of Cheap Money 1931–1932', in S. Pollard (1970) (ed.), *The Gold Standard and Employment Policies Between the Wars*, Methuen and Co., London.

Newton, S. and Porter, D. (1988), *Modernisation Frustrated: The Politics of Industrial Decline in Britain Since 1900*, Unwin Hyman, London.

O'Donnell, G. (2002), 'Merrill Lynch Presentation', Speech 'On The UK's Macro-Economic Framework – Redressing the Attention Deficit', 17/9/02. http://www.hm-treasury.gov.uk

Oatley, T. H. (1997), *Monetary Politics: Exchange Rate Co-Operation in the European Union*, University of Michigan Press, USA.

Peden, G. C. (1988), *Keynes, the Treasury and British Economic Policy*, Macmillan, London.

Peden, G. C. (1991), *British Economic and Social Policy: Lloyd George to Margaret Thatcher*, Second Edition, Macmillan, London.

Phillips, G. A. (1976), *The General Strike: The Politics of Industrial Conflict*, Weidenfeld and Nicolson, London.

Picciotto, S. (1991), 'The Internationalisation of the State', Capital and Class, No. 43.

Pollard, S. (1969), 'Trade Union Reactions to the Economic Crisis', in S. Pollard (1970) (ed.), *The Gold Standard and Employment Policies Between the Wars*, Methuen, London.

Pollard, S. (1976), *The Development of the British Economy 1914–1967*, Second Edition, Edward Arnold, London.

Ponting, C. (1994), *Churchill*, Sinclair-Stevenson, London.

Poulantzas, N. (1973), *Political Power and Social Classes*, New Left Books.

Pressnell, L. S. (1978), '1925: The Burden of Sterling', Economic History Review, No. 31.

Rawnsley, A. (2001), *Servants of the People: The Inside Story of New Labour*, Penguin, London.

Redmond, J. (1984), 'The Sterling Overvaluation in 1925: A Multilateral Approach', Economic History Review, 37 (4).

Renshaw, P. (1975), *The General Strike*, Eyre Methuen Ltd., London.

Roemer, J. (1986) (ed.), *Analytical Marxism*, Cambridge University Press, Cambridge.

Rose, M. B. (1995), 'Britain and the International Economy', in S. Constantine, M. W. Kirby, and M. B. Rose (eds), *The First World War in British History*, Edward Arnold, London.

Rowthorn, B. (1977), 'Inflation and Crisis', in B. Rowthorn (1980), *Capitalism, Conflict and Inflation: Essays in Political Economy*, Lawrence and Wishart, London.

Rubin, I. I. (1975), *Essays on Marx's Theory of Value*, Black Rose Books, Quebec.

Savvides, A. (1990), 'Real Exchange Rate Variability and the Choice of Exchange Rate Regime by Developing Countries', Journal of International Money and Finance, 9.

Sayers, R. S. (1960), 'The Return to Gold, 1925', in S. Pollard (1970), (ed.), *The Gold Standard and Employment Policies Between the Wars*, Methuen, London.

Sayers, R. S. (1976), *The Bank of England 1891–1914. Vol. 1*, Cambridge University Press, Cambridge.

Scammel, W. M. (1965), 'The Working of the Gold Standard', in B. Eichengreen (1985) (ed.), *The Gold Standard in Theory and History*, Methuen, London.

Skidelsky, R. (1969), 'Gold Standard and Churchill: The Truth', The Times 17/3/69.

Smith, D. (1992), *From Boom to Bust: Trial and Error in British Economic Policy*, Penguin, London.

Snowden, P. (1934), *An Autobiography. Vol. II 1919–1934*, Ivor Nicholson and Watson Ltd., London.

Sohnen, E. (1969), *Flexible Exchange Rates*, University of Chicago Press, Chicago.

Soule, G. (1947), *Prosperity Decade: From War to Depression 1917–1929*, Harper and Row, New York.

Stephens, P. (1996), *Politics and the Pound: The Conservatives' Struggle With Sterling*, Macmillan, London.

Strachey, J. (1925), *Revolution by Reason*, Leonard Parsons, London.

Taylor, R. (1994), 'Employment and Industrial Relations Policy', in D. Kavanagh and A. Seldon (eds), *The Major Effect*, Macmillan, London.

Thatcher, M. (1993), *The Downing St. Years*, HarperCollins, London.

Thompson, H. (1995), 'Joining the ERM: Analysing a Core Executive Policy Disaster', in R. A. W. Rhodes and P. Dunleavy (eds), *Prime Minister, Cabinet, and Core Executive*, Macmillan, London.

Tolliday, S. (1987), 'Steel and Rationalisation Policies, 1918–1950', in B. Elbaum and W. Lazonick (eds), *The Decline of the British Economy*, Clarendon Press, Oxford.

Tomlinson, J. (1990), *Public Policy and the Economy Since 1900*, Clarendon Press, Oxford.

Tower, E. and Willett, T. D. (1976), *The Theory of Optimal Currency Areas and Exchange Rate Flexibility*, Special Papers in International Economics No. 11. Princeton University.

Townsend, I. (2003), 'Economic Indicators', House of Commons Library Research Paper 03/57, 1/07/03.

Trichet, J-C. (2001), 'The Euro After Two Years', Journal of Common Market Studies, 39(1).

Tsoukalis, L. (1997), *The New European Economy Revisited*, Oxford University Press, Oxford.

Turner, J. (1984), 'The Politics of Business', in J. Turner (ed.), *Businessmen and Politics: Studies of Business Activity in British Politics, 1900–1945*, Heinemann, London.

United Nations (2000), *Options for Exchange Rate Policy*, Economic and Social Commission for Asia and the Pacific Least Developed Countries Series, No. 3, United Nations, New York.

Van Der Pijl, K. (1984), *The Making of an Atlantic Ruling Class*, Verso, London.

Vaubel, R. (1990), 'Currency Competition and European Monetary Integration', The Economic Journal, 100.

Walsh, J. I. (1994), 'Politics and Exchange Rates: Britain, France, Italy, and the Negotiation of the European Monetary System', Journal of Public Policy, 14.

Walsh, J. I. (2000), *European Monetary Integration and Domestic Politics: Britain, France, and Italy*, Lynne Rienner, London.

Westaway, P. (2003), *Modelling the Transition to EMU*, HM Stationery Office, London.

Williams, D. (1959), 'Montagu Norman and Banking Policy in the Nineteen Twenties', Yorkshire Bulletin of Economic and Social Research, 11.

Williamson, J. (1983), *The Exchange Rate System*, Institute for International Economics, London.

Williamson, J. (2000), *Exchange Rate Regimes for Emerging Markets: Reviving the Intermediate Option*, Institute for International Economics, Washington D. C.

Williamson, P. (1984), 'Financiers, The Gold Standard and British Politics, 1925–1931', in J. Turner (ed.), *Businessmen and Politics: Studies of Business Activity in British Politics,1900–1945* Heinemann, London.

Williamson, P. (1999), *Stanley Baldwin: Conservative Leadership and National Values*, Cambridge University Press, Cambridge.

Winch, D. (1969), *Economic and Policy: A Historical Study*, Hodder and Stoughton, London.

Wootton, B. (1925), 'Banking, Credit and Currency', in H. Tracey (ed.), (1930), *The Book of the Labour Party: Its History, Growth, Policy, and Leaders*. Vol. II Caxton Publishing, London.

Wren-Lewis, S. (2003), *Estimates of Equilibrium Exchange Rates for Sterling Against the Euro*, HM Stationery Office, London.

Wrigley, C. (1990), *Lloyd George and the Challenge of Labour: The Post-War Coalition 1918–1922*, Harvester Wheatsheaf, London.

Youngson, A. J. (1960), *The British Economy 1920–1957*, George Allen and Unwin Ltd., London.

Index